URBAN INEQUALITY

Politics and Society in Urban Africa

Politics and Society in Urban Africa is a unique series providing critical, in-depth analysis of key contemporary issues affecting urban environments across the continent. Featuring a wealth of empirical material and case study detail, and focusing on a diverse range of subject matter – from informal economies to urban governance, infrastructure to gender dynamics – the series is a platform for scholars to present thought-provoking arguments on the nature and direction of African urbanisms.

Other titles in the series:

URBAN INEQUALITY

Theory, Evidence and Method in Johannesburg

Owen Crankshaw

ZED

LONDON • NEW YORK • OXFORD • NEW DELHI • SYDNEY

ZED BOOKS
Bloomsbury Publishing Plc
50 Bedford Square, London, WC1B 3DP, UK
1385 Broadway, New York, NY 10018, USA
29 Earlsfort Terrace, Dublin 2, Ireland

BLOOMSBURY and Zed Books are trademarks of Bloomsbury Publishing Plc

First published in Great Britain 2022
This paperback edition published 2023

Copyright © Owen Crankshaw, 2022

Cover image: Johannesburg, South Africa. (© Dean Hutton/Bloomberg/Getty Images)

A catalogue record for this book is available from the British Library.

Library of Congress Cataloging-in-Publication Data
Names: Crankshaw, Owen, author.
Title: Urban inequality: theory, evidence and method in Johannesburg / Owen Crankshaw.
Other titles: Politics and society in urban Africa.
Description: New York: Zed Books, an imprint of Bloomsbury Publishing, 2022. |
Series: Politics and society in urban Africa | Includes bibliographical references and index.
Identifiers: LCCN 2021036860 (print) | LCCN 2021036861 (ebook) |
ISBN 9781786998941 (hardback) | ISBN 9781786998910 (epub) |
ISBN 9781786998934 (pdf) | ISBN 9781350237032
Subjects: LCSH: Equality–South Africa–Johannesburg. | Labor market–South
Africa–Johannesburg. | Johannesburg (South Africa)–Economic conditions. |
Johannesburg (South Africa)–Social conditions.
Classification: LCC HN801.J64 C74 2022 (print) | LCC HN801.J64 (ebook) |
DDC 307.76096822/15–dc23
LC record available at https://lccn.loc.gov/2021036860
LC ebook record available at https://lccn.loc.gov/2021036861

ISBN: HB: 978-1-7869-9894-1
       PB: 978-1-7869-9895-8
       ePDF: 978-1-7869-9893-4
       ePUB: 978-1-7869-9891-0

Series: Politics and Society in Urban Africa

Typeset by Integra Software Services Pvt. Ltd.

To find out more about our authors and books visit www.bloomsbury.com
and sign up for our newsletters.

CONTENTS

LIST OF FIGURES

LIST OF TABLES

ACKNOWLEDGEMENTS

This study was undertaken when I was employed at the University of Cape Town and affiliated to the African Centre for Cities. I could not have completed this research without the expert assistance of the following colleagues and friends:

Nicholas Lindenberg and Thomas Slingsby at the Geographic Information Systems Unit, Faculty of Engineering and the Built Environment, University of Cape Town. They taught me how to use the ArcMap software application and solved many technical problems.

Andrew Kerr, Takwanisa Machemedze and Lynn Woolfrey at the DataFirst Research Unit, University of Cape Town for providing me with statistical data.

Mike Bergh at OLSPS, Cape Town, for his statistical advice.

Jean-Paul Solomon for his assistance with acquiring and mapping the Population Census results for 1996 and 2011.

Philip J. Stickler for the cartography.

Adrian Frith for his useful website that matches the 2001 and 2011 Population Census Subplace names with their boundaries on Google Earth Pro: https://census2001.adrianfrith.com/ and https://census2011.adrianfrith.com/.

This research was supported financially by the National Research Foundation (Grant Numbers 85462 and 119126) and by the University of Cape Town.

Cover Image: Photograph by Dean Hutton, Getty Images. Aerial view of the central business district of the new edge city of Sandton, with the original central business district of Johannesburg on the skyline.

Chapter 1

INTRODUCTION: THEORIES OF URBAN INEQUALITY

Introduction

This book is a study of the changing nature of social inequality in Johannesburg over the last twenty to forty years. In conducting this research, my approach was to produce a case study that was guided by and would contribute to the development of international theories of urban inequality. The theories that attracted my interest were those concerned with understanding inequalities in the labour and housing markets of cities. This urban studies literature has a different approach to mainstream economic theory because of its interest in the occupational class structure of employment and its relationship to the changing geography of inequality. The first of these theoretical debates is the social polarization debate, which is concerned to describe the changing occupational structure and how it has resulted in changing patterns of earnings inequality. The second theoretical debate in the urban studies literature concerns the post-Fordist spatial order of cities. This debate is concerned to describe and measure the changing geography of inequality by examining the relationship between the changing occupational structure and the housing market. Both debates also address how the changing occupational structure of employment and the geography of inequality have influenced changes in racial earnings inequality and racial residential segregation.

Theories of labour market inequality in cities: Social polarization or professionalization?

The debate over the occupational class structure of the post-industrial city has been dominated by two different theories, namely the 'social polarization' theory and the 'professionalization' or 'skills mismatch' theory (Bailey and Waldinger, 1991; Burgers and Musterd, 2002; Hamnett, 1994). The theory of social polarization is probably best known from its application to the study of economic restructuring in global cities (Friedmann and Wolff, 1982; Hamnett, 2003; Sassen, 2001). However, it has also been applied more widely, to the study of deindustrializing non-global cities (Nijman and Wei, 2020; Stanback and Noyelle, 1984) and even entire countries (Goos and Manning, 2007; Harrison and Bluestone, 1988; Wright and Dwyer, 2003).

Proponents of the social polarization theory argue that the distributional structure of employment is becoming more polarized in terms of occupations and the earnings that they attract. Specifically, they argue that there has been more employment growth among highly skilled and highly paid occupations, on the one hand; and among low-skilled, low-paid occupations, on the other. Correspondingly, they argue that there has been slower growth of semi-skilled, middle-income jobs. The theory therefore claims that workers are becoming more concentrated at the extremes of the earnings distribution.

In the urban studies literature, the theory of occupational 'professionalization' was advanced, at least partially, as a response to the social polarization theory (Esping-Anderson *et al.*, 1993; Hamnett, 1994; Hamnett, 2020). These scholars argued that de-industrialization did not result in the occupational and income polarization among the employed workforce. Instead, they argued that de-industrialization led to increased employment in high-income managerial and professional occupations, with substantially less growth in all other occupations. These scholars also argue that professionalization of the occupational structure has been accompanied by high levels of unemployment among low-skilled workers. This theory therefore argues that employed workers are increasingly concentrated at the high-income end of the earnings distribution, while the growth of poverty is caused largely by unemployment rather than the growth of low-skilled jobs.

In the United States of America, a separate debate on the fate of low-skilled workers living in the inner cities entailed a similar argument. Wilson (1996) and Kasarda (1989) both argued that chronic unemployment among low-skilled inner-city workers was caused by de-industrialization. The decline of manufacturing employment and the growth of service sector jobs resulted in growing demand for highly educated workers and the decline in demand for poorly educated workers. This change in the demand for labour is therefore argued to be an important cause of unemployment among poorly educated workers. This theory is also known as the 'mismatch' theory because it identifies the skills disparity or 'mismatch' between the demand for highly skilled workers and the supply of low-skilled workers as the cause of rising levels of unemployment. So, in contrast to the social polarization argument, Wilson and Kasarda argued that the growth of service sector employment led to fewer low-skilled manual jobs and to the growth of highly skilled non-manual jobs. The 'professionalization' or 'mismatch' theory of urban inequality therefore argues that de-industrialization causes inequality through the growing number of low-skilled unemployed workers, on the one hand, and growing number of highly paid, highly skilled employed workers, on the other.

Unlike the social polarization theory, the professionalization theory provides a coherent explanation for rising unemployment: It is theoretically consistent to argue that the decline in the demand for low- and middle-income jobs can lead to unemployment among less-educated workers. But it is not consistent to argue that unemployment among low-skilled workers is caused by, or is consistent with, social polarization. This is because social polarization entails an increase in the numbers of low-income service sector jobs. Since these are low- and semi-skilled jobs, their growth will result in the increased demand for poorly educated workers, which, all things being equal, is not consistent with growing unemployment among low-skilled workers.

Racial and class inequality in the post-Fordist spatial order

The debate concerning the changing occupational structure of cities has been used by scholars to understand the changing geography of racial and class inequality in post-industrial cities. The proponents of the social polarization and professionalization theories both agree that the post-industrial or post-Fordist spatial order is more residentially segregated by both race and class than the industrial or Fordist order that preceded it. However, they disagree on the specific nature of this increased racial and class segregation.

Both these schools of thought agree that the growth of the high-income managerial, professional and technical class has gone together with residential suburbanization, on the one hand, and inner-city gentrification, on the other. The result is that the occupational structure of suburban residents has become increasingly middle class. This is especially the case in the new 'edge city' developments. By contrast, the occupational composition of the residents of inner-city neighbourhoods has become increasingly working class (Castells, 2002: p.299). This is not to say that the residents of inner cities have become homogeneously working class. Since the de-industrialization of inner-city economic activities, inner-city residential neighbourhoods have become more attractive to professionals, managers and technicians. The result has been the expansion of middle-class enclaves of the inner city into erstwhile working-class neighbourhoods in a process known as 'gentrification' (Castells, 2002: p.300; Hamnett, 2003: p.171).

These two schools of thought also agree on the racial characteristics of the post-Fordist spatial order. The argument is that white residents have been the main beneficiaries of employment growth in high-income managerial, professional and technical jobs. By contrast, black residents have not been upwardly mobile to the same extent. This increasing class differentiation by race is also argued to have been accompanied by deepening racial residential segregation. In US cities, black residents tend to live in the poorer inner-city neighbourhoods, whereas white residents increasingly live in the wealthier suburbs and edge cities (Beauregard and Haila, 2000: p.29). More recent migrants, largely Latinos, are also argued to be concentrated in the inner city (Castells, 2002: p.299; Sassen, 1990b: pp.85–7; Sassen, 2001: p.325; Soja, *et al.*, 1983: pp.219–20).

At this point, agreement between the polarization and professionalization schools of thought comes to an end. For the social polarization theorists, poverty among inner-city black residents is largely due to their displacement from middle-income manual jobs and their concentration in the growing number of low-skilled and low-paid service jobs (Sassen, 2001: pp.324–5). By contrast, the professionalization theorists argue that post-Fordist poverty among poorly educated inner-city black residents was caused by growing unemployment which was caused, in turn, by the decline in all manual jobs in the inner city (Kasarda,

1989: pp.27–9; Kasarda, 1995: pp.246–52; Wilson, 1996: pp.26–30). This debate is complicated somewhat by the claim among social polarization theorists that inner-city poverty was caused by both the growth of low-wage jobs and rising unemployment (Sassen, 2001: p.325), which are usually understood to be contradictory trends.

This debate over the nature and causes of racial inequality has direct relevance for our understanding of racial inequality in Johannesburg. South Africa and the USA both had a history of racial oppression during the twentieth century. Both countries also went through a period of political struggle in which black citizens achieved equal political rights with white citizens. However, despite this political equality, urban poverty among black residents in the USA increased during the 1970s and 1980s. In South African cities, the post-*Apartheid* period was also characterized by the persistence of poverty among black residents. In both countries, the main characteristic of this poverty was the increasing rate of unemployment in the racial ghettos of the major cities. Scholars have responded to this phenomenon with a range of competing theories. In the USA, some scholars argued that the growth of black unemployment was due to contemporary racism and the continuing racial oppression of blacks (Wilson, 1987: p.10). Wilson's criticism of this theory was that it is contradicted by two important social features of US cities after 1970. The first is that the growth of black poverty in cities took place after, rather than before the victories that were achieved by the civil rights movement. The second is that there was the expansion in the size of the high-income black middle class after 1970, which contradicts the argument that racial discrimination persisted in the post-civil rights era (Wilson, 1987: p.11).

Wilson therefore argues that to understand post-1970 racial inequality in US cities, we need to distinguish between the effects of historical racial oppression during the Jim Crow era and the contemporary racism of the post-civil rights struggle era (Wilson, 1987: pp.10–11). He argues that in US cities, historical racism had the effect of restricting many black workers to unskilled and semi-skilled manual jobs and restricted black residents to inner-city racial ghettos. However, he argues that the growth of unemployment among poorly educated black ghetto residents after 1970 was largely caused by the interaction of these effects of historical racism with contemporary changes in the occupational structures and economic geographies of cities (Wilson, 1987: p.39). He argues that if the growth of poverty among blacks in the 1970s and 1980s was due solely to contemporary racism, then how could the growth of the black middle class during this period be explained (Wilson, 1987: p.11)? So his explanation for the rise of urban black poverty entails an understanding of how the effects of historical racial discrimination were reinforced by later changes in the urban economy that disadvantaged poorly educated black residents of the inner cities.

Scholars who support the professionalization theory argue that there were two main features of this urban economic transformation (Kasarda, 1989: p.31; Kasarda, 1995: p.235; Wilson, 1996: pp.27–39; Wilson, 2009: p.40). The first was the decline in the number of manual jobs for workers without a high-school education and the increase in the number of jobs for workers with at least some university education. The second is that this decline of employment for manual workers was specific to the inner cities, where most poorly educated black residents lived. This change in the division of labour was caused not only by deindustrialization and restructuring within economic sectors, but also by the relocation of many inner-city businesses to edge cities. This changing demand for labour therefore resulted in high levels of unemployment among poorly educated black residents of the inner cities.

This urban economic transformation had unequal consequences for black residents. For black residents with university educations, high-paid jobs were available not only in the inner cities, but also in the edge cities. The passage of the Fair Housing Act of 1968 facilitated their exodus from the inner cities to the suburbs (Clark, 2007: p.309; Wilson, 1987: pp.49–55). The result was that the inner-city ghettos lost many of their high-income middle-class residents. The overall consequence was a dilution of the multi-class character of ghettos, which became increasingly dominated by low-skilled manual workers with high rates of unemployment.

This transformation of the inner-city black population, from a multi-class workforce with low unemployment, to a solely working-class workforce with high unemployment has been characterized as the transformation from the racial ghetto to the 'excluded ghetto'. So whereas the racial ghetto of the Fordist period was characterized by enforced racial segregation of black residents and their racial oppression, the excluded ghetto of the post-Fordist period is characterized by their exclusion from the city's economy (Marcuse, 1997: pp.3–4; Marcuse and van Kempen, 2000: pp.4 and 19).

This professionalization or skills mismatch account stands in contrast to that of the social polarization theory. Sassen argues that racial inequality in deindustrializing cities was caused by the growing demand for low-skilled workers: a demand that was met by low-skilled black and Latino immigrants (Sassen, 2001: p.321). This theory therefore opposes the argument that the growth of low-skilled jobs in the inner city was caused by the large supply of low-skilled immigrants. To the contrary, Sassen argues that the growth of the post-Fordist economy is such that it has entailed the decline of middle-income, full-time jobs in the manufacturing industry and the expansion of low-income, part-time and casual jobs in the service sector (Sassen, 2001: p.291). It was therefore the growth of the post-Fordist economy that caused the growth of low-wage jobs among low-skilled black inner-city residents. In this account, there is usually some mention of rising unemployment among low-skilled inner-city residents (Sassen, 2001: p.301). However, Sassen makes no attempt to explain how an increasing rate of unemployment among low-skilled workers is compatible with growing numbers of low-skilled jobs.

The social polarization debate, racial inequality and migration

The professionalization and social polarization theories both agree that de-industrialization and the growth of service-sector employment have increased racial earnings inequality. However, the two theories offer quite distinct descriptions of the changing nature of racial inequality and its causes. Sassen argued that social polarization resulted in the growth of low-wage jobs. This growing demand for workers in low-wage jobs was at least partly met by poorly educated foreign migrants (Sassen, 1990b: p.128). In the global cities of New York and Los Angeles, these post-1970s migrants were largely 'non-white' [sic] Latino residents who migrated from Mexico and countries in Central America and the Caribbean (Clarke, 2003: pp.31–2; Waldinger and Bozorgmehr, 1996: p.15). So the social polarization theory emphasizes the growth of low-wage jobs and argues that 'non-white' [sic] migrants tend to be concentrated in these low-wage jobs rather than in declining middle-income jobs (Baum, 1997: p.1897; Chiu and Lui, 2004: p.1868; Harrison and Bluestone, 1988: p.70; Sassen, 1990b: pp.83–4).

The professionalization or skills mismatch theory has been applied in the United States to explain the growth of black unemployment in cities. This theory argues that black farmworkers who urbanized during the 1950s and 1960s were concentrated in manual, middle-income manufacturing jobs that did not require a tertiary education. Unlike European migrants who arrived much earlier in the century, many poorly educated black migrants were forced into unemployment by deindustrialization (Kasarda, 1989: p.33; Wilson, 1996: p.30). By contrast, the growth of high-income jobs is argued to have largely benefitted the better-educated native population, most of whom are white residents of European descent. Similarly, in studies of Western European cities, authors have argued that the professionalization of the employed workforce has tended to cause higher unemployment among poorly educated workers. To the extent that immigrants from Africa, Asia and the Caribbean were poorly educated and restricted to manual occupations, they were over-represented among the unemployed (Kesteloot, 2000: pp.199–201). So it is the educational achievements of immigrants rather than solely their immigrant status that influences their position in the labour market. This interpretation is supported by Hamnett (2003: pp.117–19) who argued that in London, immigrants from Africa, Asia and the Caribbean were not homogeneously poorly educated and concentrated in low-skilled jobs. He demonstrated that there was considerable diversity of educational achievement and upward occupational mobility among immigrants and their London-born offspring.

Labour market inequality, housing markets and residential segregation

The geographical segregation of residents by occupational class is understood to be a product of the operation of both the housing market and the labour market. The relationship between these two markets is a contingent interaction: although each market is partly created by autonomous social forces, they are also created in relation to each other. So changes in the structure of the labour market will lead to changes in the demand for different kinds of housing in different locations (Hamnett and Randolph, 1986: p.223–4).

In the housing market, the choice of residential neighbourhood is therefore strongly influenced by the ability of homeowners and tenants to pay for housing.

The price of housing is determined by a variety of features. The first is the distinction between more expensive housing that is purchased by homeowners at market prices and cheaper houses that are sponsored (or subsidized) by the state (Randolph, 1991: p.27). In the case of the former, such houses may be inhabited by their owners but may equally be inhabited by tenants who pay market rents. The second distinction, which is usually related to the first, concerns the size and amenity of houses. Houses built for sale to homeowners are generally larger with more amenities, whereas state-sponsored houses are by their nature designed to be cheaper and are therefore smaller with less amenity.

Unequal earnings in the labour market can therefore be the main cause of residential segregation, depending on the segmentation of the housing market (Storper and Walker, 1983: p.32). Generally, high-income middle-class residents are homeowners and manual workers and the unemployed live in public housing (Lee and Murie, 1999: p.626; Hamnett and Randolph, 1986: p.237). In many cities of the USA and Europe, inner-city residents were generally poorer than their counterparts in the suburbs. In London, the main cause of this distinction is argued to be the concentration of state-sponsored or public housing in the inner city and the concentration of home ownership in the suburbs (Fieldhouse, 1999: p.1593; Hamnett and Randolph, 1986: pp.233–4). In Chicago and many other US cities, state-sponsored housing was also concentrated in black inner-city ghettos, which resulted in the concentration of poor black residents in these neighbourhoods (Wacquant, 2008: pp.75–8).

But state-sponsored or public housing is not, of necessity, restricted to inner-city neighbourhoods. Although public housing is usually located in cheap locations, these may also be found in the suburbs (Kesteloot, 2005: p.342). In Sydney, for example, public housing was concentrated in the western suburbs rather than the inner city, while high-income residents were concentrated in the eastern suburbs and on the north shore (Badcock, 2000: p.219; Grimes, 1996: pp.181–2). Similarly, post-war developments in Copenhagen resulted in middle-class residents leaving the central city to buy detached houses in the northern and north-western suburbs while public housing for poorer residents was built largely in the western and south-western suburbs (Andersen *et al.*, 2000: p.73).

Conceptualizing housing markets in terms of the distinction between public and private housing and their geographical distribution therefore provides us with an understanding of how unequal housing markets and an unequal labour market can combine to cause geographical, racial and class segregation. This approach is particularly relevant to understanding the geography of racial inequality in Johannesburg, where state-sponsored housing was a central tool in creating racial residential segregation during the *Apartheid* period.

Explanations for social polarization

Scholars who support the social polarization hypothesis propose several different explanations for the polarization of the occupational and income structure of employment. The first, and most important, explanation is that of deindustrialization, or what is often called 'economic restructuring'. In this explanation, it is argued that the manufacturing sector has a larger share of semi-skilled middle-income jobs than the service sector. Employment in the service sector is therefore argued to have a more polarized occupational and income structure than the manufacturing sector. The growth in service sector employment and the stagnation or even decline in manufacturing sector employment therefore results in the overall polarization of the occupational and income distribution of all employment (Sassen, 2000: pp.125–8).

This explanation for the polarization of the occupational structure is not solely concerned with the income distribution of employment. An important feature of the explanation lies in the changing nature of economic activities and their associated occupations. Specifically, the argument is that the dominant economic activities in the manufacturing sector are concerned with the production of goods, and that this kind of production entails mostly middle-income manual, skilled and semi-skilled occupations. The decline of manufacturing employment therefore results in the loss of these skilled and semi-skilled manual or 'blue-collar' jobs. So, the decline of middle-income jobs is caused by the decline of employment in particular occupations, namely the jobs of skilled artisans, and of semi-skilled machine operators, assemblers and drivers. In turn, this decline of middle-income manual employment is caused by the decline of employment in manufacturing activities.

This understanding of the nature of manufacturing occupations therefore provides one explanation for the decline of manufacturing sector employment itself. Scholars have volunteered several explanations for de-industrialization, the most important of which is that employment growth in the manufacturing sector has fallen behind that of the service sector because many manufacturing jobs were more readily mechanized and automated.

Similarly, the polarized nature of service sector employment is also understood in terms of the economic activities of this sector. Specifically, the growth of producer services, which provide specialist financial services has therefore entailed the growth of high-income managerial and professional jobs, on the one hand (Hamnett, 1994: p.401), and the growth of low-income personal service jobs on the other (Sassen, 2001: p.250).

Another explanation for social polarization has been advanced by Hamnett (2020: p.12), who proposed that social polarization is caused by the large supply of poorly educated low-skilled workers, who are usually immigrants. This explanation directly contradicts Sassen's theory, which argues that the growth of low-income jobs is caused by the demand for labour resulting from the growing service sector and downgrading of erstwhile middle-income manufacturing jobs. This explanation has been advanced in studies of Beijing (Gu, 2001: p.25; Gu and Liu, 2002: p.210; Gu *et al.,* 2006: p.285) and Brussels (Kesteloot, 1994: p.207).

Hamnett has also argued that social polarization can only take place under conditions where low-skilled workers are not provided with long-term unemployment benefits. He argues that the payment of a 'social wage' to unemployed workers has the effect of reducing the supply of workers in low-income jobs simply because it gives low-skilled workers the option of turning down low-paid and unpleasant manual jobs. Hence, cities in the United States, which has a less-developed welfare state, have a more polarized occupational structure than cities in Western Europe which are characterized by strong welfare states (Hamnett, 1996: pp.1425–6).

Types of causal explanation

These two different, if related, explanations for the changing division of labour rely on correspondingly different types of causal logic. The deindustrialization explanation of social polarization is what Sayer (2010: p.86) has called an 'instrumentalist' type of explanation. This kind of explanation refers solely to the quantitative distributions of occupations in the manufacturing and service sectors and how the growth of employment in the service sector and corresponding decline of employment in the manufacturing sector produces a quantitative (and polarizing) change in the overall occupational structure of employment. As an explanation for the polarization of the occupational structure, it makes no reference to the causal mechanism that explains the decline in manufacturing employment. As such, Sayer argues that this kind of explanation is effectively a quantitative 'calculating device' that describes statistical relationships (Sayer, 2010: p.86).

The second explanation, namely mechanization, follows a different type of causal logic. In this case, the explanation involves a 'causal mechanism' that causes changes in the division of labour by replacing manual workers with machinery. Scholars have argued that manufacturing employment has declined, and service sector employment has grown because routine manual jobs are much more amenable to mechanization and automation than most non-routine manual jobs and non-routine non-manual jobs that require cognitive activity and social interaction (Autor *et al.*, 2003, 2006; Goos and Manning, 2007). Whereas most goods-producing routine manual jobs can be mechanized, many cleaning, serving, professional and managerial jobs are more difficult, if not impossible, to mechanize. So this kind of explanation is quite different from an 'instrumentalist' explanation because changes in the occupational structure are not due solely to quantitative changes in the sectoral composition of employment. Instead, the explanation relies on descriptions of the qualitative nature of production and the qualitative changes in the methods by which goods are produced and services are provided. By describing a change in the method of production as a 'qualitative' change, I am referring to the change that is described in terms of its character or its properties, as opposed to how many times it occurs.[1]

---

1 This stands in contrast to the way that the term 'qualitative' is used in the literature in economics and sociology to refer to attitudes and ideas rather than to the qualitative nature or the properties of social relationships, physical objects and social practices.

Although this second type of explanation is based on the qualitative description of a causal mechanism, it is commonly used in studies that rely solely on quantitative evidence. In other words, statistical associations (correlations or regularities) are used as evidence for the existence of a causal mechanism, the nature of which is hypothesized in qualitative terms. This kind of explanatory reasoning has been termed the 'deductive-nomological model' of reasoning (Manicas, 2006: p.11). Critics of the deductive-nomological model of causation argue that it uses a logical sleight of hand that relies on conceptual descriptions of the qualitative nature of a causal mechanism, yet privileges statistics as the only source of evidence for the existence of the causal mechanism (Fleetwood, 2001: p.202; Porpora, 2008: p.199). In other words, evidence that takes the form of a conceptual description of the qualitative nature of the causal mechanism is treated as merely 'anecdotal', whereas the statistics that measure the events produced by the causal mechanism is considered as solid evidence. This positivist approach therefore ignores the fact that statistical associations can only be evaluated with conceptual descriptions of the causal mechanism that produces them.

In contrast to this deductive-nomological model, another type of explanation relies on evidence concerning the description of the qualitative properties of a causal mechanism in order to demonstrate that it is the cause of a phenomenon. This type of explanatory logic is termed the 'causal-explanatory model' of explanation and it relies on evidence for causation that is found, not in statistical correlations, but in qualitative descriptions that conceptualize the properties of social structures and the causal powers and liabilities that result from these properties (Crankshaw, 2014: pp.499–503; Manicas, 2006: pp.9–12; Sayer, 2010: p.120). In this model of causation, statistical correlations are understood in two different ways. First, a statistical correlation can be evidence for the existence of a causal mechanism. As such, the statistical correlation is therefore evidence of a phenomenon that needs to be explained. Second, once we have a description of the qualitative nature of a causal mechanism, statistical correlations can provide evidence of the extent to which the causal mechanism was activated in order to produce an effect (Crankshaw, 2014: pp.512–13).

The role of evidence in theoretical debates

In his review of the social polarization debate, Hamnett argues that the work of many influential scholars has generated 'a conventional wisdom regarding the inevitability of polarization and inequality in global cities', which is based on 'sloppy thinking' in terms of both conceptualizations and statistical evidence (Hamnett, 2010: p.20). One of the reasons for this kind of conceptual vagueness and ambiguity is the philosophical idea that such theories concerning the real world are rhetorical rather than descriptive (Hamnett, 1998: p.168). As such, these theories are used to persuade audiences by virtue of their moral, emotional and symbolic value rather than their ability to describe reality. By contrast, my own approach is to avoid using rhetorical devices, such as moral outrage. Instead, my style will come across as rather dispassionate. The aim of such an approach is to allow the reader to focus on the logical connections between method, evidence and theoretical descriptions.

Hamnett's observations raise an important methodological point concerning the relationship between our concepts of reality, evidence for our concepts and phenomena in the real social world. I would therefore like to advance this argument by discussing the relationship between concepts and their relationship to evidence and the real social world.

Before I do that, I would like to clarify what I mean when I use the terms 'theory' and 'empirical'. In its most general sense, the term 'theory' simply refers to an idea as opposed to the thing itself. By contrast, the term 'empirical' is used by philosophers of science to refer to observable evidence.[2] In the context of social science, however, a theory is not simply an idea. It is an idea or an interpretation that is based upon some form of evidence concerning the real social world. By contrast, a 'hypothesis' is an idea about the real world that has not been tested against the evidence.

This definition of 'theory' might seem uncontroversial to most readers, but it needs to be emphasized. Consider, for example, the distinction that scholars often make between 'theoretical' and 'empirical' contributions to knowledge. If theories are evidence-based ideas about the real world, then this distinction between 'theoretical' and 'empirical' contributions falls away because such theories must entail a discussion of empirical findings or evidence. It therefore does not make sense to separate theoretical descriptions from empirical descriptions. So, when I discuss 'theory', I am discussing the conceptual descriptions of social reality that are based upon empirical evidence. These conceptualizations can entail descriptions of the qualitative nature of social phenomena, such as the description of an economic activity. They can also take the form of explanations that describe the operation of causal mechanisms. But they can also take the form of statistical descriptions that measure the quantitative extent of a phenomenon, such as the frequency distribution of employment by occupations.

There are several possible reasons why scholars make this distinction between theoretical and empirical aspects of research. The main one is that they have been wittingly or unwittingly influenced by positivism, which still forms the bedrock of most popular and scholarly thought. One of the philosophical assumptions of positivism is the idea that social reality can be observed for what it is without us having to develop concepts about it. In other words, if we clear our minds of our preconceived ideas of reality, then we can see reality for what it really is (Doyal and Harris, 1986: p.2). Now, while there is merit in not imposing our preconceived ideas onto our observations of reality, this is not the same as saying that we can perceive reality without using concepts. Yet this is precisely what positivism

---

2 Some critical realists use the term 'empirical' to refer only to statistical evidence, reserving the term 'concept' when referring to evidence of a qualitative nature (Porpora, 2008). I think that this is both unhelpful and inconsistent with the usual use of the terms.

implies. The logic is as follows. First, we develop hypotheses or untested ideas about social reality. Then, we test our hypotheses against our observations (our evidence) by making measurements. If our observations support our hypotheses, then our knowledge is no longer theoretical: it is factually true. So, in positivism, it makes perfect sense to distinguish between theory (as hypothesized ideas about reality) and facts (as reality).

This philosophical assumption of positivism has been subject to substantial criticism in recent decades. Sayer (2010) argues that we need to abandon this positivist distinction between theories as thought objects (in our minds) and facts (as real objects). Instead, we should make a distinction between facts as objects in the real social world and facts as our observations of the real social world. In Sayer's formulation, a factual observation is, like a theory and a concept, a thought object that exists in our minds. This approach, which emphasizes our conceptually mediated perception of reality, rejects the argument that facts are the same thing as reality and that our fact-based knowledge of reality is therefore infallible. Equally, however, this approach also rejects the argument that there is no such thing as truth. Instead, it argues that evidence-based observations and interpretations can lead us to at least a partially true, yet fallible understanding of social reality. This critical realist understanding of facts as thought objects should not be seen as controversial. It simply makes explicit what is commonly practised, even in the field of labour statistics. Although employment statistics are treated as facts, the basic principles of probability sampling make it perfectly clear that measurements, such as the percentage of professionals in the workforce, are distinct from the actual population of professionals. This is evident from the use of the term 'estimate' to describe measurements based on probability samples. It is also evident from the reasoning that the accuracy of a statistical estimate is described by a 'confidence interval' that measures the range on either side of the statistical estimate within which the true value of the parameter in the population is likely to be found (Moser and Kalton, 1971: pp.69–74). So the way that probability theory conceptualizes statistics makes it perfectly clear that statistics produced by survey samples are distinct from the real populations that the survey is measuring.

This critical realist ontology allows us to understand how evidence-based knowledge (theory) develops and changes – for example, when we reject an established theory because new research has generated different facts that require a new interpretation, or when different statistical analyses of the same data files produce different estimates. This is logically possible because our fact-based knowledge of reality is not the same thing as reality itself: an ontological assumption that positivists implicitly reject. This approach helps us to make sense of the debates that will be addressed in this study. Specifically, the social polarization debate is characterized by much disagreement over the statistical evidence of trends in the occupational structure of employment. In many cases, these different statistical findings are due to different conceptualizations of occupational groups, which then result in different measurements. The problem, therefore, is that many contributors to the debate have not fully understood that the social polarization theory can only be properly tested by statistical evidence that is based on concepts that are consistent with the conceptual claims of the hypothesis.

A case study of Greater Johannesburg

Greater Johannesburg lends itself as a test case for the social polarization debate because it meets all the criteria that should have resulted in the occupational polarization of employment. First, as measured by employment, the economy of greater Johannesburg has undergone substantial de-industrialization. Second, this period of de-industrialization corresponded with large-scale in-migration of migrants from the countryside. Third, the South African State does not offer a long-term social wage to unemployed workers. So if social polarization has not occurred under these conditions, as specified by contributions to the debate, then this case study should provide some valuable insights to the social polarization debate.

Conversely, the application of the terms of the social polarization and post-Fordist spatial order debates to understanding inequality in greater Johannesburg brings a fresh approach to the literature on urban inequality in South Africa. With only some exceptions, most studies of inequality in South African cities focus on the role of *Apartheid* State policies in creating racial inequality, and on the failure of post-*Apartheid* State policies to redress racial inequality. As Seekings (2011, p.536) has observed, explanations for the perpetuation of racial inequality in the post-*Apartheid* period have been largely concerned with the way that the ANC Government is said to have betrayed the promises of the Reconstruction and Development Programme by adopting neoliberal policies that introduced cost-recovery charges for municipal services in poor neighbourhoods. Whatever the merits of these claims, the point is that explanations for the persistence of racial inequality in cities have tended to focus solely on State policy rather than on the changing urban labour market and its relationship to the housing market. By researching inequality in Johannesburg through reference to the concepts and theories of the social polarization and post-Fordist spatial order debates, my aim is to provide some new insights into the character and causes of trends in racial inequality that go beyond the analysis of State policy alone.

This study covers the period from 1970 to 2011 and its major contribution lies in the use of official statistics to measure trends in various kinds of social inequality. In this respect, the study was designed to ensure that very long-term trends were measured so that there could be no doubt that the findings represented real, structural changes and were not the result of short-term shifts or even survey errors. Although I would have preferred more up to date statistics, this was not possible because the latest population census was conducted in 2011. More recent labour market statistics are available, but I would not be able to match them with the changing geographical distribution of occupational inequality as measured by the population censuses between 1996 and 2011. So to allow for a coherent presentation of findings concerning both the long-term employment trends and changes in the geography of inequality, I opted for ending the study in 2011.

As a study, in part, of the changing pattern of racial inequality, this book entails the use of terms and concepts to describe the racial classification of Johannesburg's population. My use of these racial terms is restricted to identifying people according to their different racially defined political and urban rights during the *Apartheid* period. I do not accept that the membership of a racial group has any other necessary significance. Like many scholars, I believe that the concept of 'race' is chaotic in the sense that it treats people of one race as if they all have the same necessary properties, when in truth they do not. Conversely, the concept of race is also used to distinguish between people of different races when they nonetheless share the same fundamental properties (Sayer, 2010: p.93). This common-sense concept of race therefore defines race as much by physical appearance as by cultural attributes and social status, which indeed was the kind of reasoning that informed the racial classification of the *Apartheid* period (Posel, 2001: p.56).

This study will challenge this common-sense meaning of race by demonstrating how the occupational class, employment status and housing circumstances of racial groups have undergone substantial changes over the past forty years. These changes make it impossible to use racial terms to sensibly describe the characteristics of a group of people. The occupational class and housing characteristics of people within each racial group are so diverse that the concept of race does not usefully distinguish groups of people. So while the concept of race can be used to describe a person's political and urban rights under *Apartheid*, it does not sensibly describe anything more than that. Therefore, to describe a group of people as 'middle-class white workers' in the post-*Apartheid* period, is to describe their occupational class in relation to their historical rights under *Apartheid*.

In using the racial classification of the *Apartheid* period, I have followed the somewhat dated convention of the anti-*Apartheid* movement of referring to African, coloured and Indian people as 'black' people. This is a coherent way to avoid the term 'non-white', which is belittling, to say the least. For readers who are not familiar with South African racial terminology, here is a short summary of *Apartheid*'s racial classification: The term 'African' refers to people descended from the indigenous population of South Africa, prior to European colonization. The category of 'coloured' refers to a rather diverse group comprising the descendants of slaves brought to South Africa from the Dutch colonies in Asia, the indigenous Khoisan population as well as descendants of inter-racial marriages. The category of 'Indian' refers to the descendants of migrants from colonial India. Finally, the term 'white' refers mostly to the descendants of colonists from a variety of European countries.

Outline of the book

I have organized the following chapters of this book into two parts, followed by a conclusion. The first part deals with the changes in the labour market, which entails the changing occupational structure and its relationship with the growing unemployment rate and racial inequality. The second part deals with the changing geography of occupational and racial inequality by examining the historical interaction of the housing and labour markets.

There are two chapters in Part 1. In the first chapter (Chapter 2), I provide a critical review of the debate over the relationship between de-industrialization and the occupational and earnings structure of employment. The aim of this review is to familiarize the reader with the theories, terms and concepts in this debate and to also make the case for the way that I have conceptualized the occupational structure to address this debate. I have also included a discussion of methodological matters and statistical sources. Finally, I present the results of my research on employment trends by occupation and trends in unemployment. My general conclusion is that trends in labour market inequality took the form of professionalization, accompanied by high levels of unemployment rather than social polarization. Furthermore, I argue that these findings depend crucially on a precise understanding of the theoretical debate and of exactly what kind of evidence is required to evaluate the competing theories.

In Chapter 3, I examine the changing relationship between racial inequality and the labour market. My general conclusion is that the stronger growth of high-income middle-class jobs and middle-income non-manual jobs benefitted well-educated workers of all races. The result was the dramatic growth of the black middle class, on the one hand, and extremely high unemployment rates among poorly educated African and coloured workers, on the other. The post-*Apartheid* labour market was therefore characterized by contradictory trends with respect to racial inequality: Racial inequality among employed workers was dramatically reduced, while extreme unemployment increased intra-racial inequality among black workers and increased inter-racial inequality, largely between African and white workers.

There are four chapters in Part 2. Chapter 4 is a discussion of the Fordist spatial order of Johannesburg as it was in the early 1970s. This sets the scene for descriptions of the geographical changes that took place in subsequent decades. There is also a discussion of the housing market and my methodological approach.

In Chapter 5, I review the literature on the changing economic geography of Johannesburg, from a Fordist to a post-Fordist spatial order. This entailed the growth of the edge city of Sandton and the excluded ghettos of the southern suburbs. I then present evidence to show that the rise of Sandton as an economic hub increased occupational class inequality by increasing the concentration of the middle class in the northern suburbs of Johannesburg. Furthermore, the northward movement of employment opportunities has increased the labour market spatial mismatch between the excluded ghettos and the new job opportunities increasingly found in Sandton. However, the development of a middle-class edge city and the spatial mismatch has been partially ameliorated by the Government policy of building State-subsidized housing in and near the northern suburbs.

Chapter 6 entails a discussion of the evidence for the transformation of Johannesburg's racial ghettos into excluded ghettos by rising unemployment. I argue that the causes of high unemployment in the excluded ghettos are to be found in the changing occupational structure of employment and the large-scale provision of State-subsidized housing in the erstwhile racial ghettos of the southern suburbs. Contrary to results elsewhere, however, poverty was not concentrated in the racial ghettos by the flight of the black middle class to the edge city of Sandton and elsewhere.

In Chapter 7, I review the literature on racial residential desegregation in Johannesburg and argue that the use of the dissimilarity index to measure segregation over time is inappropriate. I present evidence to show that the extent of racial desegregation in Johannesburg's formerly whites-only neighbourhoods is substantially more than is generally accepted. I also present evidence to show that the geographical pattern of racial desegregation was shaped by the differentiated formerly whites-only housing market and the substantial growth of the black middle class. I summarize the overall methodological and theoretical conclusions in the final chapter.

Part I

DE-INDUSTRIALIZATION AND THE LABOUR MARKET

Chapter 2

THE CHANGING OCCUPATIONAL STRUCTURE: SOCIAL POLARIZATION OR PROFESSIONALIZATION?

The social polarization debate

The social polarization debate has been largely concerned with the question of measuring the changing occupational structure of the labour market and how it has affected the earnings distribution. The debate has therefore drawn upon the scholarly debates concerning the occupational class structure and how it should be conceptualized. In turn, these debates about the occupational class structure have relied upon the International Standard Classification of Occupations (ISCO) (ILO, 2012: p.65), most notably the 'Major Groups' of occupations (Table 2.1).

Table 2.1 The International Standard Classification of Occupations: Major Groups of Occupations

1-Digit Code	Major Group
1	Managers
2	Professionals
3	Technicians & Associate Professionals
4	Clerical Support Workers
5	Services & Sales Workers
6	Skilled Agricultural, Forestry and Fishery Workers
7	Craft and Related Trades Workers
8	Plant and Machine Operators and Assemblers
9	Elementary Occupations
0	Armed Forces Occupations[1]

Source: ILO (2012: p.65).

1 In most applications of the International Standard Classification of Occupations taxonomy, the Armed Forces, which includes only rank-and-file members, are included in 'Services and Sales Workers'.

The idea of the occupational class structure has been developed and used by scholars from very different philosophical and political persuasions. They range from Goldthorpe, who considers himself a 'liberal' proponent of Rational Action Theory (Goldthorpe, 1996) to Wright (1997), who is concerned with debates in Marxist class theory. Although these scholars have produced very different theories of social class, they nonetheless used similar classifications of the occupational class structure.

Goldthorpe's class scheme classifies two of his occupational classes as belonging to the 'salariat' or 'service class' (Goldthorpe and Knight, 2006: p.110). These two occupational classes are the (i) 'Professional, Administrative, and Managerial Employees, Higher Grade' and (ii) 'Professional, Administrative, and Managerial Employees, Lower Grade; Technicians, Higher Grade'. These two social classes are distinguished from all other wage workers on the grounds that employees in these occupational classes have higher and more stable earnings, greater upward career mobility and lower risks of unemployment when compared to other occupations (Goldthorpe and Knight, 2006: p.112). Goldthorpe classifies the remaining occupations into 'independent', 'intermediate' and 'working class' groups. The 'independents' are small employers and self-employed workers. The white-collar 'intermediate' workers are those employed in routine non-manual jobs such as sales, service and clerical workers. The blue-collar 'intermediate' workers are those employed as lower grade technicians and supervisors of manual workers. Finally, the 'working class' are those workers employed in routine, lower grade non-manual jobs and semi-skilled and unskilled manual jobs (Goldthorpe and Knight, 2006: p.110).

Scholars engaged with Marxist class theory have also been concerned to distinguish the high-income 'middle class' from other occupational classes. Marxist theory, which understands the capitalist class structure as a relationship to the means of production, posits two main classes, namely the capitalist class and the working class. In between these major classes, are the 'traditional middle class' or small capitalist class (the *petit bourgeoisie*) of self-employed traders, artisans and professionals and the 'new middle class' of technicians, professionals and managers who are employees rather than being self-employed.

In his neo-Marxist theory of class structure, Wright proposes a classification that is not unlike that of Goldthorpe's class scheme. In his strict classification of the working class, Wright classifies employees in managerial, supervisory, 'expert' professional, semi-professional, technical and craft (or artisan) occupations as belonging to contradictory class locations between the capitalist class and the working class (Wright, 1997: pp.23–6, p.76). In his extended definition of the working class, he included technical, semi-professional and craft occupations in the working class rather than the middle class (Wright, 1997: pp.52–4). All other occupations, namely clerical, sales and service occupations, and machine operators and unskilled labourers, were classified as working class.

These debates over social class have permeated the social polarization debate in different ways. It is therefore helpful to have a good understanding of the concepts used in the occupational class structure and how they relate to concepts of social class. Most notably, European scholars have used the concept of the 'middle class' to describe the highly skilled and high-income managerial, professional and technical occupations. Readers should note that most US scholars use the term 'middle class' to refer to middle-income manual occupations associated with manufacturing activities, specifically Craft and Related Trades Workers and Plant and Machine Operators and Assemblers (Sassen, 2000: p.5). So, when Sassen uses the term 'middle class', she is referring to what European scholars would call middle-income <u>working-class</u> occupations.

The social polarization debate takes as its starting point an earnings structure that distinguishes between high-income, middle-income and low-income occupational classes. The result is that there has been much debate about which occupational groups belong in these three income groups. This is an important debate because it makes an explicit link between earnings and the occupational class structure, rather than simply conceptualizing inequality in terms of earnings alone. The purpose of studying earnings inequality in terms of the occupational class structure is to provide explanations for changes in the earnings distribution. So, for example, the decline of employment in middle-income jobs can be explained by our understanding of how automation and mechanization have replaced many manual craft and machine-operating jobs in manufacturing activities.

In this study, my approach is to treat occupational class as a concept to describe the division of labour rather than to describe social classes. In other words, following Sayer and Walker (1992: p.19), my view is that social divisions that are described by occupations do not constitute a social class division. They argue that Marxist social classes are understood in terms of their ownership or non-ownership of the means of production. By contrast, the Marxist concept of the 'division of labour' describes the occupational class structure, which refers to the different kinds of tasks performed by workers in the labour process (Sayer and Walker, 1992: pp.24–9). So, by studying the occupational class structure, I am not endorsing the Weberian theory of social classes (see Goldthorpe and Knight, 2006), which treats occupational groups as different social classes while ignoring relationships of ownership (Sayer and Walker, 1992: p.27).

To provide an example, the differences between professionals and machine operators should rather be understood in terms of the Marxist concept of the 'division of labour'. The division of labour can describe how and why professionals have more control over their work and are able to demand better working conditions than machine operators. It is therefore not necessary to burden the Marxist concept of social class with these kinds of divisions between workers. Instead, social classes and the division of labour should be treated as distinct social structures that interact with each other. I have therefore taken the somewhat unorthodox practice of referring to all employees as 'workers'.

Conceptualizing high-income, middle-income and low-income occupations

The initial contributions to the debate by Friedmann and Wolff (1982) and Sassen-Koob (1984) conceptualized managerial, professional and technical occupations as high-income jobs. Middle-income occupations were conceptualized as all manual jobs in the manufacturing sector while low-income jobs were conceptualized as unskilled jobs in the service sector (Friedmann and Wolff, 1982: pp.320–2; Sassen-Koob, 1984: pp.157 and 162). Friedmann and Wolff did not describe the nature of these low-paid service occupations but Sassen argues that they entail jobs such as cleaners, residential building attendants, errand runners and low-wage jobs in gourmet food and other specialty shops (Sassen-Koob, 1984: p.157). The employment growth of low and high-income jobs was contrasted with the decline in the number of middle-income jobs, which are described as blue-collar (manual) jobs in the manufacturing sector rather than in solely occupational terms (Friedmann and Wolff, 1982: p.320; Sassen-Koob, 1984: p.146). In another contribution to this debate, Harrison and Bluestone (1988: p.71) argued that low-paid jobs included workers such as cashiers, janitors, truck drivers, waiters, nurse's aides, orderlies, kindergarten and elementary school teachers, chambermaids, doormen, department store clerks [i.e. sales workers] and building custodians.

These early contributions to the debate were therefore clear about the composition of the high-skilled and high-income occupational groups, namely the managerial, professional and technical occupations. However, there was less clarity on the composition of the middle and low-income occupational groups. Initially, middle-income occupations were argued to be manual or blue-collar jobs that are strongly represented in the manufacturing sector. The assumption of the social polarization argument was that the occupational distribution of the service sector was more polarized than the manufacturing sector that it was replacing. On the strength of this assumption, research tended to focus on the growth of low-income service-sector occupations rather than on middle-income service occupations. In most contributions, the implicit assumption was that, apart from highly paid managerial, professional and technical occupations, most service sector jobs were low-income occupations. This assumption was then used to classify the major occupational groups into high-, middle- and low-income groups. Since statistics on the occupations of employees are usually classified according to the International Standard Classification of Occupations (ISCO) (ILO, 2012), this resulted in the following classification of major groups of occupations:

1. The major occupational groups of 'Managers', 'Professionals' and 'Technicians and Associate Professionals' were classified as high-income occupations.
2. The groups of skilled and semi-skilled manual occupations, namely, 'Craft and Related Trades Workers' and 'Plant and Machine Operators and Assemblers' were classified as middle-income workers, as were the non-manual occupational group of 'Clerical Support Workers'.
3. The major groups of 'Elementary Occupations' (which include unskilled manual occupations found predominantly in the services sector, such as domestic servants and office cleaners) and 'Services and Sales Workers' were classified as a low-income group. (Baum, 1997; Chiu and Lui, 2004).

This classification of 'Services and Sales Workers' as a low-income group by many scholars is controversial. They were probably taking their cue from earlier contributions, which argued that certain sales jobs, such as 'cashier' and 'salespersons' were low-income rather than middle-income jobs (Harrison and Bluestone, 1988: p.71; Sassen, 1998: p.143). Whatever the reason, the result of including the employment of 'Services and Sales Workers' in their calculation of low-income job growth had significant consequences: it meant that these studies produced results that showed more polarization of the occupational and income structure than would have been the case if this occupational group was classified as middle-income.

So scholars who researched employment trends in Hong Kong (Chiu and Lui, 2004) and Sydney (Baum, 1997) interpreted their evidence to argue that social polarization, rather than professionalization, had taken place. Conversely, Clark and McNicholas (1996: p.62) argued that if the employment numbers of sales workers were classified as middle-income, then their results for employment change in Los Angeles revealed that professionalization had taken place. Similarly, Hamnett's review of Atzema and de Smidt's (1992) research on the Randstad, argued that professionalization had taken place, even when it was assumed that 'commercial' (sales) and 'services' occupations were low-income jobs rather than middle-income jobs (Hamnett, 1994: pp.410–12). Finally, Debnar *et al.* (2014: p.30), in their study of Tokyo, defined sales and service workers as low-income workers and found large increases in low-income employment but not in high-income employment. Another important contribution to the debate – finding evidence in favour of occupational professionalization – also classified sales workers as middle-income earners. At the same time, however, these authors expressed some doubt as to whether at least some of the workers in these occupational groups were low-income earners (Esping-Andersen *et al.*, 1993: p.46).

This question was addressed directly by Borel-Saladin and Crankshaw, whose research on Cape Town showed that the average earnings of 'Services and Sales Workers' was slightly higher than those of middle-income 'Craft and Related Trades Workers' and 'Plant and Machinery Operators and Assemblers' (Borel-Saladin and Crankshaw, 2009: p.655). Reviewing the findings presented by Baum (1997) and Chiu and Lui (2004), Borel-Saladin and Crankshaw argued that these studies made the mistake of assuming that the earnings of 'Services and Sales Workers' were closer to the earnings of low-income 'Elementary Workers', when their own evidence showed that their average earnings were closer to those of middle-income, blue-collar workers rather than low-income elementary workers (Borel-Saladin and Crankshaw, 2009: p.649; Hamnett, 2010: p.24; Hamnett, 2012: p.365).

Later research on greater Johannesburg presented further evidence that the earnings of 'Services and Sales Workers' mostly fell into the 4th to 8th earnings deciles, rather than into the lowest three earnings deciles (Crankshaw, 2017: p.1618). These findings for greater Johannesburg also demonstrated that routine white-collar workers typical of the service sector, namely 'Clerical Support Workers' and 'Services and Sales Workers' earned roughly the same as middle-income blue-collar (or manual) jobs typical of the manufacturing sector, namely 'Craft and Related Trades Workers' and 'Plant and Machine Operators and Assemblers'. The major occupational group that dominated employment in the lowest three earnings deciles was that of 'Elementary Occupations' (Crankshaw, 2017: p.1618).

Earnings polarization and occupational polarization

What evidence was advanced in support of this kind of occupational and income polarization at this stage of the debate? Friedmann and Wolff (1982: p.322) provided some estimates of the numbers employed in these occupational classes but did not present evidence on changes in their size over time. Sassen provided evidence of social polarization by citing Stanback and Noyelle (1984) whose research showed evidence of earnings polarization by economic sector. Their research on some major US cities over the period from 1960 to 1976 argued that earnings polarization was largely due to the growth of service sector employment. Harrison and Bluestone (1988: pp.70–1) relied on secondary evidence of projected employment growth to argue that there was more growth of low-income jobs than high-income jobs, which is obviously not evidence that both high-income and low-income jobs were increasing more than middle-income jobs.

So, at this initial stage of the debate, there was still no clear conceptualization of the nature of middle- and low-income occupations, and no evidence that there was occupational polarization of employment. There was evidence of the polarization of earnings, but there was no research to show that this change in the earnings distribution was due largely to changes in the occupation structure of employment.

Sassen's later contributions to this debate did not provide evidence of occupational polarization. Instead, she presented evidence of household earnings polarization and of a decline in average individual wages over the 1970s and 1980s (Sassen, 2000: pp.125–9). In the case of the former, evidence of earnings polarization does not prove that there was occupational polarization. Earnings polarization may have a variety of causes, of which occupational polarization is merely one. In the case of the latter, evidence of declining individual earnings is evidence of growing poverty and not of earnings and occupational polarization. In other words, increasing poverty is evidence of the growing proportion of poor households rather than evidence of growing numbers of poor and rich households. As Hamnett (2010: p.20) has noted, the concepts of inequality in earnings (the earnings gap) and social polarization are not interchangeable.

So even a decade after the social polarization hypotheses were first advanced, firm evidence concerning the occupational polarization of employment, which was the proposed cause of earnings polarization, had not been produced. The main weakness of these earlier contributions was not only that the authors failed to produce any evidence at all, but also that the nature of the evidence did not correspond to the concepts entailed in the social polarization hypothesis.

By the 1980s, there were some important contributions to this debate that presented evidence that favoured the theory of professionalization rather than social polarization. Hamnett's (1986: p.394) research showed that between 1961 and 1981, employment among managers, professionals and associate professionals grew dramatically, compared with a decline in almost all other occupations (except for relatively small employment growth among non-professional, self-employed workers). Hamnett's later research on London covered the period from 1981 to 1991, where he found a similar professionalizing trend in employment. Employment in managerial, professional and semi-professional occupations grew in absolute terms, while employment in all other occupations declined (Hamnett, 2003: pp.65–6). Similar results were found for New York City over the period from 1970 to 1980, where employment among managers and professionals grew substantially in absolute terms, compared with declining employment in all other occupational groups (except for relatively small employment growth in service occupations). On the basis of these results, Bailey and Waldinger (1991: pp.51–2) concluded that 'The overall trend was toward occupational upgrading, not polarization'.

The results of these studies of New York and London presented solid evidence in support of professionalization because they were not encumbered by large increases in sales and services occupations. The numbers of clerical and sales workers had declined in absolute terms and the small amount of growth in service jobs was so much less than the growth in managerial, professional and semi-professional jobs, that it could not be considered a polarizing trend, even if such jobs were conceptualized as low-income occupations.

Many scholars who made later contributions to this debate did not pay attention to this early conceptualization of the relationship between the major groups of occupations and earnings. The result was that they conceptualized occupations in a manner that was entirely inconsistent with the social polarization theory. Tai tested the social polarization hypothesis in Singapore, Hong Kong and Taipei and concluded that the occupational structure in these cities was undergoing a trend of professionalization rather than polarization. However, these results were produced by a classification in which 'Managers' and 'Professionals' were defined as high-income earners, 'Technicians and Associate Professionals' as middle-income earners and all other occupational groups as low-income earners (Tai, 2006: pp.1747–9). This classification therefore places Sassen's middle-income manual occupations in the same group as her low-income service sector occupations. It also classifies technicians and associate professionals as middle-income rather than high-income occupations. In a different study of Taipei, Tai (2005: p.157) followed a similar classification. The results of these studies therefore do not coherently address the social polarization theory.

More recently, van Ham *et al.* (2020) presented evidence on employment trends between 1980 and 2011 in New York, London and Tokyo. On the basis of their findings, they also argued that the occupational structure in these three cities had undergone professionalization rather than social polarization: in all three cities, employment in high-income occupations increased substantially in relative terms, whereas relative employment in low-income jobs declined. Employment in middle-income jobs declined slightly in relative terms in both New York and London but increased slightly in Tokyo.

Van Ham *et al.* (2020) relied on earnings evidence from sample surveys to classify occupations into high-, middle- and low-income groups. Employment in these occupations was then measured using census data. The classification of occupations into high-, middle- and low-income occupations was done using a combination of occupational status (as defined by the International Standard Classification of Occupations hierarchy), earnings and the consistency of the relationship between earnings and status for each city over time. So these authors used status and earnings as the basis for deciding on the cut-offs between high-, middle- and low-income occupations. The flaw in this approach is that it ignored the valuable way that Sassen conceptualized the changing occupational structure. Sassen's argument highlights that social polarization entails the transformation of the occupational structure – from one characterized by large numbers of middle-income workers (engaged in manual jobs typical of factory work in the manufacturing sector) to one characterized by growing numbers of higher-income workers such as managers and professionals on the one hand, and lower-income service workers on the other. It is perfectly clear from her reasoning that middle-income workers should be conceptualized not simply in terms of the statistics of the earnings distribution, but in terms of the occupational definition of craft workers and machine operators and assemblers.

The earnings criteria used by Van Ham *et al.* (2020: Supplementary information) meant that they classified craft workers and machine operators and assemblers in different ways. Sometimes they are middle-income workers, but mostly they are low-income workers, depending on the earnings of the sample surveys for the relevant years. The result of this conceptualization is that their measurements do not adequately test Sassen's theory as far as the growth of employment in low-income service occupations is concerned. This is because the growth in low-income jobs is not consistently isolated from the growth of middle-income manufacturing jobs.

This review of the way that scholars have classified the major occupational groups into high-, middle- and low-income groups demonstrates the need for a logically coherent classification that is consistent with both the terms of the social polarization debate and the earnings evidence.

Absolute and relative changes in the occupational structure of employment

In 1994, an important contribution to this debate was made by Hamnett (1994) that provided substantial evidence of changes in the occupational structure in the global city of Randstad in Holland.[2] Hamnett's contribution also improved the precision of Sassen's concept of social polarization, which was ambiguous about whether social polarization entailed relative or absolute changes in

2 An earlier study by Hamnett did present evidence on occupational restructuring in London, but it was not a direct engagement in the social polarization debate (Hamnett, 1986).

employment. On his understanding of Sassen's hypothesis, Hamnett argued that social polarization should be understood as the absolute rather than the relative growth of employment at the opposite poles of the earnings and occupational distribution (Hamnett, 1994: p.405). This might seem a trivial distinction, but it is not. Relative polarization entails the increased percentage share of low- and high-income jobs and a declining share of middle-income jobs. This relative measurement of polarization can be the result of the absolute decline in middle-income jobs, with no change at all in the absolute numbers of low- and high-income jobs. Relative polarization therefore does not conform to Sassen's original proposal that social polarization is caused by absolute employment growth in the service sector (Sassen-Koob, 1984: 139). This version of Sassen's definition of social polarization is clearly making a case for absolute employment growth: 'Along with a sharp decline in the number of middle-income blue- and white-collar jobs, there has been a modest increase in the number of high-wage professional and managerial jobs and a vast expansion in the supply of low-wage jobs' (Sassen, 1998: p.46).

Many contributions to this debate have ignored this distinction and have presented statistical evidence of relative polarization, which is not a direct test of Sassen's hypothesis. Studies that used relative employment change as evidence of social polarization include Esping-Anderson *et al.* (1993), Clark and McNichols (1996) and Kloosterman (1996). Studies that used absolute employment trends include Baum's studies of Sydney (Baum, 1997) and Singapore (Baum, 1999), Bailey and Waldinger's (1991) study of New York, Chiu and Lui's (2004) study of Hong Kong and Van Ham *et al.*'s (2020) study of New York, London and Tokyo. Clearly, if Sassen's theory of social polarization is to be adequately tested, it should be done by measuring absolute rather than relative employment trends.

Earnings polarization

Some authors have tested the social polarization hypothesis by producing evidence concerning the polarization (or not) of the earnings distribution rather than of the occupational distribution (Kloosterman, 1996: p.472). Such studies obviously do not address the claim that the polarizing earnings distribution is caused by the polarizing occupational distribution. The social polarization theory is not simply concerned with the changing distribution of earnings. It is a theory that is concerned with the explanation of the changing distribution of earnings through reference to the changing division of labour. In other words, the theory proposes that the polarization of the earnings distribution is brought about by changes in the occupational structure of employment. It does not, for example, propose that the growth of low-wage jobs was caused by the decline of wages for middle-income jobs, thereby transforming them into low-wage jobs. The social polarization theory should therefore be tested by examining the employment trends of occupational groups that are classified according to both their economic activities and their earnings.

Method and sources

If a theory is to be tested with new evidence, then it should be obvious that such evidence must be appropriate to the claims made by the theory. As I have discussed in the introduction, the social polarization debate should be tested by evidence that directly addresses the following claims (see Borel-Saladin, 2012: p.27).

1. Social polarization is the phenomenon in which the occupational structure becomes polarized by the absolute employment growth of high-income and low-income occupations and the absolute decline of middle-income jobs.
2. Middle-income jobs are those manual occupations that are usually associated with manufacturing production, namely skilled artisans (craft and related trades workers), and semi-skilled plant and machine operators and assemblers. Low-income jobs are those occupations that earn less than middle-income manual jobs. High-income jobs are those occupations that earn more than middle-income, manual jobs.
3. Social polarization is caused by deindustrialization, which is the decline of employment in manufacturing activities and the rise of employment in service activities. This cause is statistical in nature: because the occupational structure of service sector employment is more polarized than that of the manufacturing sector, employment growth in the former and employment decline in the latter will result in an overall trend towards income and occupational polarization.

Sources of labour market statistics

This chapter entails a case study of employment trends in the South African Province of Gauteng, which comprises the metropolitan cities of Johannesburg, Tshwane and Ekurhuleni and the smaller district municipalities of Sedibeng and West Rand. There are two reasons why this larger, greater Johannesburg boundary was selected for study rather than the boundary of the City of Johannesburg. The first reason is that Johannesburg is functionally part of all the cities in Gauteng: The Gauteng Province is composed almost entirely of a continuous urban conurbation that is linked by railways and motorways. Gauteng is also geographically isolated from the other major urban centres and therefore forms a single, geographically contiguous urban area. In this geographical context, employment trends in Johannesburg could, in principle, be caused by geographical changes within the Province, such as the movement of certain kinds of jobs from Johannesburg to Pretoria. This problem was avoided by studying employment trends in the whole Province. The second reason is that the employment statistics provided by earlier population censuses and all the household surveys do not contain variables that indicate the city in which the household was enumerated or sampled. Instead, only the Magisterial District or the Province of residence is supplied in the data files.[3] Furthermore, the sample design of the household surveys does not allow for statistical generalization for geographical areas within the provinces.

The sources of employment statistics are the official population censuses and household surveys. The population censuses are for the years 1970, 1980, 1991, 1996, 2001 and 2011. The household surveys are for the years 1994 to 2011. The data for both the population censuses and household surveys and relevant documentation were provided by the DataFirst Research Unit at the University of Cape Town.[4] Both these sources of data are in the form of case-by-variable matrixes that allow for the recoding of variable categories and the production of cross-tabulations.

Apart from the 1980 population census and one part of the 1970 census, the census data provided by DataFirst are in the form of 5 per cent or 10 per cent samples that were drawn from the results of the full count. These are therefore very large samples that fall within the range of 200,000 to 400,000 individual cases. As such, they provide high levels of statistical reliability and precision. The household surveys are sample surveys with smaller sample sizes. These samples were designed to provide statistical estimates at the level of individual provinces and sample sizes for Gauteng range from roughly 3,500 to 20,000 individuals. These large sample sizes were achieved by aggregating the bi-annual and quarterly surveys for each year. These samples are probability samples, which mean that the statistical counts in the samples can be extrapolated to the population of Gauteng. These statistical estimates, being based on probability samples, are subject to random error. However, the extent of this random error can be calculated as the standard error at specific levels of reliability (Moser and Kalton, 1971). All the statistical results presented here are provided with the standard error at the 95 per cent level of probability. This is shown in graphs as the 'confidence interval', which is the measure of the standard errors on both sides of the statistical estimate.

Since the boundaries of the Gauteng only came into existence in 1994, population census data for earlier years were obtained by collating data for the Magisterial Districts that fall within the modern boundaries of Gauteng. Magisterial Districts are areas under the jurisdiction of a magistrate. These jurisdictional districts have been used by the state as the geographical units for the presentation of population census statistics. Because their boundaries remained more-or-less stable over many years, Magisterial Districts are best suited for comparing different censuses (StatsSA, 2007). In the case of Gauteng, using the Magisterial District boundaries provided by Statistics South Africa, I have defined the boundaries of Gauteng with the Magisterial Districts of Alberton, Benoni, Boksburg, Brakpan, Bronkhorstspruit, Cullinan, Germiston, Heidelberg, Johannesburg (including Soweto), Kempton Park, Krugersdorp, Nigel, Oberholzer, Pretoria, Randburg,

3 The 'Subplace' or neighbourhood of the households were provided only in the Supercross Tables supplied for the 1996, 2001 and 2011 Population Censuses. See chapters 5 to 7 for an analysis of neighbourhood-level statistics.

4 https://www.datafirst.uct.ac.za/

Randfontein, Roodepoort, Shoshanguve, Springs, Vanderbijl Park, Vereeniging, Westonaria and Wonderboom.

The population censuses from 1970 to 1991 did not use the International Standard Classification of Occupations to measure employment by occupation. Nonetheless, the occupations were classified into many narrowly defined groups that were sufficiently detailed to allow me to recode them into Major Groups of occupations.

The household survey data were in the form of the Post-Apartheid Labour Market Series (PALMS) Version 2.1 dataset. This is a cross-sectional data file created by merging the results from thirty-nine national sample surveys of households conducted by Statistics South Africa (StatsSA) from 1994 to 2012. They comprise the October Household Surveys from 1994 to 1999, the biannual Labour Force Surveys from 2000 to 2007 and the Quarterly Labour Force Surveys from 2008 to 2012 (Kerr, *et al.*, 2014; Kerr and Wittenberg, 2020). The Post-Apartheid Labour Market Series data file is preferable to the original survey data files because it includes: (1) corrected sample weights that allow for more precise longitudinal measurement of trends in employment and income; and (2) a consistent measure of income, which was lacking in the original surveys (Kerr, 2013). The sample sizes for Gauteng range from about 3,000 to 4,500 individual cases for each survey, which provides adequately precise annual statistical estimates with a reliability of 95 per cent. In years where more than one survey was conducted, the survey results were averaged to provide one estimate per year. As a result, the sample sizes for these years were much larger and provided greater precision and reliability.

These statistics on employment are based on household interviews and are not surveys of businesses or institutions. The labour market statistics therefore include all individuals who pursued an economic activity in the week prior to the surveys. So, the statistics include all full-time, part-time, casual and temporary employment as well as self-employment and informal sector activities.

The deindustrialization of employment in greater Johannesburg

The employed workforce of greater Johannesburg has undergone substantial deindustrialization over the past forty years. According to the evidence from the population censuses, manufacturing employment grew strongly throughout the 1970s, peaking in 1980. Thereafter, manufacturing employment declined precipitously for the subsequent two decades (Figure 2.1 and Table 2.2). By contrast, service sector employment grew steadily throughout this period. After 2001, manufacturing employment increased again but did not catch up with the high and growing levels of service sector employment. In relative terms, employment in the manufacturing sector therefore declined from 25 per cent of all employment in 1980 to only 10 per cent in 2011 (Table 2.3). Unlike many other deindustrializing cities, Johannesburg was once dominated by a large gold-mining industry. As late as the 1950s, the mining and quarrying sector was the single

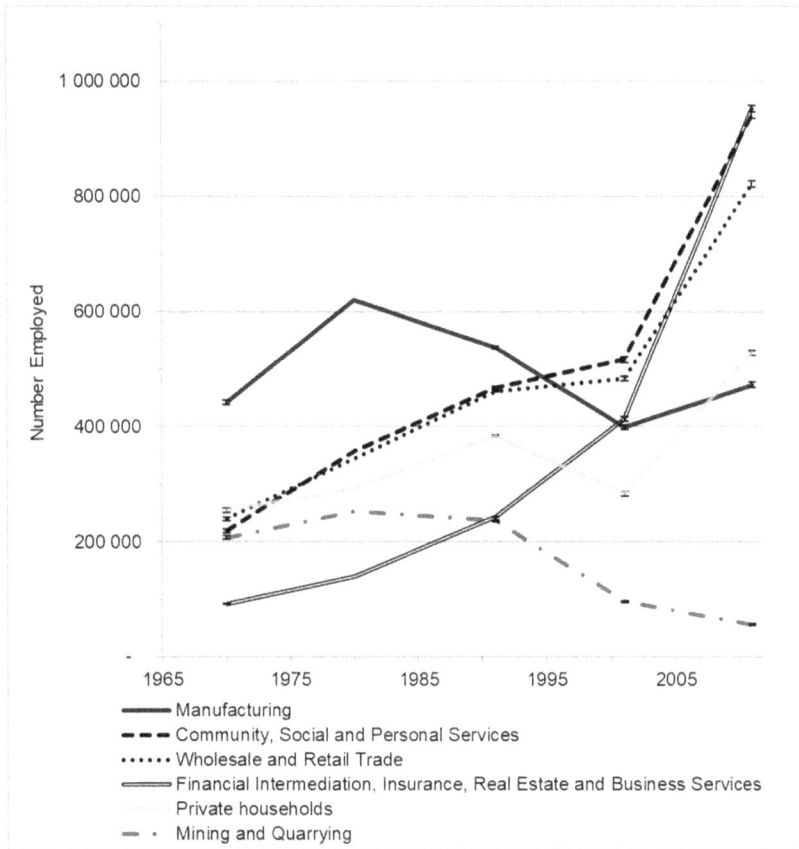

Figure 2.1 Employment by Selected Economic Sectors in Gauteng, 1970–2011[5]
Error bars indicate the 95 per cent confidence intervals.
Sources: Author's Analysis of Population Census Data Files, DataFirst Research Unit, University of Cape Town. See Table 2.2.

largest sector by employment (Crankshaw and Parnell, 2004: p.357). However, employment in this sector declined steadily as the Witwatersrand gold mines were depleted of gold ore and eventually closed.

Over the same period, employment in all service sectors grew substantially. Absolute employment in the large economic sectors of Community, Social and Personal Services and Wholesale and Retail trade tripled between 1970 and 2011

5 The data points for the 1996 Population Census are omitted in this graph because they do not fit the long-term trends and are therefore probably wrong because such increases and decreases over a relatively short period are impossible. Also, they make reading the trends difficult. Refer to the tables for the 1996 employment estimates.

Table 2.2 Employment by Main Economic Sector in Gauteng, 1970–2011

Main Economic Sector	1970	1980	1991	1996	2001	2011
Agriculture, Hunting, Forestry and Fishing	74,590	67,040	66,946	35,732	67,988	67,625
Mining and Quarrying	207,273	253,185	236,452	54,497	96,671	56,641
Manufacturing	441,661	619,680	537,447	322,330	399,142	472,829
Electricity, Gas and Water Supply	16,865	23,103	33,977	34,266	21,763	37,413
Construction	112,724	113,191	156,440	154,199	161,283	359,939
Wholesale and Retail Trade	239,624	345,023	461,600	351,789	483,148	821,995
Transport, Storage and Communication	90,867	132,093	169,402	166,845	170,792	323,095
Financial Intermediation, Insurance, Real Estate and Business Services	92,271	140,805	243,091	323,790	412,941	951,870
Community, Social and Personal Services	218,833	357,873	467,912	416,486	516,439	940,617
Private Households	254,833	293,942	384,463	319,598	283,252	527,899
Activity Inadequately Described or Other	75,665	96,259	100,855	274,348	283,076	4,129
Total	1,825,206	2,442,194	2,858,585	2,453,878	2,896,495	4,564,052

Sources: Author's Analysis of Population Census Data Files, DataFirst Research Unit, University of Cape Town.

(Table 2.2). The most dramatic increase was in the Finance, Insurance, Real Estate and Business Services sector, in which employment grew ten-fold. So whereas the Manufacturing sector was by far the largest employer in 1970, by 2011, it was the fourth-largest economic sector (Table 2.2). Correspondingly, whereas Financial Intermediation, Insurance, Real Estate and Business Services were the fourth smallest employer in 1970, by 2011 it was the largest. Other important service sectors, namely Wholesale and Retail Trade and Community, Social and Personal Services, each employed only half the numbers of the Manufacturing sector in 1970. By 2011, they each employed roughly twice as many workers as the Manufacturing sector (Table 2.2).

This evidence shows that economic activities in greater Johannesburg have been substantially restructured since the 1970s. This restructuring can be described as deindustrialization, with the accompanied rise of employment in the service sector, most notably in the Financial Intermediation, Insurance, Real Estate and Business Services sector. This decline in Manufacturing employment was also accompanied by the decline of employment in the other major goods-producing sector of Mining and Quarrying. According to the social polarization theory, deindustrialization

Table 2.3 Percentage Distribution of Employment by Main Economic Sector in Gauteng, 1970–2011

Main Economic Sector	1970	1980	1991	1996	2001	2011
Agriculture, Hunting, Forestry and Fishing	4	3	2	1	2	1
Mining and Quarrying	11	10	8	2	3	1
Manufacturing	24	25	19	13	14	10
Electricity, Gas and Water Supply	1	1	1	1	1	1
Construction	6	5	5	6	6	8
Wholesale and Retail Trade	13	14	16	14	17	18
Transport, Storage and Communication	5	5	6	7	6	7
Financial Intermediation, Insurance, Real Estate and Business Services	5	6	9	13	14	21
Community, Social and Personal Services	12	15	16	17	18	21
Private Households	14	12	13	13	10	12
Activity Inadequately Described or Other	4	4	4	11	10	0
Total	100	100	100	100	100	100

Sources: Author's Analysis of Population Census Data Files, Data First Research Unit, University of Cape Town.

Note that the totals do not always add up because of rounding off.[6]

6 The estimates are rounded off because all the data files, except for the 1980 Population Census, were composed of samples rather than full counts. The estimates must therefore be multiplied by sample weights that are accurate to many decimal points with the result that the estimates are decimal or fractional numbers and not integers.

results in the social polarization of the occupational and income structure of employment. So, with such dramatic de-industrialisation, we should expect to find that the occupational structure of greater Johannesburg has undergone social polarization, with employment growth in low- and high-income occupations, and a decline or at least stagnation in employment in middle-income occupations.

Relating occupational groups to the earnings distribution

The first step in generating statistics to test the social polarization theory must be to establish the relationship between occupational groups and the distribution of earnings. Scholars who have used statistics to measure changes in the occupational structure have relied on occupational classifications with about six to ten main groups of occupations (Table 2.4). Most official employment statistics rely on this kind of occupational classification that is roughly the same as the International Standard Classification of Occupations (ILO, 2012: p.65). This classification has great utility because it presents statistical trends while simultaneously providing descriptions of these occupational groups. A more finely tuned occupational classification with a great many occupational groups would not present useful results on employment trends because there would be too many trends to make any sense of changes in the occupational structure.

One might reasonably ask why the social polarization theory should not be tested simply with earnings data. The answer – as discussed above – is that the social polarization theory is not solely a theory of the polarization of earnings. This theory also proposes that the polarization of earnings is caused by changes in the occupational structure. So, for this reason, research that tests this theory should entail a study of how changes in the occupational structure are related to changes in the distribution of earnings.

Authors who have evaluated the social polarization hypothesis by using this occupational classification generally classify Managers, Professionals, Technicians and Associate Professionals as high-income workers. Skilled Agricultural, Forestry and Fishery Workers, Craft and Related Trades Workers and Plant and Machine Operators and Assemblers are classified as middle-income workers. Finally, Elementary Workers are classified as low-income workers. The position of Clerical Support Workers and Services and Sales Workers is usually debated as being either a middle-income or low-income occupational group. Scholars have usually based this classification on the average incomes of these Major Groups of occupations.

The question of whether Services and Sales Workers are a middle-income or low-income group is especially pertinent because some scholars have argued that this is the occupational group that has seen the growth of low-income workers that earn less than middle-income factory workers. Since this is an occupational group with large numbers of workers, scholars who classify it as a low-income group may be over-estimating the growth of low-wage employment. Conversely, those

Table 2.4 A Comparison of Occupational Class Schemes

ISCO Classification of 1-digit Major Groups (ILO, 2012)	United Kingdom Socio-Economic Groups (Rose and Pevalin, 2005: p.60)	Hamnett (2003)	Clark and McNicholas (1996)
1 Managers	1.1 Employers in Industry (large establishments)	Managers	Professional Technical & Administrative
	1.2 Managers (large establishments)		
	2.1 Employers in Industry (small establishments)		
	2.2 Managers (small establishments)		
	13 Farmers (employers and managers)		
2 Professionals	3 Professional Workers (self-employed)	Professionals	
	4 Professional Workers (employees)		
3 Technicians & Associate Professionals	5.1 Intermediate non-manual workers (ancillary workers and artists)	Intermediate	Clerical
4 Clerical Support Workers	5.2 Intermediate non-manual workers (foremen and supervisors non-manual)		
5 Services & Sales Workers	6 Junior non-manual workers		Service
	7 Personal service workers		Sales
6 Skilled Agricultural, Forestry and Fishery Workers	15 Agricultural workers	Semi-Skilled Manual	Skilled
	14 Farmers (own account)	Skilled Manual	
7 Craft and Related Trades Workers	8 Foremen and supervisors (manual)		
	9 Skilled manual workers		
	12 Own-account workers other than professional		
8 Plant and Machine Operators and Assemblers	10 Semi-skilled manual workers	Semi-Skilled Manual	Unskilled
9 Elementary Occupations	11 Unskilled manual workers	Unskilled Manual	Household Service
0 Armed Forces Occupations	16 Members of armed forces	Armed Forces	

who classify it as a middle-income group may be under-estimating the growth of low-income employment.

This question can be resolved by calculating the average pre-tax earnings of occupational groups at a very fine '4-Digit' or 'Unit Group' classification. The result gives over 300 'Unit Group' occupations that can then be categorized into deciles according to their average earnings.[7] These deciles can then be cross-tabulated with the Major Groups of occupations to show the distribution of employment in the Major Groups across the earnings deciles. The results will then show the distribution of Services and Sales Workers across the earnings deciles. This will be much more accurate than calculating the average earnings for the whole Major Group.

The results from the Post-Apartheid Labour Market Series for 2011 show that almost all employment (84 per cent) in manual occupations associated with the manufacturing sector that are claimed to be middle-income jobs fell into the middle four earnings deciles, namely deciles four to seven (Figure 2.2). Correspondingly, almost half (45 per cent) of all middle-income employment was in the occupations of Craft and Related Trades Workers and Plant and Machine Operators and Assemblers. On these grounds, it is therefore reasonable to argue that other occupations falling within earnings deciles four to seven should also be considered middle-income occupations. These other occupations are in the Major Groups of Clerical Support Workers and Services and Sales Workers, which make up 29 and 15 per cent of all middle-income employment, respectively. The remaining employment in the middle-income deciles is made up of Technicians and Associate Professionals (7 per cent) and Elementary Occupations (4 per cent) (Figure 2.2).

Almost all employment (91 per cent) in the Major Groups of Managers, Professionals and Technicians and Associate Professionals fell into the highest three earnings deciles, namely deciles eight to ten. Correspondingly, employment in these two Major Groups contributed 88 per cent to all employment in the highest three earnings deciles. The remaining employment of about 11 per cent was in the Major Groups of Clerical Support Workers and Services and Sales Workers, which fell mostly into decile eight (Figure 2.2). The most numerous specific Unit Group occupations were secretaries, statistical finance clerks, production clerks and firefighters.

Those occupations that earned less than middle-income manual occupations fell into earnings deciles one to three. Most employment (68 per cent) in these low-income deciles was in the Major Group of Elementary Workers, which is mainly composed of domestic workers and gardeners, street vendors, porters, office cleaners, garbage collectors and other unskilled manual labourers

---

7 Average earnings for each Unit Group occupation were calculated by using all the surveys from 1996 to 2011. This method was used because it gave the most consistent results and also ensured that every Unit Group occupation had earnings data to allow the calculation of an average.

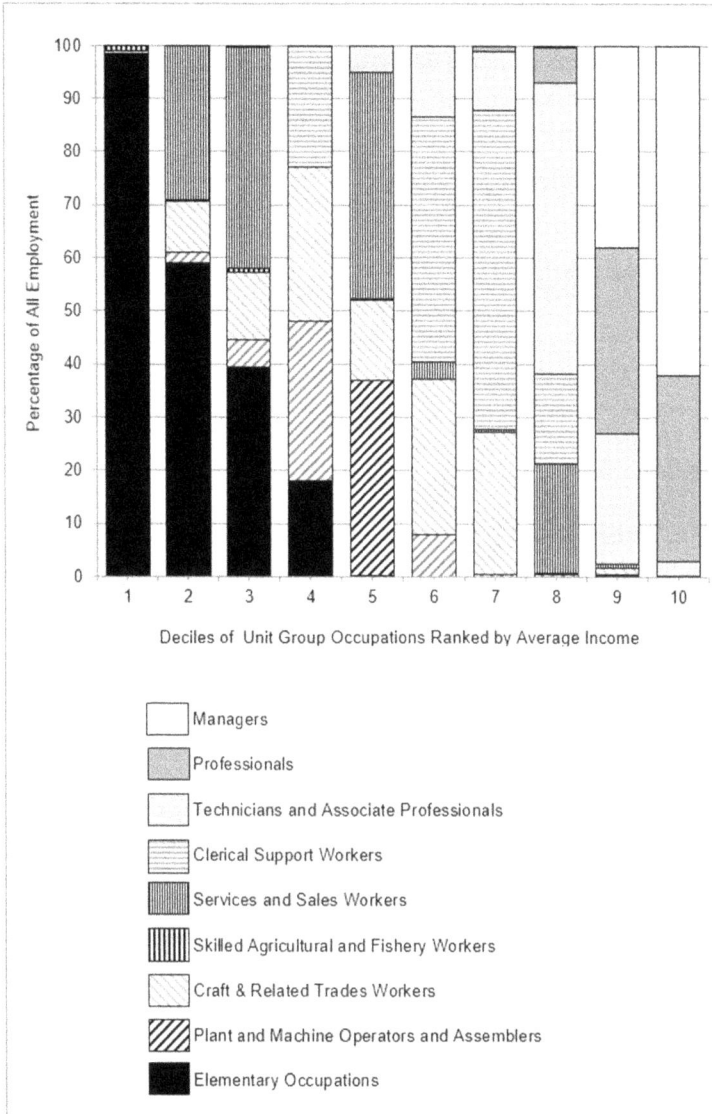

Figure 2.2 Percentage Employment in Major Groups of Occupations by Pre-Tax Earnings Decile, Gauteng 2011

Sources: Author's Analysis of the Post-Apartheid Labour Market Series Data Files, DataFirst Research Unit, University of Cape Town. See Table 2.5.

(Table 2.6). Correspondingly, almost all (93 per cent) employment in the Major Group of Elementary Workers fell into these low-income deciles (Table 2.7). In addition, almost all employment (82 per cent) in the Major Group of Skilled Agricultural and Fishery Workers fell into the low-income deciles.

Table 2.5 Percentage Employment in Major Groups of Occupations by Deciles Based on Average Earnings of Unit Group Occupations, Gauteng 2011

	Earnings Deciles Based on the Average Earnings of Unit Group Occupations									
	1	2	3	4	5	6	7	8	9	10
Managers	0	0	0	0	0	0	0	0	38	62
Professionals	0	0	0	0	0	0	1	7	35	35
Technicians and Associate Professionals	0	0	0	0	5	13	11	55	25	3
Clerical Support Workers	0	0	0	23	0	46	60	17	0	0
Services and Sales Workers	0	29	42	0	43	3	1	21	1	0
Skilled Agricultural and Fishery Workers	1	0	1	0	0	0	0	0	0	0
Craft & Related Trades Workers	0	10	13	29	15	29	27	0	1	0
Plant and Machine Operators and Assemblers	0	2	5	30	37	8	0	0	0	0
Elementary Occupations	99	59	39	18	0	0	0	0	0	0
Total	100	100	100	100	100	100	100	100	100	100

Sources: Author's Analysis of the Post-Apartheid Labour Market Series Data Files, DataFirst Research Unit, University of Cape Town.

So these results support the argument that employment in low-income occupations can be measured by using the Major Groups of Elementary Workers and Skilled Agricultural and Fishery Workers. However, a substantial percentage of low-income occupations (22 per cent) were in the Major Group of Services and Sales Workers. The remaining employment in low-income occupations (9 per cent) was in the Major Groups of Skilled Craft and Related and Plant and Machine Operators and Assemblers (Table 2.6).

These results therefore suggest that employment classified by the Major Groups of occupations can be used to measure trends in the earnings distribution while simultaneously providing a description of the economic activities provided by occupational descriptions. However, there is substantial employment among Services and Sales Workers that falls into the low-income deciles. Therefore, using this Major Group to estimate employment in middle-income jobs will under-estimate the amount of employment growth in low-income jobs. This flaw, which is caused by measuring employment by Major Groups of occupations, can be solved by measuring employment by deciles of the average earnings of Unit Group occupations instead of by Major Groups of occupations. However, it is methodologically important to group these earnings deciles into low-, middle- and high-income groups rather than simply to measure employment trends by earnings decile. One reason for doing this, as I argued above, is to ensure that the

Table 2.6 Employment in Major Groups of Occupations by High, Middle and Low Deciles Based on Average Pre-Tax Earnings of Unit Group Occupations, Gauteng 2011 (Column Percentage Distribution)

	Low-Income Occupations (Deciles 1–3)	Middle-Income Occupations (Deciles 4–7)	High-Income Occupations (Deciles 8–10)
Managers	0	0	36
Professionals	0	0	27
Technicians and Associate Professionals	0	7	25
Clerical Support Workers	0	29	5
Services and Sales Workers	22	15	6
Skilled Agricultural and Fishery Workers	1	0	0
Craft & Related Trades Workers	7	24	0
Plant and Machine Operators and Assemblers	2	21	0
Elementary Occupations	68	4	0
Total	100	100	100

Sources: Author's Analysis of the Post-Apartheid Labour Market Series Data Files, DataFirst Research Unit, University of Cape Town.

Table 2.7 Employment in Major Groups of Occupations by High, Middle and Low Deciles Based on Average Pre-Tax Earnings of Unit Group Occupations, Gauteng 2011 (Row Percentage Distribution)

	Low-Income Occupations (Deciles 1–3)	Middle-Income Occupations (Deciles 4–7)	High-Income Occupations (Deciles 8–10)	Total
Managers	0	0	100	100
Professionals	0	1	99	100
Technicians and Associate Professionals	0	24	75	100
Clerical Support Workers	0	88	12	100
Services and Sales Workers	47	40	14	100
Skilled Agricultural and Fishery Workers	82	18	0	100
Craft and Related Trades Workers	20	79	1	100
Plant and Machine Operators and Assemblers	8	91	1	100
Elementary Occupations	93	7	0	100

Sources: Author's Analysis of the Post-Apartheid Labour Market Series Data Files, DataFirst Research Unit, University of Cape Town.

measurement of employment change tests the social polarisation theory by using the appropriate concepts. The second reason for doing so is that this will also allow us to maintain a description of earnings deciles in terms of their occupational composition. So in the light of the discussion of the statistical relationship between earnings deciles and Major Group occupations, I created a new variable in which I re-categorized the Major Group occupations according to the earnings deciles into which their constituent Unit Group occupations fell.[8] This resulted in three main groups of earnings deciles:

1. Low-Income Group (Deciles 1–3): Mainly composed of Elementary Workers and some Services and Sales Workers, and all Skilled Fishery and Agricultural Workers.
2. Middle-Income Group (Deciles 4–7): Mainly composed of Clerical Support Workers, Services and Sales Workers, Craft and Related Trades Workers and Plant and Machinery Operators and Assemblers with a small proportion of other occupational groups.
3. High-Income Group (Deciles 8–10): Mainly composed of Managers, Professionals and Technicians and Associate Professionals, with a small proportion of Clerical Support Workers and Services and Sales Workers, with a small proportion of other occupational groups.

This method could only be used with the Post-Apartheid Labour Market Series statistics because the surveys from 1996 to 2011 collected consistent information on Unit Group occupations and their earnings. The population censuses did not collect consistent information on Unit Group occupations and their earnings, so their results were not suitable for applying this method.

In the following section, the results of these two different methods are presented, using the population census statistics for the years 1980 and 2001, and the Post-Apartheid Labour Market Series statistics for 1996 and 2011. I have relied on the statistics from 1996 to 2011 instead of from 1994 to 2011 because prior to 1996 information on Unit Group occupations was not collected by the surveys. This statistical analysis aimed to achieve two goals. The first was to confirm that any changes in the occupational structure were consistent, long-term trends. This is the reason why I have taken the trouble to analyse the results of five population censuses conducted over a period of forty years and thirty-eight surveys conducted over a period of eighteen years. The second aim was to measure these employment changes to test the social polarization theory. Both kinds of evidence are relevant for a rigorous test of the theory. By necessity, employment change must be measured by comparing employment at two points in time. However, these two points in time must be shown to be the outcome of a consistent long-term trend or their comparison would be meaningless.

8 This was calculated by using earnings data from all the surveys over the period from 1996 to 2011.

Changes in the division of labour: Polarization or professionalization?

a) Measurement of employment change using the major groups of occupations
According to the results of the population censuses, the size of the employed workforce more than doubled between 1970 and 2011. However, the absolute number of middle-income, manual workers grew only slightly (Figure 2.3). Specifically, the employment of Craft and Related Trades Workers, and Plant and Machine Operators and Assemblers grew at an average growth rate of only 0.6 per cent per year (Table 2.8). By contrast, there was more employment growth in both high-income, highly skilled jobs and low-skilled, low-income jobs. Absolute employment in the high-income jobs of Managers, Professionals and Technicians and Associate Professionals grew at an average annual rate of 3.2 per cent. Similarly, employment in low-income elementary jobs grew at an average annual rate of 1.5 per cent. On the face of it, this seems to suggest that the occupational structure of employment has become polarized, with more growth among high-income and low-income jobs and less growth among the manual middle-income jobs that are associated with manufacturing activities. However, the evidence also shows that there was dramatic growth among middle-income, white-collar jobs that has more than made up for the slow growth in middle-income blue-collar jobs. Specifically, the absolute employment of Clerical Support Workers and Services and Sales Workers grew at an average rate of 4.3 per cent per year, making it the fastest-growing occupational group over this period (Table 2.8).

The occupational class structure of employment was therefore substantially restructured over the four decades from 1970 to 2011. In 1970, employment in middle-income, blue-collar jobs was greater than any other single occupational class. By 2011, this class of Craft and Related Trades Workers and Plant and Machine Operators and Assemblers was the smallest of all the occupational classes (Figure 2.3). By contrast, employment in middle-income, white-collar employment grew dramatically. In 1970, Clerical Support Workers, Services and Sales Workers was the smallest occupational class. By 2011, it had grown in number to become the largest occupational group (Figure 2.3).[9] Similarly, the employment of high-income Managers, Professionals, Technicians and Associate Professionals grew dramatically, taking them from being the second-smallest occupational group in 1970 to the second-largest in 2011 (Figure 2.3). Employment in low-income manual jobs also grew, but not as fast as the high and middle-income jobs.

The results from the analysis of the PALMS produced similar results for the matching period from 1994 to 2011. The only substantial difference is that the estimates for the employment of high-income Managers, Professionals, Technicians and Associate Professionals from 2007 onwards were higher than the

---

9 The employment estimate for Clerical, Sales and Services workers by the 1991 Population Census, which is inconsistent with the long-term employment trend, is almost certainly due to an error in the compilation of the full count or in the drawing of the sample from the full count. It is not due to an error in the sampling weights.

estimates for middle-income Clerical Support Workers and Services and Sales Workers (Figure 2.4).

The above discussion of the long-term employment trends in the division of labour can be summarized as follows. The employment of middle-income, manual workers grew only slightly, with much faster growth in high-income, low-income and non-manual middle-income occupational groups. Having established that the

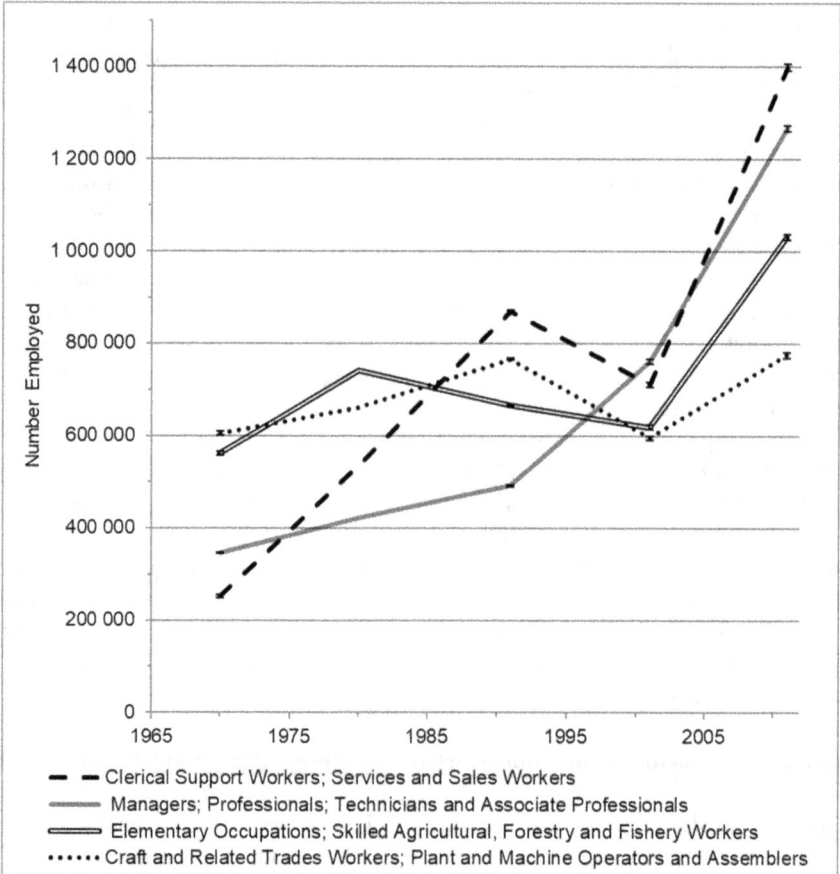

Figure 2.3 Employment in Major Groups of Occupations in Gauteng, 1970–2011[10]
Error bars indicate the 95 per cent confidence intervals.
Sources: Author's Analysis of Population Census Data Files, DataFirst Research Unit, University of Cape Town. See Table 2.8.

10 The data points for the 1996 Population Census are omitted from this graph because they are probably wrong and make reading the trends difficult. Refer to Table 2.5 for the 1996 employment estimates.

Table 2.8 Employment by Major Groups of Occupations in Gauteng, 1970–2011

	1970	1980	1991	1996	2001	2011	Average Annual Percentage Growth Rate
Managers; Professionals; Technicians and Associate Professionals	346,436	421,482	491,362	583,911	759,766	1,267,125	3.2%
Clerical Support Workers; Services and Sales Workers	251,859	534,126	869,916	509,308	710,586	1,398,736	4.3%
Craft and Related Trades Workers; Plant and Machine Operators and Assemblers	604,909	659,741	765,770	559,881	595,468	774,526	0.6%
Elementary Occupations; Skilled Agricultural, Forestry and Fishery Workers	561,327	741,663	665,267	539,417	618,482	1,030,742	1.5%
Occupation Not Specified	60,675	85,182	66,272	261,361	212,194	1,072	
Total	1,825,206	2,442,194	2,858,587	2,453,878	2,896,496	4,472,201	2.2%

Sources: Author's Analysis of Population Census Data Files, DataFirst Research Unit, University of Cape Town.

changes in the division of labour between 1970 and 2011 are the result of long-term and consistent trends, we are now able to ask if these changes in employment resulted in a more polarized income and occupational structure. The best way to establish this is to calculate the extent of the changes in the occupational structure over the periods of study. This will tell us whether the occupational structure has a polarized distribution and if there is a polarized pattern of absolute employment growth.

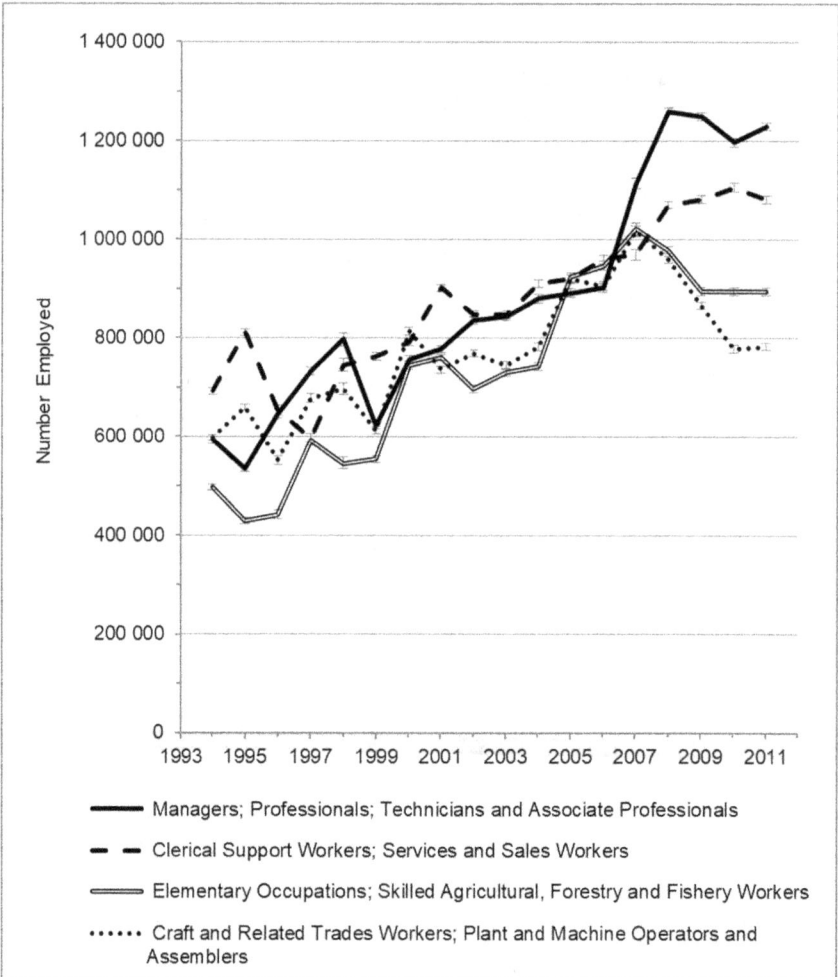

Figure 2.4 Employment in Major Groups of Occupations in Gauteng, 1994–2011
Error bars indicate the 95 per cent confidence intervals.
Sources: Author's Analysis of the Post-Apartheid Labour Market Series Data Files, DataFirst Research Unit, University of Cape Town. See Table 2.9.

Table 2.9 Employment by Major Group Occupations in Gauteng, 1994–2011

	1994	1995	1996	1997	1998	1999	2000	2001	2002	2003	2004	2005	2006	2007	2008	2009	2010	2011
Managers; Professionals; Technicians and Associate Professionals	593,141	534,423	646,005	732,545	797,011	621,778	755,589	777,605	835,072	843,130	880,086	891,367	902,635	1,113,381	1,259,999	1,249,434	1,196,933	1,229,687
Clerical Support Workers; Services and Sales Workers	692,063	811,683	639,842	592,084	736,555	758,246	785,979	891,897	841,377	835,225	897,899	913,057	954,769	961,165	1,058,611	1,071,151	1,096,124	1,074,157
Craft and Related Trades Workers; Plant and Machine Operators and Assemblers	597,820	659,079	551,584	677,897	697,184	612,266	813,773	735,924	768,995	745,119	782,555	920,094	905,330	1,016,644	959,999	865,554	778,265	782,908
Elementary Occupations; Skilled Agricultural, Forestry and Fishery Workers	496,328	428,841	455,158	595,720	553,640	557,100	751,165	770,875	703,162	742,581	755,233	931,309	951,205	1,029,228	989,065	903,731	903,529	901,449
Occupation Not Specified	-	330,579	291,252	80,096	60,306	475,913	18,710	14,833	26,379	20,238	7,407	5,477	9,600	17,357	433	-	-	-
Total	2,379,352	2,764,605	2,583,841	2,678,342	2,844,696	3,025,303	3,125,215	3,191,134	3,174,984	3,186,292	3,323,179	3,661,303	3,723,538	4,137,773	4,268,107	4,089,870	3,974,850	3,988,200

Sources: Author's Analysis of the Post-Apartheid Labour Market Series Data Files, DataFirst Research Unit, University of Cape Town.

The results of the population censuses for the period from 1970 to 2011 show that there was no occupational polarization. Instead, the greatest absolute employment growth took place in middle-income occupations, followed closely by employment growth in high-income occupations. The least employment growth, by a large margin, took place among low-income occupations (Figure 2.5). The results of the Post-*Apartheid* Labour Market Series for the period from 1994 to 2011 show that most of the employment growth was in high-income jobs, followed closely by the growth in middle-income jobs. Employment growth was lowest in low-income jobs (Figure 2.6).

If we break down the employment growth of middle-income jobs, the results from both the population censuses and the labour market surveys show that most of the growth was due to increases in the employment of non-manual middle-income Clerical Support Workers and Services and Sales Workers.

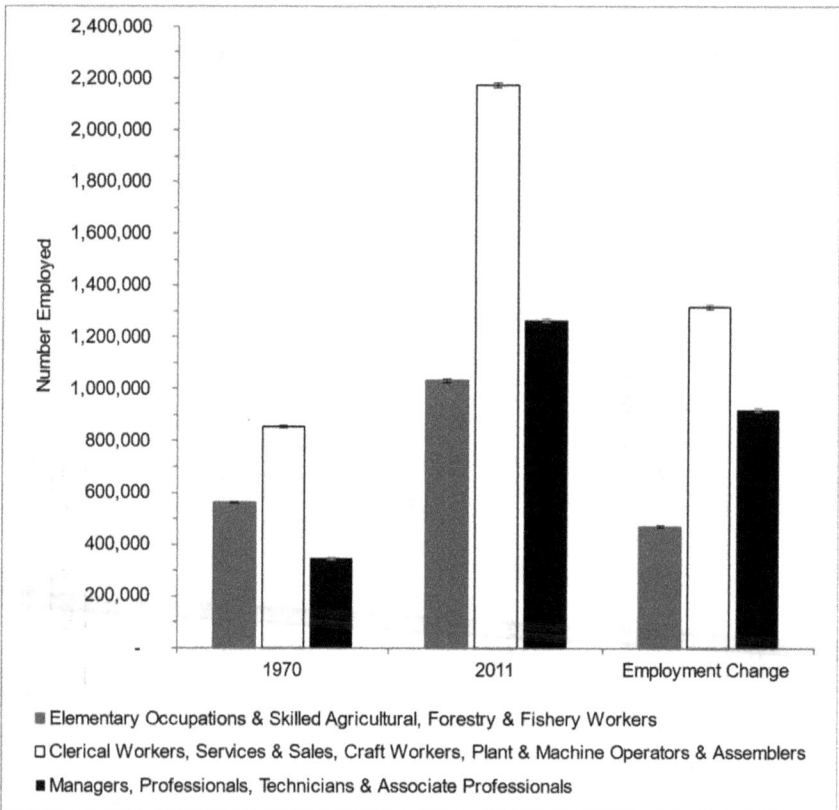

Figure 2.5 Employment Change by Low-, Middle- and High-Income Occupational
              Groups in Gauteng, 1970–2011 (Based on Major Groups of Occupations)
Error bars indicate the 95 per cent confidence intervals.
Sources: Author's Analysis of Population Census Data Files, DataFirst Research Unit, University of Cape Town. See
       Table 2.10.

Table 2.10 Employment Change by Low-, Middle- and High-Income Occupational Groups in Gauteng, 1970–2011 (Based on Major Groups of Occupations)

	1970	2011	Employment Change		Employment Change
Managers, Professionals, Technicians & Associate Professionals	346,436	1,267,125	920,689	High-Income Occupations	920,689
Clerical Support Workers & Services & Sales Workers	251,859	1,398,736	1,146,877	Middle-Income Occupations	1,316,494
Craft & Related Trades Workers, Plant & Machine Operators & Assemblers	604,909	774,526	169,617		
Elementary Occupations & Skilled Agricultural, Forestry & Fishery Workers	561,327	1,030,742	469,415	Low-Income Occupations	469,415
Occupation Not Specified	60,675	1,072	−59,603		−59,603
Total	1,825,206	4,472,201	2,646,995		2,646,995

Sources: Author's Analysis of Population Census Data Files, DataFirst Research Unit, University of Cape Town.

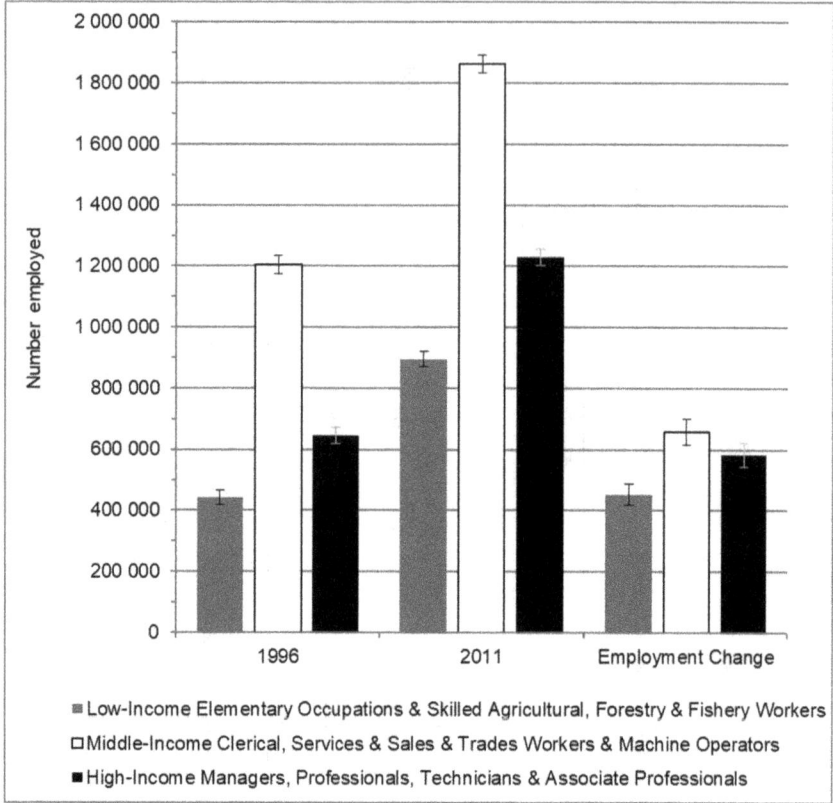

Figure 2.6 Employment Change by Low-, Middle- and High-Income Occupational
            Groups in Gauteng, 1996–2011 (Based on Major Groups of Occupations)
Error bars indicate the 95 per cent confidence intervals.
Sources: Author's Analysis of the Post-Apartheid Labour Market Series Data Files, DataFirst Research Unit, University
      of Cape Town.

Employment growth in manual middle-income jobs was extremely low (Figure
2.7 and Figure 2.8).

The differences between the estimates of employment change by these two sources
are mostly due to the different periods over which the change was measured. In
1970 the occupational group of clerical, services and sales workers was the second-
smallest group by employment size. By 1991, it had grown to become the largest
occupational group by absolute employment size. So the change in employment
among Clerical Support Workers and Services and Sales Workers from 1996 to
2011 was therefore less than the change from 1970 to 2011 because by 1996, the size
of employment among clerical, services and sales jobs was already large.

These measurements of the extent of employment change in high-, middle- and
low-income occupations do not support the social polarization theory. The growth
of low-income jobs was roughly half the growth of high-income, managerial,
professional and technical jobs. In this respect, the results lend some support to

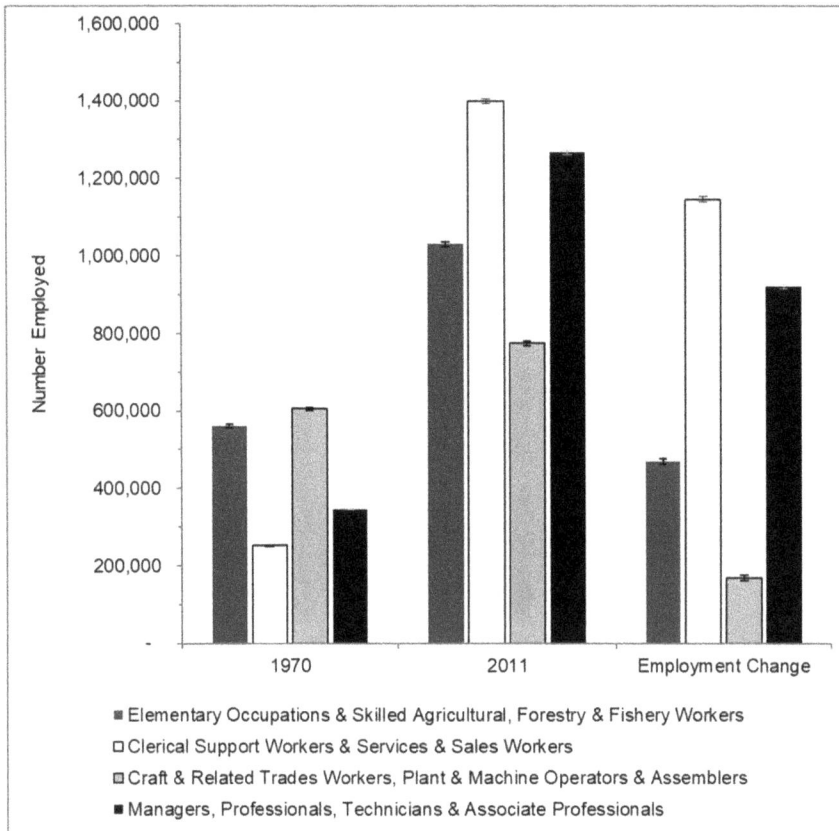

Figure 2.7 Employment Change by Four Low-, Middle- and High-Income Groups of
Occupations in Gauteng, 1970–2011
Error bars indicate the 95 per cent confidence intervals.
Sources: Author's Analysis of Population Census Data Files, DataFirst Research Unit, University of Cape Town.

Hamnett's professionalization theory, which argues that there has been much more employment growth among high-income, middle-class jobs than in any other occupational groups. However, these results also show that employment growth in high-income jobs was matched and even exceeded by growth in middle-income clerical, services and sales jobs.

b) Measurement of employment change using groups of earnings deciles
The main difference between the results based on groups of earnings deciles and the results based on Major Groups of occupations is that the former show more employment in low-income occupations and less employment in middle-income occupations. The estimates of high-income employment trends are roughly the same for both methods (compare Figure 2.4 with Figure 2.9). The main reason for this is that many Services and Sales Workers were reclassified from the middle-income group to the low-income group.

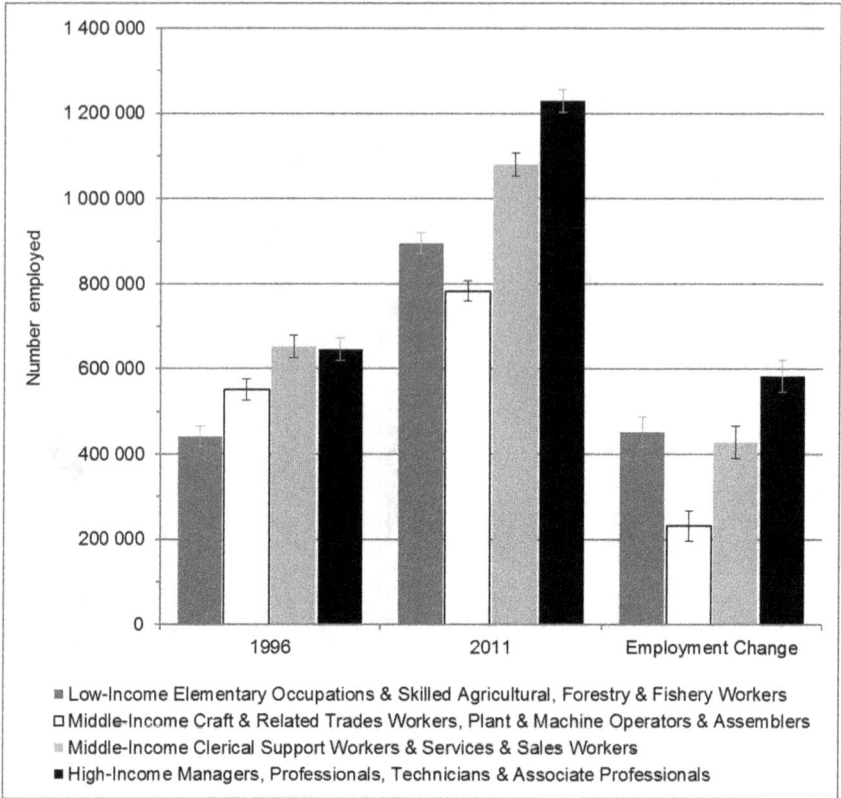

Figure 2.8 Employment Change by Four Low-, Middle- and High-Income Groups of Occupations in Gauteng, 1996–2011

Error bars indicate the 95 per cent confidence intervals.

Sources: Author's Analysis of the Post-Apartheid Labour Market Series Data Files, DataFirst Research Unit, University of Cape Town.

Has this larger estimate of employment in low-income occupations resulted in substantially different estimates of changes in the occupational structure? The results using this method also show that there was no occupational and income polarization. Over the period from 1996 to 2011, employment changes in low-, middle- and high-income occupations were roughly the same (Figure 2.10). Although the survey estimates show that more employment growth took place in high-income occupations than in low- and middle-income occupations, the differences between these estimates are not statistically significant.[11] Although the

11 These estimates are based on probability sample surveys, the results of which are subject to random error, which is measured by the confidence interval at the 95 per cent level of probability. In this case, the confidence intervals of all the estimates of employment change overlap with one another, which means that the differences between the estimates of employment change cannot be distinguished from differences caused by random error.

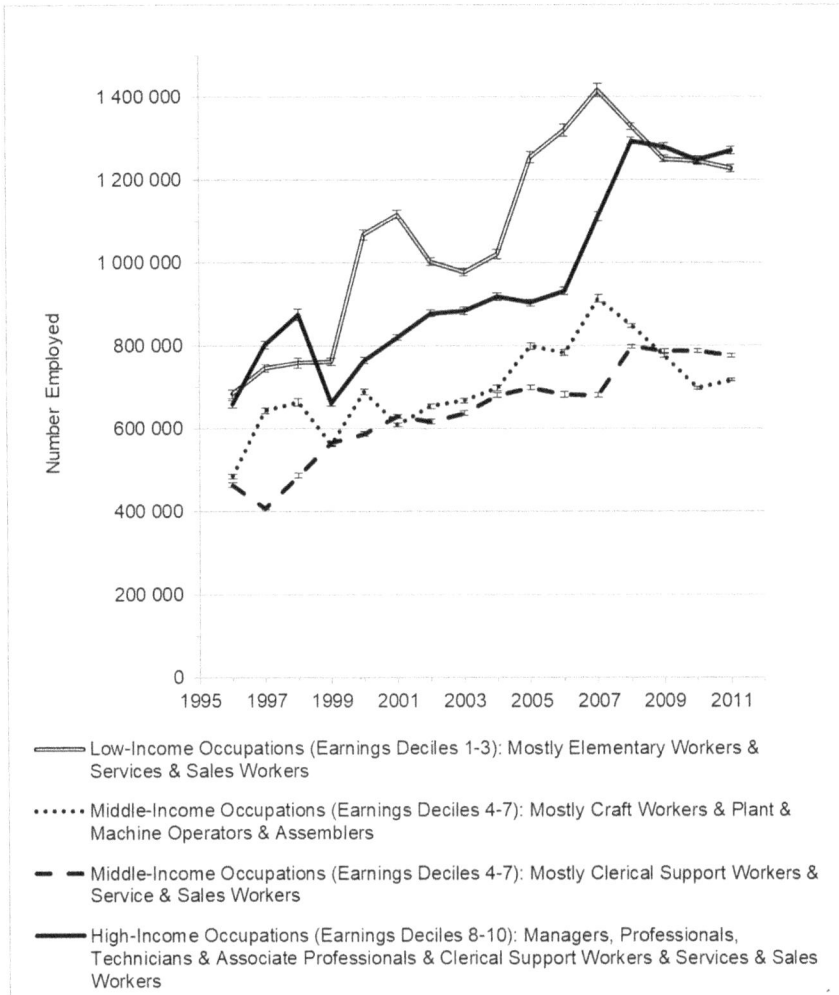

Legend:

━━━ Low-Income Occupations (Earnings Deciles 1-3): Mostly Elementary Workers & Services & Sales Workers

•••••• Middle-Income Occupations (Earnings Deciles 4-7): Mostly Craft Workers & Plant & Machine Operators & Assemblers

— — Middle-Income Occupations (Earnings Deciles 4-7): Mostly Clerical Support Workers & Service & Sales Workers

━━━ High-Income Occupations (Earnings Deciles 8-10): Managers, Professionals, Technicians & Associate Professionals & Clerical Support Workers & Services & Sales Workers

Figure 2.9 Employment in Groups of Deciles Based on the Average Earnings of Unit Group Occupations in Gauteng, 1996–2011
Error bars indicate the 95 per cent confidence intervals.
Sources: Author's Analysis of the Post-Apartheid Labour Market Series Data Files, DataFirst Research Unit, University of Cape Town. See Table 2.11.

absence of statistically significant differences might seem to be an inconclusive finding, the small confidence intervals actually demonstrate that the real differences between the employment changes in low-, middle- and high-income occupations are very small. Therefore, the overall finding based on this method is that, over the period from 1996 to 2011, there was no substantial change to the occupational structure. So, although these trends show no pattern of professionalization, they also do not demonstrate the polarization of the occupational structure. However,

Table 2.11 Employment Change by Groups of Deciles Based on the Average Earnings of Unit Group Occupations in Gauteng, 1996–2011

	1996	1997	1998	1999	2000	2001	2002	2003	2004	2005	2006	2007	2008	2009	2010	2011
Low-Income Occupations[1]	682,662	745,558	757,936	761,308	1,067,310	1,115,979	1,001,409	977,341	1,020,398	1,255,273	1,319,655	1,415,363	1,328,419	1,250,422	1,244,438	1,226,949
Middle-Income Manual Occupations[2]	484,818	642,043	663,043	561,339	688,430	609,549	653,415	667,533	696,976	798,819	782,571	914,070	847,319	773,874	696,243	716,284
Middle-Income Non-Manual Occupations[3]	464,045	407,160	486,931	564,926	586,846	629,863	616,191	636,995	680,194	697,883,	681,083	679,542	797,121	785,331	786,390	774,141
High-Income Occupations[4]	658,262	801,550	874,876	661,817	763,747	820,436	877,591	884,082	917,086	903,295	930,630	1,111,443	1,293,642	1,280,187	1,247,780	1,270,827
Occupation or Earnings Not Specified	299,040	82,029	78,559	475,913	18,883	15,308	26,380	20,341	8,525	6,032	9,600	17,357	1,606	57	–	–
Total	2,588,827	2,678,340	2,861,345	3,025,303	3,125,215	3,191,134	3,174,984	3,186,291	3,323 179	3,661,301	3,723,538	4,137,774	4,268,107	4,089,870	3,974,850	3,988,201

1 Earnings Deciles 1–3: Mostly Elementary Workers and some Services and Sales Workers.

2 Earnings Deciles 4–7: Mostly Craft Workers and Plant and Machine Operators and Assemblers.

3 Earnings Deciles 4–7: Mostly Clerical Support Workers and Services and Sales Workers.

4 Earnings Deciles 8–10: Mostly Managers, Professionals, Technicians and Associate Professionals, with some Clerical Support Workers and Services and Sales Workers.

Sources: Author's Analysis of the Post-Apartheid Labour Market Series Data Files, DataFirst Research Unit, University of Cape Town.

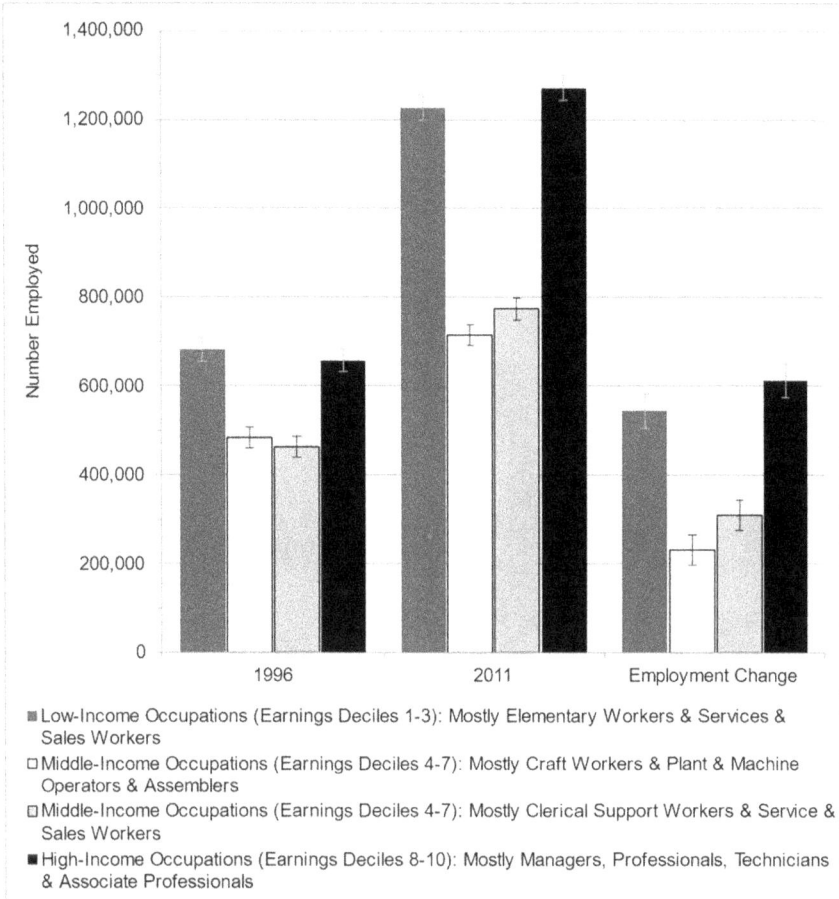

Low-Income Occupations (Earnings Deciles 1-3): Mostly Elementary Workers & Services & Sales Workers

Middle-Income Occupations (Earnings Deciles 4-7): Mostly Craft Workers & Plant & Machine Operators & Assemblers

Middle-Income Occupations (Earnings Deciles 4-7): Mostly Clerical Support Workers & Service & Sales Workers

High-Income Occupations (Earnings Deciles 8-10): Mostly Managers, Professionals, Technicians & Associate Professionals

Figure 2.10 Employment Change by Low-, Middle- and High-Income Occupations in Gauteng, 1996–2011 (Based on Deciles of the Average Earnings of Unit Group Occupations)

Error bars indicate the 95 per cent confidence intervals.

Sources: Author's Analysis of the Post-Apartheid Labour Market Series Data Files, DataFirst Research Unit, University of Cape Town.

using this method, the results for the period from 1996 to 2012 do show a marginally professionalizing trend (Crankshaw, 2017: p.1619).

If we break down this employment change to distinguish between the middle-income manual jobs of mostly Craft and Related Trades and Plant and Machine Operators and Assemblers, on the one hand, and the middle-income non-manual jobs of mostly Clerical Support Workers and Services and Sales Workers, we can confirm the earlier results, which showed that more of the growth in all middle-income jobs was due to the growth of non-manual clerical, services and sales jobs rather than the growth of manual jobs (Figure 2.11).

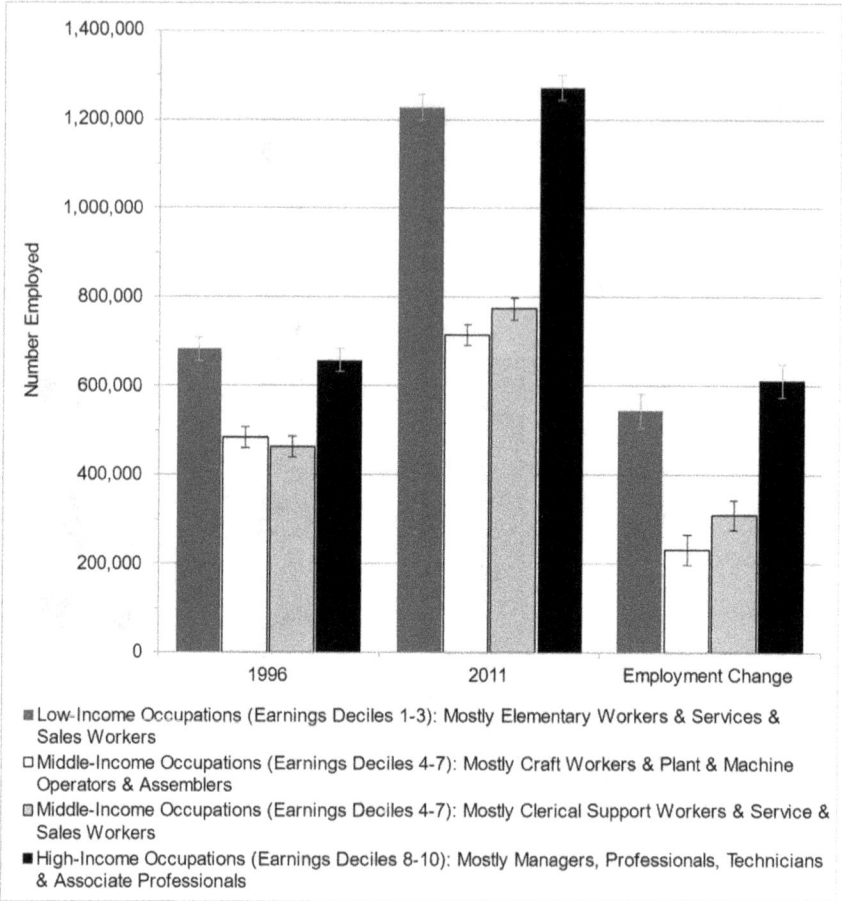

Figure 2.11 Employment Change by Four Groups of Low-, Middle- and High-Income
               Occupations in Gauteng, 1996–2011 (Based on Deciles of the Average
               Earnings of Unit Group Occupations)
Error bars indicate the 95 per cent confidence intervals.
Sources: Author's Analysis of the Post-Apartheid Labour Market Series Data Files, DataFirst Research Unit, University
    of Cape Town.

Unfortunately, this method of modifying the Major Groups of occupations
using earnings deciles of Unit Groups occupations cannot be applied to the
population census data because they do not include the precise earnings of Unit
Group occupations. However, the results can be used make rough corrections to
the longer-term trends produced by the analysis of the population census results.
The findings suggest that 22 per cent of all Services and Sales Workers, 7 per cent
of all Craft and Related Trades Workers and 2 per cent of all Plant and Machine
Operators and Assemblers should be classified as low-income workers rather than
middle-income workers (Table 2.6). We can apply this correction to the population
census results to compensate for the underestimation of low-income workers by

transferring 29 per cent of the employment in middle-income occupations to the employment of low-income occupations for both 1980 and 2011. This re-calculation decreases the employment growth in middle-income occupations from 1,019,164 to 877,759 and increases employment growth between 1980 and 2011 in low-income occupations from 309,382 to 525,314 (Table 2.10). However, this correction does not substantially change the outcome. This adjusted estimate of the increase in the number of low-income jobs is still only 60 per cent of the employment increases in both middle- and high-income jobs (Table 2.10). So even when we adjust for the main shortcoming of using Major Group occupations to measure employment changes in low-, middle- and high-income occupations, the results from the population censuses do not support the social polarization theory. Instead, the results support the professionalization theory, which argues that high-income employment has grown much more than low-income employment.

Unemployment

The professionalization of the occupational structure between 1970 and 2011 was accompanied by the substantial increase in the rate of unemployment. According to the population censuses, from 1970 to 1980, the strict unemployment rate was just under 5 per cent.[12] From 1980 to 2001, unemployment increased dramatically to 36 per cent and then declined to 26 per cent by 2011 (Figure 2.12). The results based on the Post-Apartheid Labour Market Series sample surveys followed a similar trend, but with lower estimates of the strict unemployment rate. According to this source, the unemployment rate increased from 19 per cent in 1994 to 29 per cent in 2002. From 2002 to 2011, the unemployment rate fluctuated between 29 per cent and 20 per cent (Figure 2.12).

These results, which show that the professionalization of the occupational structure was accompanied by rising and chronic unemployment, suggest that the changing occupational structure may be one of the causes of long-term unemployment in greater Johannesburg. Scholars have argued that the professionalization of the occupational structure produces a skills mismatch, in which there is growing demand for workers with a completed secondary and tertiary educations and a declining demand for workers who have not completed high school (Kasarda, 1989). The extent to which this skills mismatch has caused

---

12 The population censuses record unemployment with a single question that defines unemployed workers as workers who are without employment and who are work-seekers. This is known as the 'official' or 'strict' definition of unemployment because it does not include workers who are unemployed but who have become discouraged and have given up looking for a job. The household surveys record unemployment with a battery of questions that define unemployed workers (by the strict definition) as workers who have actively looked for work or tried to start a business in the month preceding the survey and who were available to start work or a business in the week prior to the survey (StatsSA, 2008: p.7).

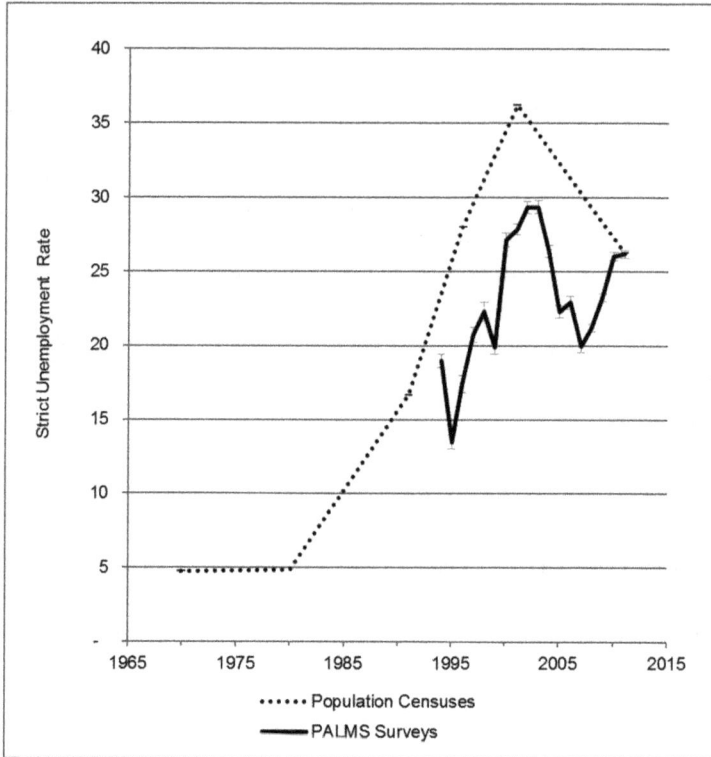

Figure 2.12 The Strict Unemployment Rate in Gauteng, 1970–2011.
Error bars indicate the 95 per cent confidence intervals.
Sources: Author's Analysis of the Population Census and Post-Apartheid Labour Market Series Data Files, DataFirst
     Research Unit, University of Cape Town.

Table 2.12 Trends in Employment, Unemployment, Total Workforce[13] and Population in
          Gauteng, 1970–2011

	Employment	Strict Unemployment	Total Workforce	Total Population	Workforce Participation Rate (%)	Strict Unemployment Rate (%)
1970	1,825,206,	91,211	1,916,417	3,930,188	49	5
1980	2,442,194	125,286	2,567,480	5,258,996	49	5
1991	2,858,586	572,538	3,431,124	6,458,333	53	17
1996	2,623,268	1,021,090	3,644,358	7,210,129	51	28
2001	2,896,496	1,643,742	4,540,238	8,830,156	51	36
2011	4,472,201	1,591,776	6,063,977	11,973,782	51	26

Sources: Author's Analysis of the Population Census and Post-Apartheid Labour Market Series Data Files, DataFirst
     Research Unit, University of Cape Town.

13 For the benefit of non-economists, the term 'workforce' refers to the sum of both
   employed and unemployed workers.

unemployment can be established for greater Johannesburg by first measuring the educational levels of workers in different occupational groups. If there are substantial education differences for workers in different occupational groups, we can then measure the extent to which changes in the occupational structure are related to changes in the demand for workers with different levels of education.

My analysis of the Post-Apartheid Labour Market Series data shows that although there was a general increase in the level of education among workers employed in all occupational groups between 1994 and 2011, there were

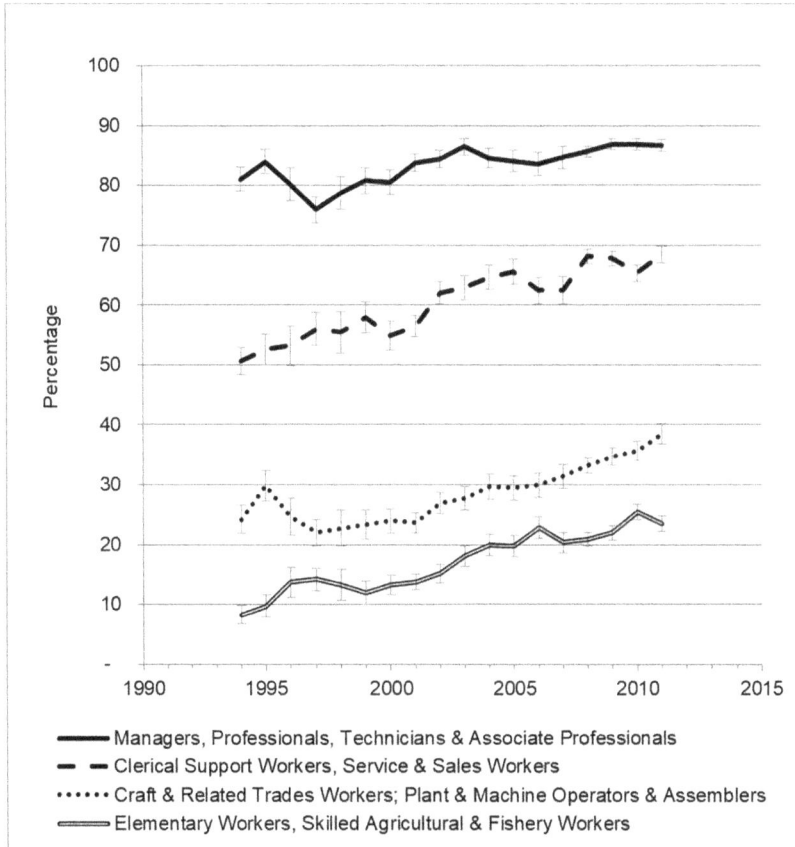

Figure 2.13 Percentage of Workers with at Least a Completed Secondary Education by Occupational Group, 1994 – 2011[14]

Error bars indicate the 95 per cent confidence intervals

Sources: Author's Analysis of the Population Census and Post-Apartheid Labour Market Series Data Files, DataFirst Research Unit, University of Cape Town.

14 This includes all employed workers with a completed secondary education plus a post-secondary diploma or certificate, a post-secondary National Technical Certificate or tertiary degree.

substantial educational differences between workers in different occupational groups. Most Managers, Professionals, Technicians and Associate Professionals, Clerical Support Workers and Services and Sales Workers had either completed their secondary education or had some form of tertiary education.[15] By contrast, most manual workers had not completed their secondary education (Figure 2.13). So the non-manual high-income and middle-income occupations, which have seen the greatest employment growth, are also those occupations that generally require either a secondary or tertiary education. By contrast, those occupations that have seen the slowest employment growth are those that generally do not require a completed secondary education.

Another method of demonstrating this skills mismatch is to measure the employment trends among workers with different educational qualifications. The

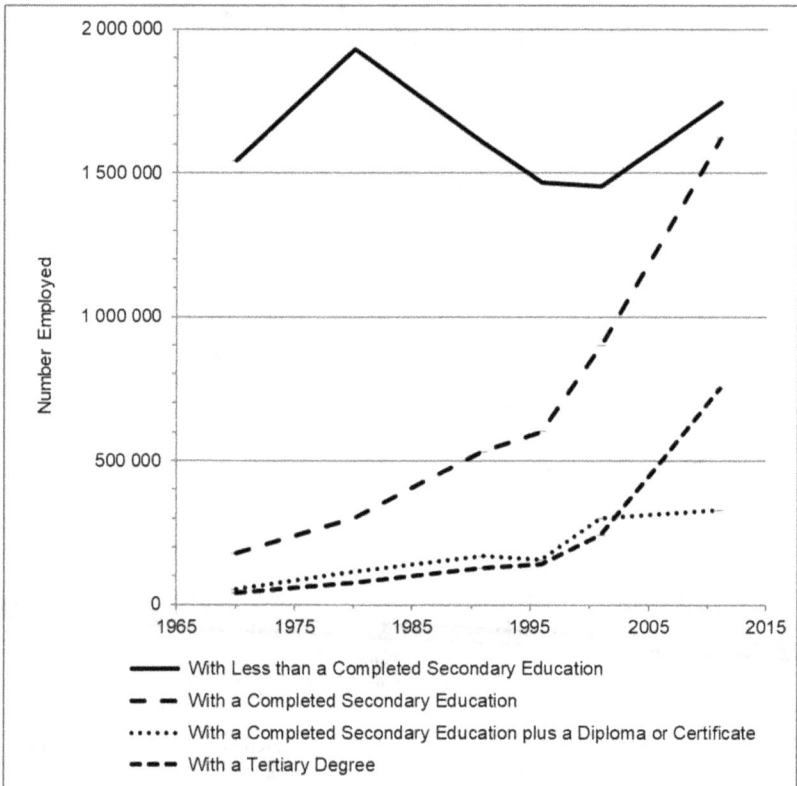

Figure 2.14 Employment Trends by Educational Level in Gauteng, 1970–2011
Error bars indicate the 95 per cent confidence intervals.
Sources: Author's Analysis of the Population Census Data Files, DataFirst Research Unit, University of Cape Town.

15 In South Africa, a completed secondary education is achieved after twelve years of schooling.

results show that from 1970 to 2011, the demand for workers with less than a completed secondary education was stagnant, increasing only slightly over a forty-year period. By contrast, the demand for workers with a completed secondary education and a tertiary degree increased dramatically (Figure 2.14).

This skills mismatch was also reflected in the dramatically different unemployment rates of workers with different levels of education. These different unemployment rates have a consistent, long-term trend from 1970 to 2011, with the level of education being inversely correlated with the unemployment rate. By 2011, the unemployment rate among workers who had not completed secondary school was 34 per cent (Figure 2.15). Among those who had completed secondary school, it was much lower, at only 24 per cent, and among

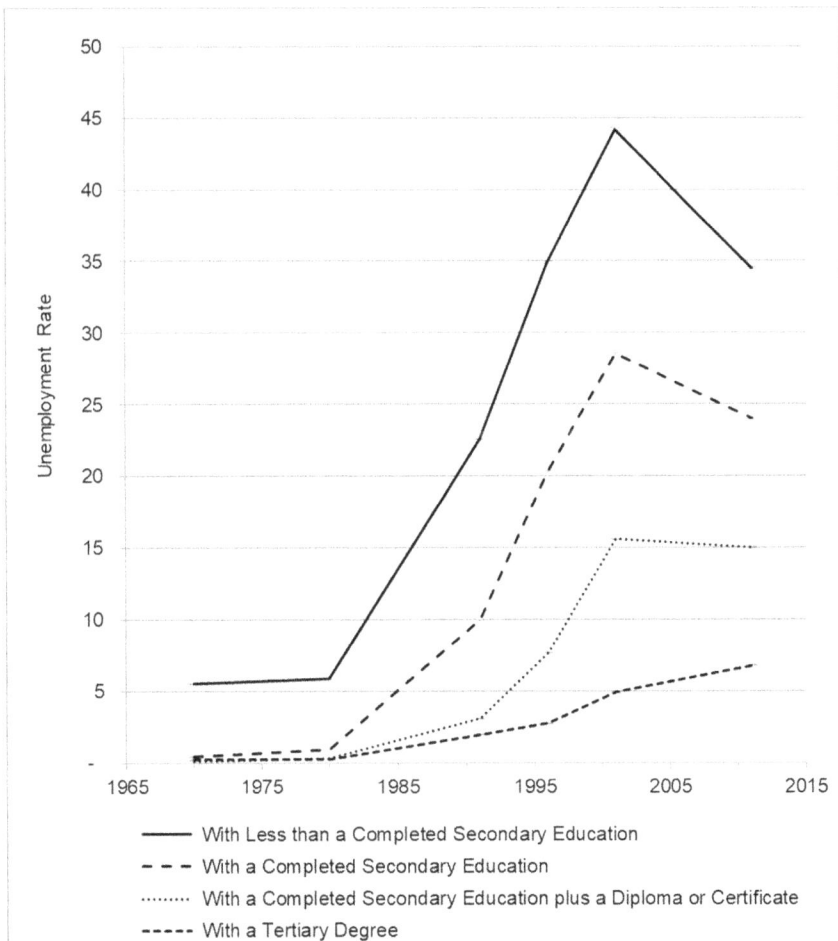

Figure 2.15 Educational Level by Strict Unemployment Rate in Gauteng, 1970–2011

Error bars indicate the 95 per cent confidence intervals.
Sources: Author's Analysis of the Population Census Data Files, DataFirst Research Unit, University of Cape Town.

those who had completed a post-school diploma or certificate, it was even lower, at 15 per cent (Figure 2.15). Among workers with at least a three-year university degree the unemployment rate was only 7 per cent (Figure 2.15). These results are convincing evidence that the increasing demand for more educated workers in non-manual occupations is one of the important causes of the high rate of unemployment.

The extent to which the changes in the occupational structure have contributed to the demand for more educated workers can be established by measuring the changes in the numbers of workers in each occupational group with at least a completed secondary education. These changes across occupational groups can then be expressed as a percentage distribution that will show how much each occupational group contributed to the overall extent of employment change. The results for employment change between 1980 and 2011 show that two-thirds (66 per cent) of all employment growth among workers with at least a completed secondary education was found in the high-income and middle-income, non-manual occupations. By contrast, only one-third (34 per cent) was due to employment growth in low- and middle-income manual jobs (Table 2.13). These results therefore suggest that the changing occupational structure of employment in Gauteng has increased the skills mismatch between the educational levels of the workforce and the educational levels that are required among employed workers. This skills mismatch was therefore a partial cause of unemployment among workers who had not completed a secondary education.

The skills mismatch is not the only likely cause of unemployment in greater Johannesburg. Another feature of the labour market over this period was that there was much higher growth in the size of the workforce (employed and

Table 2.13 Employment Change among Workers with a Completed Secondary or Tertiary Education, 1980 and 2011

Workers with a Completed Secondary or Tertiary Education	1980	2011	Employment Change 1980–2011	Percentage of Employment Change 1980–2011
Managerial, Professional, Technical & Associate Professional Workers	280,684	979,206	698,522	31.6
Clerical Support Workers & Services & Sales Workers	153,046	923,602	770,556	34.8
Craft & Related Trades Workers & Plant & Machine Operators & Assemblers	46,045	372,929	326,884	14.8
Elementary Workers & Skilled Fishery & Agricultural Workers	4,681	425,289	420,608	19.0
Occupation Not Specified	5,610	662	−4,948	−0.2
Total	490,066	2,701,688	2,211,622	100.0

Sources: Author's Analysis of the Population Census Data Files, DataFirst Research Unit, University of Cape Town.

unemployed workers) than in the size of employment (Figure 2.16).[16] From 1970 to 1980, the increase in the size of the workforce was matched by employment growth: both grew at an annual average rate of 3 per cent (Table 2.14). However, over the two decades from 1980 to 2001, employment growth was substantially less than the growth of the whole workforce. Whereas employment grew at an annual average rate of only 0.8 per cent, the workforce grew at a much higher rate of 2.8 per cent (Table 2.14). As a result, unemployment increased dramatically

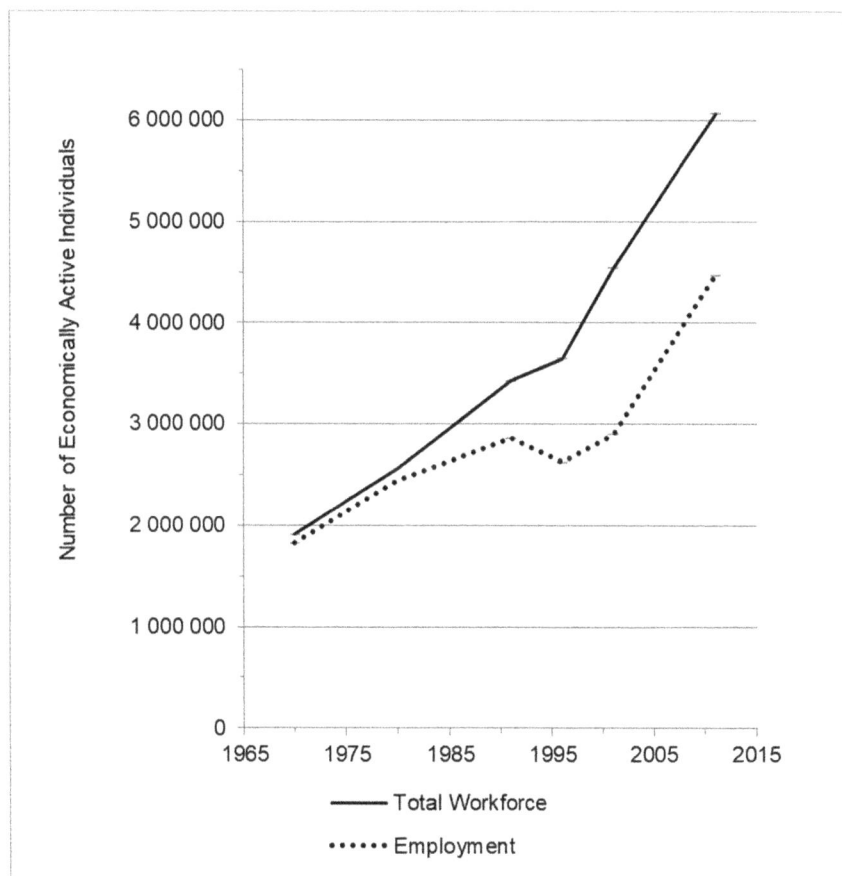

Figure 2.16 Trends in the Workforce and Employment in Gauteng, 1970–2011[17]
Error bars indicate the 95 per cent confidence intervals.
Sources: Author's Analysis of the Population Census Data Files, DataFirst Research Unit, University of Cape Town.

16 See Hodge (2009) for a similar finding concerning national employment and workforce trends.

17 This includes all employed workers with a completed secondary education plus a post-secondary diploma or certificate, a post-secondary National Technical Certificate or tertiary degree.

Table 2.14 The Average Annual Rates of Growth in Employment, Unemployment and the
Total Workforce in Gauteng, 1970–2011 (Percentage)

	Employment	Strict Unemployment	Total Workforce
1970 to 1980	3.0	3.2	3.0
1980 to 2001	0.8	13.0	2.8
2001 to 2011	4.4	-0.3	2.9
1970 to 2011	2.2	7.2	2.8

Sources: Author's Analysis of the Population Census Data Files, DataFirst Research Unit, University of Cape Town.

over this period: the number of unemployed workers grew at an annual average
rate of 13 per cent (Table 2.14). In the subsequent decade, from 2001 to 2011, the
annual average rate of employment growth increased to 4.4 per cent, exceeding the
rate of growth in the total workforce of both employed and unemployed workers
(Table 2.14). So, over the period from 2001 to 2011, the gap between the size of
the workforce and employment decreased slightly, but not enough to reverse the
level of unemployment that was created in earlier decades. This is an important
result for the debate over professionalization, since it suggests that the high levels
of unemployment were not solely caused by changes in the occupational structure
of employment: it was also the interaction of the high rate of population growth
and low employment growth that contributed to the rise in unemployment. This
interpretation would explain why the rate of unemployment is highest, not only
among poorly educated workers, but also among younger workers who entered
the labour market during the period when the employment growth was much
lower than in earlier decades (Branson, 2006: pp.14–17).

Causes of occupational restructuring

Deindustrialization or mechanization across all economic sectors?

Sassen's main explanation for increasing social polarization in cities is the
deindustrialization of employment, namely the decline of employment in
manufacturing activities and the rise of employment in service sector activities,
most notably in producer services (Sassen, 2000: pp.62–5). She argues that
deindustrialization causes social polarization because the service sector has a
more polarized occupational structure than the manufacturing sector. However,
studies of employment trends in greater Johannesburg by Borel-Saladin (2012)
and Crankshaw and Borel-Saladin (2014) found that deindustrialization was
not the main cause of changes to the overall occupational structure. Although
their results showed that the decline of middle-income manual jobs from 1980
to 2000 was mostly due to the decline of manufacturing employment, this was
not the case for the period from 2000 to 2010. The growth in high-income jobs

from 1980 to 2010 was caused mostly by changes within economic sectors and not by the greater growth of the service sector relative to other economic sectors. Similarly, the changes in low-income employment from 1980 to 2010 were due to the combination of both the changing sectoral composition of employment and changes in the occupational structure within each economic sector (Borel-Saladin, 2012: pp.103–10; Crankshaw and Borel-Saladin, 2014: pp.1864–7). Borel-Saladin and Crankshaw therefore argued that the overall pattern of professionalization was largely due to the pattern of employment change within most economic sectors rather than to deindustrialization (Crankshaw and Borel-Saladin, 2014: p.1868). In this respect, their findings agree with results for New York (Bailey and Waldinger 1991: p.51), Amsterdam and Rotterdam (Kloosterman, 1996: p.474), which all showed a professionalizing trend that was not caused mainly by the decline of employment in manufacturing activities.

It therefore makes sense to understand the decline of middle-income manual jobs in terms of the decline of certain kinds of occupational tasks that are carried out across a range of economic sectors, rather than the decline of solely manufacturing activities. From this perspective, the question should then be on the labour processes characteristic of middle-income manual jobs and the way that it has changed to reduce the demand for manual workers.

Evidence from case studies of companies in Gauteng shows that a variety of different causes resulted in managers taking steps to increase productivity by mechanization and intensifying production through multi-skilling. This causal mechanism is one of the important explanations for the relatively slow growth of employment in middle-income manual jobs. This causal mechanism could therefore partly explain both the absolute decline of middle-income manual jobs in the manufacturing sector and the slow rate of employment growth of these same jobs in other economic sectors.

During the *Apartheid* period, the shortage of white artisans was one of the reasons why managers accelerated the mechanization of the labour process and the fragmentation of the skilled trades into semi-skilled operative tasks. They pursued this strategy because they were legally allowed to employ black workers on semi-skilled manual tasks but not on skilled craft tasks, which were reserved for white workers (Crankshaw, 1990; Crankshaw, 1997; Webster, 1985). Apart from the skill shortage, there were other compelling reasons for employers to adopt capital-intensive methods of production during the *Apartheid* period (Black and Hasson, 2016: pp.290–8). Firstly, up until the late 1980s, low interest rates made it relatively cheap for employers to invest in mechanization, encouraging them to opt for capital-intensive production rather than labour-intensive production methods. Secondly, cheap electricity favoured the development of heavy industry such as iron ore smelting and other capital-intensive industries. Thirdly, state investment in strategic industries, such as producing oil from coal to reduce dependence on oil imports, led to the development of highly capital-intensive manufacturing in the chemicals industry generally (Crompton, 1995). Finally, the *Apartheid* Government provided many incentives for companies that promoted capital-intensive production methods. These were tax incentives, depreciation allowances on capital expenditure, debt financing, subsidized interest rates and the provision of supporting utilities and infrastructure (Black and Hasson, 2016: p.295).

These Government policies facilitated the expansion of the highly capital-intensive cement industry during the 1980s. Examples were the large factories that were established in Kaalfontein by Blue Circle Cement and in Germiston by Pretoria Portland Cement (Ngoasheng, 1995: p.44). Similarly, companies in the brick industry tended to favour increasingly capital-intensive production during the 1980s. Examples include the two 'super-modern' brick factories that were built in Rietvlei, near Pretoria, and in Midrand by Corobrick and Cullinan Brick, respectively. These factories manufactured bricks using mechanized 'tunnel' kilns that dried and then fired bricks in a continuous process that was controlled by computers. These new factories reduced the production process from ninety days to only four days. Such was the level of automation that only twelve workers were required on each shift (Ngoasheng, 1995: p.110).

In the post-*Apartheid* period, employers pursued mechanization for similar reasons. After 1994 the new African National Congress Government pursued macroeconomic policies that further liberalized international trade (Roberts, 2014: pp.186–7). This resulted in cheap imports that caused the closure of many manufacturing businesses, especially those engaged in labour-intensive production (Nattrass, 1998; p.84). For example, factories producing household appliances relied on tariff barriers that gave an effective protection rate of 35 to 50 per cent on most appliances and a protection rate of 500 per cent on television sets. These industries required a protection rate of at least 20 per cent in order to survive (Bauman, 1995: pp.70–1). When tariff barriers were lowered during the mid-1990s, such companies faced new competition from cheaper imports and many were forced to close, with the loss of middle-income manual jobs. In one example, the closure of the Kelvinator refrigerator factory in 1999 was blamed on the competition from cheap imports from Swaziland once the tariff barriers were lifted (Barchiesi, 1999: p.68, Barchiesi, 2005: p.177; Vlok, 1999: p.64).

Post-*Apartheid* industrial policy also promoted capital-intensive production to such an extent that capital-intensive production increased at an even faster rate than before (Black and Hasson, 2016: p.290). This policy aimed to reduce earnings inequality by supporting high-productivity factories that could afford to pay higher wages to manual workers. In this way, this post-*Apartheid* policy aimed to encourage manufacturing companies to move away from a vicious cycle of low-wage, low-skill and low-productivity (Joffe *et al.*, 1995: p.214). This policy was achieved by raising the minimum wage across entire industries, which led to the closure of many labour-intensive factories that could not afford higher wages (Nattrass and Seekings, 2019: p.165). By contrast, companies that adopted capital-intensive methods of production were able to thrive under this new policy. The end result of these policies was therefore fewer middle-income manual jobs than there would otherwise have been.

An example of this drive to capital-intensive production was the augmentation of the packaging factory at the South African Breweries in Alrode, Alberton. This new factory used such technologically advanced machinery that the company required the best-performing machine operators to take a trade test in order to become fully trained artisans (i.e. craft workers). These artisans were then promoted to 'process operators', which meant higher wages but more flexible and productive workers (Mager, 2010: p.132–3). This highly mechanized production process meant that 18 per cent of the workers had tertiary educations and almost half (49 per cent) were skilled artisans with apprenticeship training that was equivalent to a completed secondary education (Webster, *et al.*, 2008: p.30). This occupational division of labour stood in stark contrast to the earlier one in which entailed the employment of semi-skilled machine operators rather than qualified artisans.

During the *Apartheid* period the motor vehicle industry was protected by effective tariff barriers of 100 per cent (Black, 1994: p.53). With the liberalization of trade policies in the post-*Apartheid* period, some companies responded by intensifying their methods of production and increasing the extent of automation. A case study of the BMW factory in Rosslyn, Pretoria, showed that productivity was increased through a combination of skills upgrading, multi-skilling, quality circles and automation. New technology entailed highly automated welding machines for body assembly and automated paint shops (Masondo, 2005: pp.158–70).

Employment in the iron and steel industry was also dramatically restructured in the post-*Apartheid* period. A case study of the ISCOR/ArcelorMittal factory in Vanderbijlpark showed that employment declined from 56,200 in 1989 to only 8,947 in 2014. Over this same period, steel output decreased by only one-third and the value of all plant, machinery and equipment increased five-fold (Hlatshwayo and Buhlungu, 2017: pp.136–7). This restructuring entailed the introduction of highly automated and computerized production processes, such as remote-controlled cranes and packaging machines (Hlatshwayo, 2015: pp.83–4; Hlatshwayo and Buhlungu, 2017: pp.134–5 and 138).

These case studies of manufacturing companies therefore suggest that an important cause of the slow growth of middle-income manual employment that generally required less than a completed secondary education was due to mechanization and automation that replaced low-income and middle-income manual work with machinery and computers. Although these case studies were drawn from manufacturing companies, these occupations are not restricted to the manufacturing sector and could also explain the slow growth of low and middle-income manual employment in other economic sectors.

The industrial conciliation system

Hamnett (1996: p.1426) and Esping-Andersen (1993: p.34) both argue that in countries where the state encourages centralized bargaining institutions, trade unions tend to be stronger and therefore more effective in raising the level of minimum wages. This phenomenon resonates strongly in the South African context where a strong trade union movement, in a political alliance with the African National Congress (the post-*Apartheid* ruling party), successfully instituted national minimum wages across a variety of manufacturing subsectors. This has incentivized employers to replace lower-paid machine operators employed in labour-intensive factories with higher-paid machine operators in capital-intensive factories (Nattrass, 2013: p.12; Nattrass, 2014: p.131). In effect, this meant employing fewer middle-income Plant and Machine Operators and Assemblers than would otherwise be the case, thus contributing to higher levels of unemployment among poorly educated workers (Seekings and Nattrass, 2015: p.232).

The social wage

Scholars have argued that social polarization has not taken place in Western European cities because their welfare states provide unemployed workers with a 'social wage'. They argue that because low-skilled workers have the right to a social wage, this reduces their compulsion to accept unpleasant and low-paid jobs, which in turn leads to fewer low-income jobs and higher unemployment. By contrast, they argue that in countries without this kind of welfare provision, cities have lower unemployment rates and higher numbers of low-income jobs (Esping-Anderson, 1993: p.35; Hamnett, 1996: p.1428).

The case of Johannesburg provides an opportunity to test the extent to which this causal mechanism might have operated because there are no substantial welfare benefits for unemployed workers in South Africa. The Unemployment Insurance Fund pays a benefit only to workers who have previously held a job, and even then, the benefit lasts for only six months (SAIRR, 2004: p.318). Furthermore, the unemployment benefit amounts to only half the wage of an unskilled manual worker (DoL, 2004: p.18). The South African unemployment benefit is therefore not a substitute for a low-wage job. Under these conditions, one would therefore expect to find the growth of low-income jobs and therefore some degree of social polarization in greater Johannesburg. The absence of social polarization in greater Johannesburg therefore suggests that these supply-side mechanisms do not operate to decrease the numbers of low-income jobs. Instead, the main causes for the slow growth of low-income jobs probably lie in the changes to production, the organization of work and a generally lower demand for low-income manual workers.

Immigration and migration

Sassen argued that the polarization of the occupational structure led to an increased demand for low-wage workers, which was met by low-skilled immigrants (Sassen, 2001: pp.311–23). This theory was contested by Hamnett (1996: p.1428), who argued that it was the high levels of low-skilled immigration to cities such as New York and Los Angeles that might explain their polarized occupational structure. In contrast to cities in Western Europe, New York and Los Angeles have much higher levels of immigration. This theory was put to the test by Borel-Saladin (2013), using a case study of greater Johannesburg. Johannesburg is a city with a rapidly growing population, caused by natural growth, migration from the countryside and immigration. Over the period from 1980 to 2001, roughly half the working-age population were migrants or immigrants (Borel-Saladin, 2013: p.12). Her findings showed that in-migrants and immigrants to Greater Johannesburg had similar occupational profiles to native residents and she therefore concluded that in-migration and immigration therefore did not contribute to changes in the occupational structure (Borel-Saladin, 2013: pp.27–8).

Conclusion

The results of this study of employment trends in Gauteng show that the occupational structure did not become more polarized in the manner that is proposed by the social polarization theory. Instead, the long-term evidence from the population census data is that the occupational structure became more professionalized over the period from 1970 to 2011. The evidence for this is that employment in both non-manual middle-income and high-income jobs grew more than employment in manual low-income jobs. The analysis of the Post-Apartheid Labour Market Series data for the latter part of this period, from 1996 to 2011, also does not provide evidence of occupational polarization or professionalization. Instead, the results show that there were no differences in employment growth among low-, middle- and high-income occupations. If these results were to conform to the predictions of the social polarization theory, we would expect the findings to show that employment growth in low- and high-income jobs had exceeded employment growth in middle-income occupations.

Consistent with the finding that there was no disproportionate growth in low- and high-income jobs, these results also show that unemployment increased dramatically from 1980 to about 2001. Part of this rise in unemployment was due to the decline in demand for manual jobs that required less than a completed secondary education. This means that the relatively higher growth in demand for non-manual middle and high-income jobs was a partial cause of growing unemployment. So the changing pattern of inequality in greater Johannesburg conforms more to the professionalization theory in which the employed workforce has become more skilled and better-paid, alongside high levels of unemployment among less-educated workers.

The social polarization theory is nonetheless correct in one respect. The theory argues that deindustrialization caused the slower employment growth of manual middle-income jobs that are largely found in the manufacturing sector. These results partly support this argument. Both the long-term results from the population censuses and the shorter-term results of the Post-Apartheid Labour Market Series data show that employment growth among manual workers in middle-income occupations was less than other middle-income jobs, such as clerical and sales jobs, and much less than the growth in low-income and high-income occupations. However, the decline in manual middle-income jobs was not restricted to the manufacturing sector and was not solely due to the decline of manufacturing activities.

These findings also demonstrate the fallacy of assuming that all Clerical Support Workers and Services and Sales Workers are employed in low-income occupations. This assumption has led many scholars to conclude that the growth of service sector employment results in occupational polarization. By contrast, this study has demonstrated that, although a substantial minority of Services and Sales Workers earn less than middle-income factory workers, most of them do not. Furthermore, Clerical Support Workers were shown to be mostly employed in middle-income occupations with only some employed in high-income occupations. The substantial growth of employment in these non-manual, middle-income jobs compensated for the slow growth of manual, middle-income jobs. The result was that, although there was slow growth in manual middle-income employment, the overall growth of middle-income jobs was roughly the same as, or exceeded, the growth in low- and high-income jobs. This growth in non-manual middle-income jobs is therefore one of the statistical reasons why changes in the occupational structure did not follow a polarizing trend.

This study has important implications for the social polarization debate by providing a comparative case study. The social and economic conditions in greater Johannesburg are such that it provides us with counterfactual conditions that are an important test of the social polarization theory. These two counterfactual conditions are (i) the absence of a social wage for unemployed workers and (ii) the presence of large-scale in-migration and immigration. Scholars have argued that these two conditions are necessary for social polarization to take place. The results for greater Johannesburg suggest that these two supply-side labour market conditions are not always enough to produce social polarization. Instead, the findings suggest that an important, if not the main cause of changes to the occupational structure lies in the changing demand for different kinds of labour. Specifically, at this stage of economic development, low-wage unskilled jobs and middle-income semi-skilled manual jobs have been more readily replaced by mechanization than routine service, sales and clerical jobs.

By conceptualizing the changing nature of earnings inequality in terms of the social polarization debate, this study has also brought a new perspective to our understanding of inequality in greater Johannesburg. Instead of understanding post-*Apartheid* earnings inequality solely in terms of the failure of the State to provide adequate welfare for poor residents, this focus on the changing occupational structure has shown that the employed workforce has become generally more educated and better-paid. Furthermore, this growing demand for non-manual clerical, sales, professional, technical and managerial workers, was accompanied by a declining demand for manual workers, which has contributed to the high unemployment levels among poorly educated workers.

Chapter 3

PROFESSIONALIZATION, UNEMPLOYMENT AND RACIAL INEQUALITY

Introduction

The social polarization debate has proposed some partial explanations for the persistence of racial inequality in urban labour markets through reference to the changing historical relationship between migration to cities, the racial division of labour and deindustrialization. Specifically, proponents of the social polarization theory have argued that racial inequality was increased by the growth of low-income jobs because much of the demand for these jobs was met by migrants of different races to the native residents. By contrast, the professionalization theory argues that the decline of manual middle-income employment in the manufacturing sector led to high levels of unemployment among poorly educated black residents whose migration to cities coincided with deindustrialization. Both these theories argue that the growth of high-income jobs has benefitted better-educated residents, who are more likely to be native white residents rather than black migrants.

In one important respect, these theories can be used to interpret the changing patterns of racial inequality. Specifically, by focusing on the changing occupational structure and how these changes may have racially unequal consequences, these theories provide a useful approach to understanding the persistence of racial inequality in greater Johannesburg during the post-*Apartheid* period. In other respects, however, these theories are not useful. The distinction in US cities between the largely white native population and the more recently arrived migrant black population does not easily correspond to the history of migration in greater Johannesburg where both black and white workers have been numerically important components of the urban population since it was first settled. Both the social polarization and professionalization theories argue that racial inequality is partly caused by the changing relationship between waves of migration and the urban labour market. If this were true, then we would expect to find that a higher percentage of whites were native to greater Johannesburg and that higher percentages of Africans, coloureds and Indians were migrants. However, Borel-Saladin's (2013) study of greater Johannesburg showed that there were high proportions of migrants among all races and that the occupational profiles of migrants and natives were not substantially different. Her findings therefore suggest that waves of migration alone are not enough to explain racial inequality in greater Johannesburg.

How have the long-term changes in the occupational structure of employment changed the character of racial inequality in greater Johannesburg's labour market? The changes in the occupational structure from 1970 to 2011 show that there was slower employment growth in manual low-income and middle-income jobs that required less-educated workers. By contrast, there was much more employment growth in non-manual middle-income and high-income jobs that required better-educated workers. In other words, the growth of jobs for Elementary Workers, Craft and Related Trades Workers and Plant and Machine Operators and Assemblers was substantially less than the growth of jobs for Clerical Support Workers, Services and Sales Workers, Managers, Professionals, Technicians and Associate Professionals.

This change in the occupational structure was accompanied by the increase in the unemployment rate to very high levels among poorly educated workers. The restructuring of the labour market therefore benefitted better-educated workers and disadvantaged poorly educated workers. This meant that the distribution of educational qualifications within each race played an important role in determining labour market inequality between races. So the aim of this chapter is to examine the extent to which the historical legacy of racial discrimination during the *Apartheid* period and the abolition of racial discrimination since 1994 interacted with the changing occupational division of labour over the period from 1970 to 2011. Specifically, evidence will be presented to address the question of the extent to which the unequal racial division of labour among employed workers was eroded or reinforced over this period. Evidence will also be presented on the racial character of unemployment and how this can be at least partly explained by the changing occupational structure of employment.

High-income employment: Managers, professionals, technicians and associate professionals

During the *Apartheid* period, less than a quarter of middle-class jobs were filled by black workers.[1] Furthermore, racially exclusive employment practices restricted black workers to middle-class jobs in institutions that served members of their own races only. This meant that although black middle-class employment did increase during the *Apartheid* period, it was largely restricted to jobs such as nursing, teaching and management within the increasing number of blacks-only hospitals, schools, universities and local government authorities (Crankshaw, 1997: pp.87–92). However, during the late and post-*Apartheid* periods, the combination of a shortage of middle-class white workers and the decline of racial discrimination in the labour market led to the steep increase in the numbers of middle-class black workers (Figure 3.1 and Table 3.1). In 1991, at the end of the *Apartheid*

---

1 For earlier studies of the black and African middle class, see Crankshaw (1986) and Simkins and Hindson (1979).

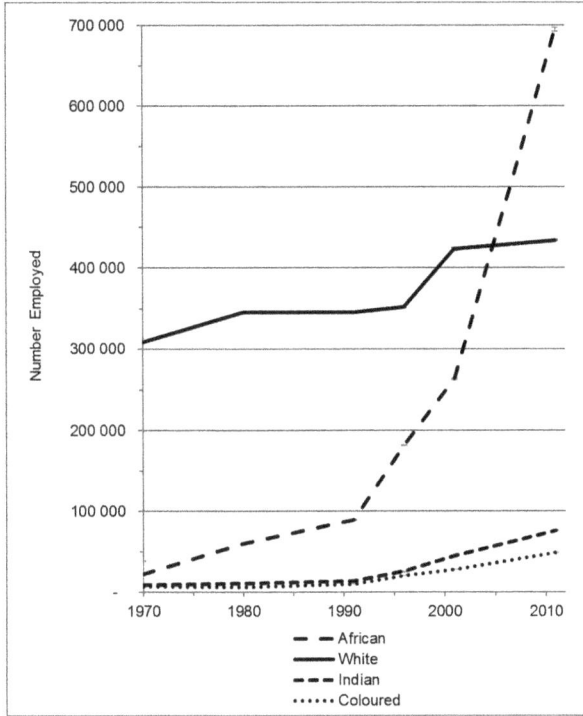

Figure 3.1 The Racial Composition of High-Income, Middle-Class* Employment in
Gauteng, 1970–2011
* Managers, Professionals, Technicians and Associate Professionals
Error bars indicate the 95 per cent confidence intervals.
Sources: Author's Analysis of Population Census Data Files, DataFirst Research Unit, University of Cape Town.

Table 3.1 Managerial, Professional, Technical and Associate Professional Employment by
Race in Gauteng, 1970–2011

	1970	1980	1991	1996	2001	2011	Average Annual Percentage Growth Rate, 1970–1991	Average Annual Percentage Growth Rate, 1991–2011
African	22,180	59,710	89,453	181,530	263,331	694,515	7	11
Coloured	7,105	6,109	10,031	20,462	28,187	49,071	2	8
Indian	8,721	10,677	13,831	25,797	44,973	76,176	2	9
White	308,430	344,986	345,184	352,177	423,274	434,172	1	1
Total	346,436	421,482	458,499	579,966	759,765	1,253,934	1	5
Black	38,006	76,496	113,315	227,789	336,491	819,762	5	10

Sources: Author's Analysis of Population Census Data Files, DataFirst Research Unit, University of Cape Town.

period, black workers made up only 25 per cent of all middle-class employment (Figure 3.2 and Table 3.2). In subsequent decades, the employment growth rate of black workers in middle-class jobs increased dramatically. Over the period from 1991 to 2011 the African middle class grew at an average annual rate of 11 per cent and the coloured and Indian middle classes grew at rates of 8 and 9 per cent, respectively (Table 3.1). By contrast, the numbers of middle-class white workers increased only marginally, growing at an average rate of only 1 per cent per year. Correspondingly, the white share of middle-class employment declined from 89 per cent in 1970 to only 35 per cent by 2011. This meant that the African share of middle-class employment grew from only 6 per cent in 1970 to 55 per cent in 2011. Similarly, the percentages of coloured and Indian workers employed in middle-class jobs doubled over this period (Figure 3.2 and Table 3.2). So although white workers were still over-represented in middle-class occupations by 2011, there was a dramatic change in the racial composition of the middle class: in both absolute and relative terms, there were more middle-class African workers than middle-class white workers.

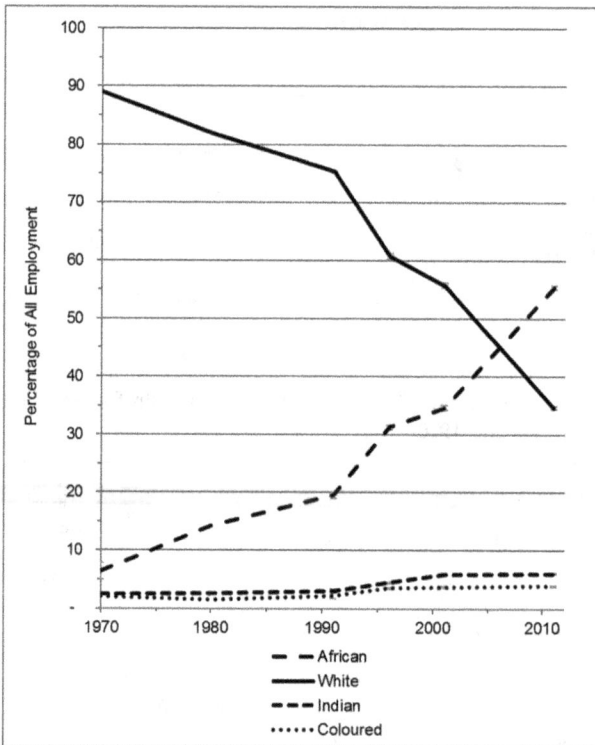

Figure 3.2 The Percentage Racial Composition of High-Income, Middle-Class* Employment in Gauteng, 1970 to 2011

* Managers, Professionals, Technicians and Associate Professionals
Error bars indicate the 95 per cent confidence intervals.
Sources: Author's Analysis of Population Census Data Files, DataFirst Research Unit, University of Cape Town.

Table 3.2 Percentage Racial Composition of Managerial, Professional, Technical and Associate Professional Employment in Gauteng, 1970–2011

	1970	1980	1991	1996	2001	2011
African	6	14	20	31	35	55
Coloured	2	1	2	4	4	4
Indian	3	3	3	4	6	6
White	89	82	75	61	56	35
Total	100	100	100	100	100	100
Black	11	18	25	39	44	65

Sources: Author's Analysis of Population Census Data Files, DataFirst Research Unit, University of Cape Town.

The post-*Apartheid* racial desegregation of schools and universities was an important cause of the growing number of tertiary-educated black workers who then became eligible for employment in professional, managerial and technical jobs. The racial desegregation of formerly whites-only schools was accompanied by policies that effectively turned them into fee-paying schools, with the possibility of fee exemptions for some pupils from low-income households (Fiske and Ladd, 2004: p.60). Despite the new fees and the restrictions on the number of pupil enrolments from outside the feeder areas, these schools desegregated steadily (Sujee, 2004: p.49). Reasons for this include the decline of the white school-going population, which had already led to the underutilization and subsequent closure of hundreds of whites-only schools before 1991 (Metcalfe, 1991: p.xi). The second reason is that the formerly whites-only neighbourhoods became racially desegregated and these new black residents sent their children to the local, formerly whites-only schools (Bell and McKay, 2011: pp.36–7). Third, following the pattern in other cities (Hunter, 2010: p.2650; Hunter, 2015: p.45) by the late 1990s, as much as 25 per cent of Sowetan households were sending their children to better schools in other parts of city, while local Sowetan schools were underutilized (de Kadt *et al.*, 2014: p.182). This meant that the desegregation of formerly whites-only schools did not completely exclude pupils from poorer black families who were excluded from the expensive property market of the formerly whites-only neighbourhoods. Similarly, the formerly whites-only universities were substantially deracialized, thereby providing the tertiary educations necessary for occupationally mobile black workers to enter careers in professional, technical and managerial occupations (Cooper, 2015: p.253).

As far as employment policies and practices were concerned, one reason for the dramatic growth of black middle-class employment was the introduction by the post-*Apartheid* Government of affirmative action law that was aimed at promoting upward occupational mobility among well-educated black workers. Specifically, the Employment Equity Act of 1998 required private businesses with more than fifty employees or with a financial turnover that exceeded specified thresholds both to set targets for and to report on their progress in appointing black workers into middle-class technical, professional and managerial jobs (Southall, 2016: p.71).

Another important piece of legislation was the Black Economic Empowerment Act of 2003, which aimed to expand the numbers of black business-owners (Seekings and Nattrass, 2005: p.343). Although the latter measure aimed at transforming racially unequal patterns of business ownership, it would also have increased the number of black employers who were recorded in official statistics as middle-class managers, professionals, associate professionals and technicians. One form of Black Economic Empowerment in large corporations entailed the sale of a portion of their shares to black-owned companies that was paid for with a loan. These deals favoured a small, politically connected group of individuals, and would have had little impact on the size of the black middle class: in 2003, as much as 72 per cent of the total value of Black Economic Empowerment deals were shared by only six individuals (Southall, 2016: p.89). However, another form of Black Economic Empowerment was the procurement policy of State Departments, which aimed to favour contracts with companies that had higher proportions of, among other things, black ownership. This form of Black Economic Empowerment therefore favoured a larger number of small black-owned companies whose owners and some employees would have been recorded as middle class in official statistics (Southall, 2016: p.88).

Another area of State intervention was in the employment practices of State departments. From the mid-1990s, it was State policy to achieve racially representative numbers of employees in the public administration. The initial targets of 50 per cent black and 30 per cent African employees were soon met: by 2004, the racial proportions of staff in Gauteng were representative of the Province's racial demography (Southall, 2016: p.75). This dramatic racial transformation of the public administration was achieved in part by voluntary retirement schemes for white senior officials that encouraged their early departure. In addition, the overall number of managers employed in the public sector was increased threefold between 1995 and 2001 (Southall, 2016: p.77). Similarly, managerial jobs in the State-owned enterprises, such as those responsible for electricity (Eskom), the railways (Transnet) and telecommunications (Telkom), with their head offices in Gauteng, were also successfully targeted by the State for affirmative action (Southall, 2016: p.79).

This expansion in the size of the black middle class did not result in the substantial displacement of the white middle class into lower-income occupational classes. The absolute size of the white middle class continued to grow during the post-*Apartheid* period (Figure 3.1) and the percentage of all white workers who were employed in middle-class jobs remained at roughly 50 per cent over the period from 1970 to 2011 (Figure 3.3, Table 3.3 and Table 3.4). The growth of the black middle class therefore took place in the context of a general increase in the number of middle-class jobs that could not be met by the supply of white workers alone. Between 1970 and 2011, only 14 per cent of the increase in middle-class employment was met by white workers. Correspondingly, 86 per cent of the increase in the number of middle-class jobs was filled by black workers, and 74 per cent by African workers alone (Table 3.5).

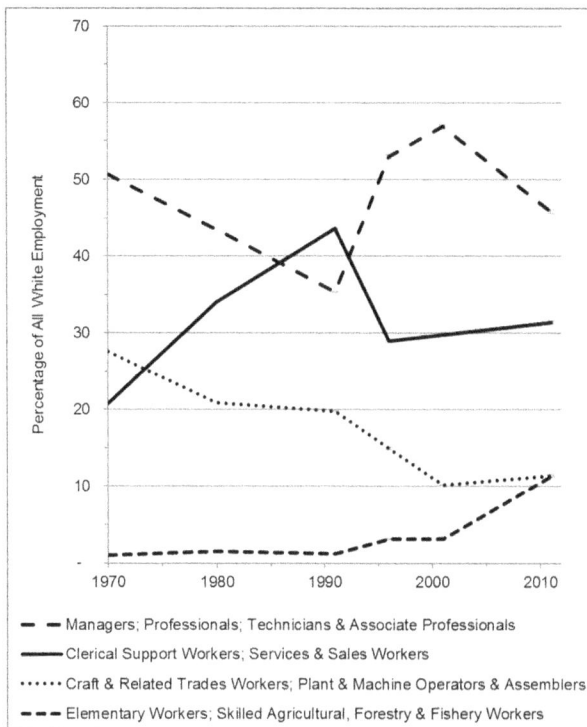

Figure 3.3 The Percentage Occupational Composition of White Employment in Gauteng, 1970–2011
Error bars indicate the 95 per cent confidence intervals.
Sources: Author's Analysis of Population Census Data Files, DataFirst Research Unit, University of Cape Town.

Table 3.3 The Occupational Composition of White Employment in Gauteng, 1970–2011

Occupational Groups	1970	1980	1991	1996	2001	2011
Managers, Professionals, Technicians & Associate Professionals	308,430	344,986	345,184	352,177	423,274	434,172
Clerical Support Workers, Services & Sales Workers	126,684	270,228	425,524	192,639	221,274	297,686
Craft & Related Trades Workers, Plant & Machine Operators & Assemblers	167,846	166,061	193,575	99,247	75,602	108,413
Elementary Workers, Skilled Agricultural, Forestry & Fishery Workers	6,249	12,203	11,830	20,761	23,511	107,404
Occupation Not Specified	14,373	11,541	32,930	103,631	76,417	222
Total	623,582	805,019	1,009,043	768,455	820,078	947,897

Sources: Author's Analysis of Population Census Data Files, DataFirst Research Unit, University of Cape Town.

Table 3.4 The Percentage Occupational Composition of White Employment in Gauteng, 1970–2011

Occupational Groups	1970	1980	1991	1996	2001	2011
Managers, Professionals, Technicians & Associate Professionals	51	43	35	53	57	46
Clerical Support Workers, Services & Sales Workers	21	34	44	29	30	31
Craft & Related Trades Workers, Plant & Machine Operators & Assemblers	28	21	20	15	10	11
Elementary Workers, Skilled Agricultural, Forestry & Fishery Workers	1	2	1	3	3	11
Total*	100	100	100	100	100	100

Sources: Author's Analysis of Population Census Data Files, DataFirst Research Unit, University of Cape Town.
* 'Occupation Not Specified' was excluded from these percentage calculations.

Table 3.5 Managerial, Professional, Technical and Associate Professional Employment Change by Race in Gauteng, 1970 and 2011

	Employment Growth, 1970–2011	Percentage of All Middle-Class Employment Growth, 1970–2011
African	672,335	74
Coloured	41,966	5
Indian	67,455	7
White	125,742	14
Total	907,498	100
Black	781,756	86

Sources: Author's Analysis of Population Census Data Files, DataFirst Research Unit, University of Cape Town.

The relatively greater increase of high-income, middle-class jobs therefore benefitted well-educated workers of all races. White workers, who benefitted from privileged access to good schools and universities during the *Apartheid* period, were given a skills advantage in the labour market. They were therefore well-placed to benefit from the growth of middle-class employment, not only during *Apartheid*, but also in the post-*Apartheid* period. The result was that white workers continued to be substantially over-represented in high-income, middle-class jobs. Although all black workers were historically disadvantaged by racial discrimination in both education and employment policies during the *Apartheid* period, in recent decades the deracialization of schools and universities has dramatically increased the numbers of well-educated black workers, mostly African workers, who have also benefitted from the growth of middle-class jobs.

So contrary to the argument that the growth of high-income jobs excluded black workers, these findings show that well-educated black workers have benefitted from the growth of middle-class employment. In Western European and some US cities where white residents are an overwhelming majority, it might be argued that the high demand for middle-class workers can be met without employing black residents. However, in the case of Johannesburg, where white residents are a very small minority; their numbers were not nearly enough to meet the strong growth in demand for middle-class workers. As a result, no amount of informal, post-*Apartheid* racial discrimination by white managers could substantially exclude black workers from middle-class jobs.

There is a flip-side to this racial demography of greater Johannesburg: although the growth of black middle-class employment dramatically changed the racial composition of the middle class, it did not have nearly as much impact on the occupational profile of black workers. This is because the black middle class forms a much smaller percentage of all black workers than it does of all middle-class workers. In 1970, only 3 per cent of all black workers were employed in middle-class jobs. By 2011, this percentage had increased to 24 per cent (Figure 3.4, Table 3.6 and Table 3.7). So when compared to the occupational profile of whites, even by 2011, the percentage of all black workers in middle-class jobs was still only about half the percentage (47 per cent) of all white workers in middle-class jobs (Figure 3.3 and Table 3.4).

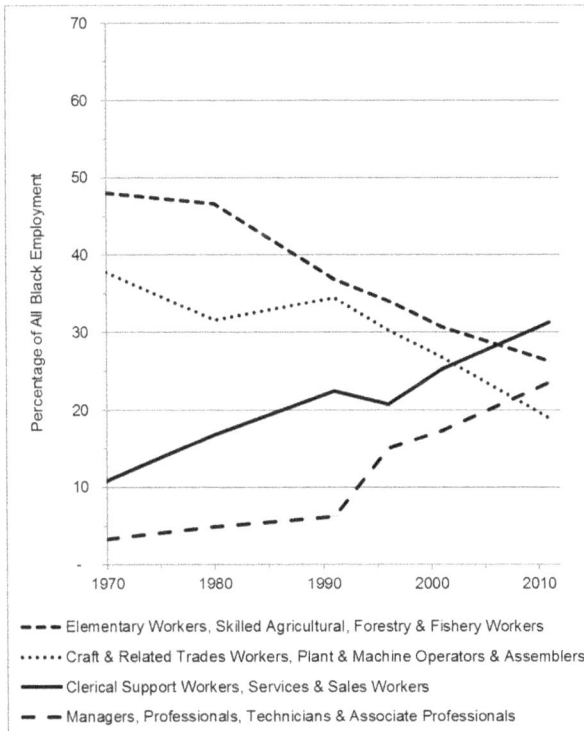

Figure 3.4 The Percentage Occupational Composition of Black Employment in Gauteng, 1970–2011

Error bars indicate the 95 per cent confidence intervals.

Sources: Author's Analysis of Population Census Data Files, DataFirst Research Unit, University of Cape Town.

Table 3.6 The Occupational Composition of Black Employment in Gauteng, 1970–2011

Occupational Groups	1970	1980	1991	1996	2001	2011
Managers, Professionals, Technicians & Associate Professionals	38,006	76,496	113,315	227,789	336,491	819,762
Clerical Support Workers, Services & Sales Workers	125,231	263,898	408,332	313,513	489,312	1,090,084
Craft & Related Trades Workers, Plant & Machine Operators & Assemblers	437,063	493,680	625,301	457,711	519,868	659,999
Elementary Workers, Skilled Agricultural, Forestry & Fishery Workers	555,078	729,460	669,256	515,295	594,971	915,314
Occupation Not Specified	46,302	73,641	33,342	155,189	135,777	850
Total	1,201,680	1,637,175	1,849,546	1,669,497	2,076,419	3,486,009

Sources: Author's Analysis of Population Census Data Files, DataFirst Research Unit, University of Cape Town.

Table 3.7 The Percentage Occupational Composition of Black Employment in Gauteng, 1970–2011

Occupational Groups	1970	1980	1991	1996	2001	2011
Managers, Professionals, Technicians & Associate Professionals	3	5	6	15	17	24
Clerical Support Workers, Services & Sales Workers	11	17	22	21	25	31
Craft & Related Trades Workers, Plant & Machine Operators & Assemblers	38	32	34	30	27	19
Elementary Workers, Skilled Agricultural, Forestry & Fishery Workers	48	47	37	34	31	26
Total*	100	100	100	100	100	100

Sources: Author's Analysis of Population Census Data Files, DataFirst Research Unit, University of Cape Town.
* 'Occupation Not Specified' was excluded from these percentage calculations.

Middle-income employment

The social polarization theory argues that deindustrialization in global cities has caused the decline of middle-income jobs, with the result that poorly educated black workers have been increasingly concentrated in low-income jobs (Sassen, 2001). The professionalization (or skills mismatch) theory argues that deindustrialization in US cities caused the decline of manual middle-income jobs, which led to high levels of unemployment among poorly educated black workers (Hamnett, 2003: pp.115–16; Kasarda, 1989; Wilson, 1987). Both these theories therefore tend to ignore the possibility of middle-income employment growth due to the increase in clerical, services and sales jobs. In the case of London, there was very little employment growth among clerical, services and sales jobs (Hamnett, 2003: p.65; Hamnett, 2015: p.241) and a study of New York showed an absolute decline (Bailey and Waldinger, 1991: p.52). In Hong Kong, Singapore, Taipei and Sydney, however, there was substantial absolute growth of these middle-income, non-manual jobs (Baum, 1997: p.1886; Baum, 1999: p.1100; Chiu and Lui, 2004: p.1870; Tai, 2006: p.1750). In greater Johannesburg, there was also a dramatic and long-term increase in the number of middle-income non-manual jobs, which has partly offset the slow growth in manual middle-income jobs.[2]

The long-term employment trends in greater Johannesburg from 1970 to 2011 show that the middle-income manual jobs of Craft and Related Trades Workers and Plant and Machine Operators and Assemblers grew at a much slower rate than other occupational groups, growing at an average rate of only 1 per cent per year from 1970 to 1991 and stagnating thereafter (Figure 3.5 and Table 3.8). Since these manual jobs were generally performed by less-educated black workers, their relative numerical decline probably did contribute to growing unemployment among poorly educated black workers. Throughout the *Apartheid* period, over 90 per cent of all machine operators and assemblers were black workers (Crankshaw, 1997: p.146; Simkins and Hindson, 1979: p.9). At the end of *Apartheid*, just over half of all the skilled trade workers were still white (Crankshaw, 1997: p.147), and by 2011, 85 per cent of these jobs were filled by black workers.[3] However, a substantial percentage of white workers were still employed as Craft and Related Trades Workers in 1970. As a result, statistically speaking, the overall percentage of white workers employed in all middle-income manual jobs was 28 per cent in 1970 (Table 3.8). This percentage declined steadily to 14 per cent by 2011, which was caused (in the statistical sense) by the slow absolute decline in the employment of white workers and a steady increase in the employment of African workers (Table 3.9). These manual occupations were therefore an important source of employment for poorly educated black, especially African, workers. This was especially true for the employment of Plant and Machine Operators and Assemblers, which grew dramatically from the 1960s until the end of 1980s through the mechanization of production in the manufacturing and construction industries (Crankshaw, 1990, Crankshaw, 1996; Crankshaw, 1997; Webster, 1985). This change in the division of labour transformed the occupational character

---

2 Note that the 1991 Population Census overestimated the employment of Services and Sales Workers and Clerical Support Workers. My investigations show that this is an error in the original full count or in the sampling of the full count. The weighting of the cases is therefore not the source of the error.

3 Author's calculation from 2011 Population Census results.

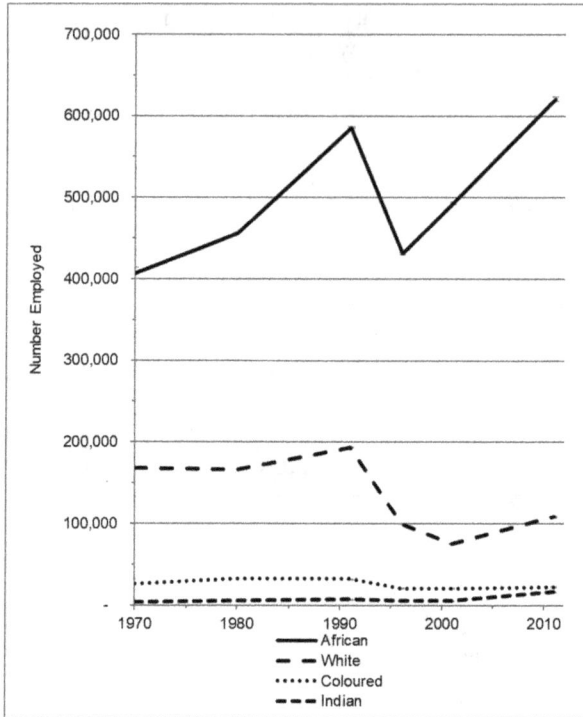

Figure 3.5 The Racial Composition of Middle-Income, Manual* Employment in
         Gauteng, 1970–2011
* Craft and Related Trades Workers, Plant and Machine Operators and Assemblers
Error bars indicate the 95 per cent confidence intervals.
Sources: Author's Analysis of Population Census Data Files, DataFirst Research Unit, University of Cape Town.

of black manual workers. In 1970, most of them were employed in low-income
unskilled jobs. By 2011, most of them were employed in middle-income, semi-
skilled jobs. The relative decline of these middle-income jobs after 1991 is therefore
a tragic irony of the post-*Apartheid* period because it has deprived poorly educated
black workers of middle-income jobs and was therefore an important cause of
their extremely high level of unemployment.

In contrast to employment trends in middle-income manual jobs, the dramatic
growth of clerical, services and sales jobs provided an alternative source of
middle-income employment opportunities, mostly for African workers. Although
a substantially greater percentage of these jobs require a completed secondary
education, their growth has nonetheless benefitted black (mostly African) workers
rather than white workers. From 1970 to 1991, about 50 per cent of these jobs
were filled by African workers. After 1991, the percentage of African workers grew
rapidly, reaching 71 per cent by 2011 (Figure 3.6 and Table 3.10). Correspondingly,
the percentage of white workers decreased from 50 per cent in 1970 to 21 per
cent in 2011 (Figure 3.6 and Table 3.10), which meant that white workers were no

Table 3.8 Employment of Craft and Related Trades Workers, Plant and Machine Operators and Assemblers by Race in Gauteng, 1970–2011

	1970	1980	1991	1996	2001	2011	Average Annual Percentage Growth Rate, 1970–1991	Average Annual Percentage Growth Rate, 1991–2011
African	406,980	455,934	585,268	431,156	493,209	620,607	2	0
Coloured	26,128	32,369	32,460	21,051	20,986	22,736	1	-2
Indian	3,955	5,377	7,573	5,504	5,673	16,656	3	4
White	167,846	166,061	193,575	99,247	75,602	108,413	1	-3
Total	604,909	659,741	818,876	556,958	595,470	768,412	1	0
Black	437,063	493,680	625,301	457,711	519,868	659,999	2	0

Sources: Author's Analysis of Population Census Data Files, DataFirst Research Unit, University of Cape Town.

Table 3.9 Percentage Racial Composition of Employment of Craft and Related Trades Workers, Plant and Machine Operators and Assemblers in Gauteng, 1970–2011

	1970	1980	1991	1996	2001	2011
African	67	69	71	77	83	81
Coloured	4	5	4	4	4	3
Indian	1	1	1	1	1	2
White	28	25	24	18	13	14
Total	100	100	100	100	100	100
Black	72	75	76	82	87	86

Sources: Author's Analysis of Population Census Data Files, DataFirst Research Unit, University of Cape Town.

longer over-represented in these occupations. This substantial deracialization of non-manual middle-income jobs was caused, in the statistical sense, by the strong absolute employment growth largely among African workers and the absolute decline in the numbers of white workers after 1991 (Figure 3.7 and Table 3.11).

So although this strong growth in non-manual middle-income employment growth is somewhat unusual among global cities, it does entail some 'upgrading' of the occupational structure in the general manner proposed by Hamnett. Furthermore, although the growth of these middle-income jobs has largely benefitted secondary-school graduates, this has not excluded black workers.

The consequence of these contradictory employment trends in all (manual and non-manual) middle-income jobs was that the percentage of all black workers who were employed in manual middle-income jobs was halved, decreasing from 38 per cent in 1970 to only 19 per cent in 2011. Over the same period, the percentage of black workers employed in non-manual middle-income jobs increased from

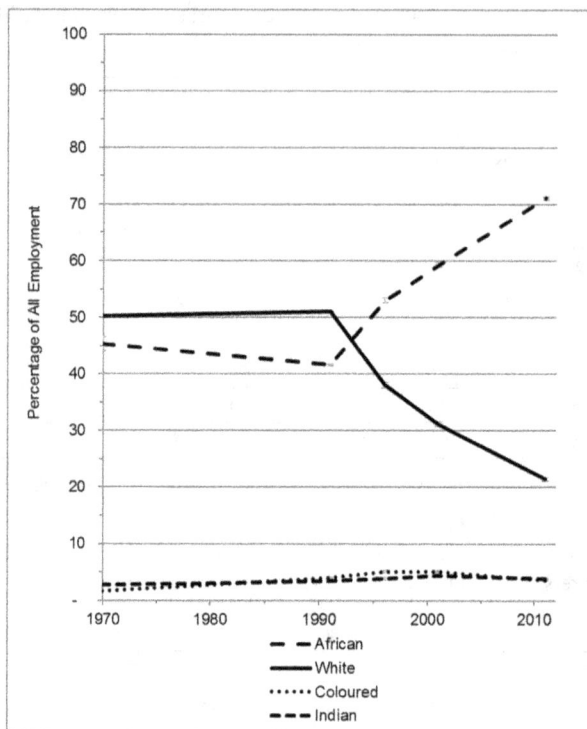

Figure 3.6 The Percentage Racial Composition of Middle-Income, Non-Manual*
            Employment in Gauteng, 1970–2011
* Clerical Support Workers and Services and Sales Workers
Error bars indicate the 95 per cent confidence intervals.
Sources: Author's Analysis of Population Census Data Files, DataFirst Research Unit, University of Cape Town.

Table 3.10 The Percentage Racial Composition of Clerical Support Workers and Services
            and Sales Workers in Gauteng, 1970–2011

	1970	1980	1991	1996	2001	2011
African	45	44	42	53	59	71
Coloured	2	3	4	5	5	4
Indian	3	3	3	4	4	4
White	50	51	51	38	31	21
Total	100	100	100	100	100	100
Black	50	49	49	62	69	79

Sources: Author's Analysis of Population Census Data Files, DataFirst Research Unit, University of Cape Town.

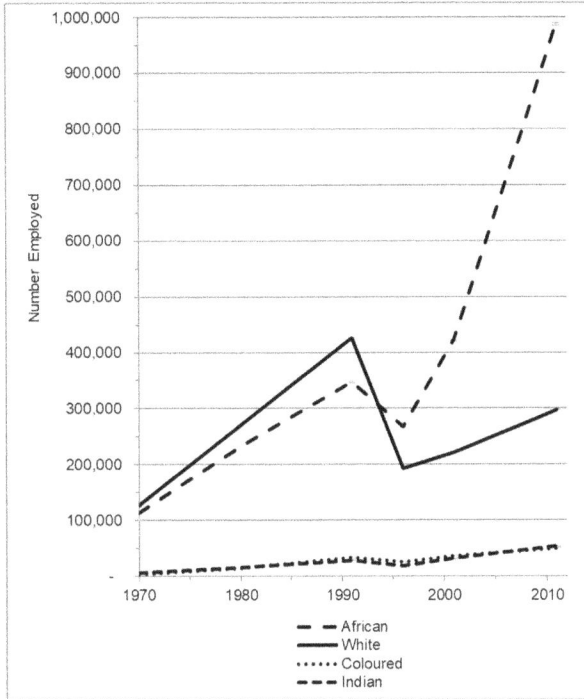

Figure 3.7 The Racial Composition of Middle-Income, Non-Manual* Employment in Gauteng, 1970–2011

* Clerical Support Workers and Services and Sales Workers
Error bars indicate the 95 per cent confidence intervals.
Sources: Author's Analysis of Population Census Data Files, DataFirst Research Unit, University of Cape Town.

Table 3.11 Employment of Clerical Support Workers and Services and Sales Workers by Race in Gauteng, 1970–2011

	1970	1980	1991	1996	2001	2011	Average Annual Percentage Growth Rate, 1970–1991	Average Annual Percentage Growth Rate, 1991–2011
African	114,020	232,617	346,823	268,163	421,227	986,479	5	5
Coloured	4,184	14,791	33,173	26,007	36,362	50,366	10	2
Indian	7,027	16,490	28,336	19,343	31,723	53,239	7	3
White	126,915	270,228	425,524	192,639	221,274	297,686	6	−2
Total	251,915	534,126	833,856	506,152	710,586	1,387,770	6	3
Black	125,231	263,898	408,332	313,513	489,312	1,090,084	6	5

Sources: Author's Analysis of Population Census Data Files, DataFirst Research Unit, University of Cape Town.

11 per cent to 31 per cent (Figure 3.4). So the restructuring of middle-income jobs from largely manual jobs to largely non-manual jobs has benefitted better-educated black workers. Conversely, the increased demand for more educated workers in middle-income clerical, sales and service jobs has therefore contributed to rising unemployment levels among less-educated black workers who would have previously been employed in middle-income manual jobs.

Low-income employment

According to the social polarization theory, racial inequality in global cities was increased by the decline of middle-income jobs and the concentration of more recent black migrants in low-income jobs rather than in manual middle-income jobs. By contrast, the professionalization theory argues that racial inequality was increased by the decline of black employment in manual middle-income jobs and the consequent rise of unemployment among poorly educated black workers.

In the case of greater Johannesburg, low-income, 'Elementary' jobs were filled almost completely by black workers during the *Apartheid* period. Only in recent years has the number of white workers in low-income jobs increased (Table 3.12). Furthermore, although there was substantial absolute growth of low-income jobs, this increase was much less than the increases in middle- and high-income jobs. We can therefore conclude that racial inequality was not increased by the relatively larger growth of low-income jobs in which black workers were concentrated. To the contrary, had there been more growth in low-income jobs, racial inequality would probably have been lessened by lower rates of unemployment among poorly educated black workers.

Table 3.12 Employment of Elementary and Skilled Agricultural, Forestry and Fishery Workers by Race in Gauteng, 1970–2011

	1970	1980	1991	1996	2001	2011	Average Annual Percentage Growth Rate, 1970–2011
African	546,720	719,633	658,345	503,774	581,870	879,011	0.05
Coloured	7,955	9,079	10,219	8,620	10,506	21,543	0.10
Indian	403	748	692	2,901	2,595	14,760	0.36
White	6,249	12,203	11,830	20,761	23,511	107,404	0.28
Total	561,327	741,663	681,086	536,056	618,482	1,022,718	0.06
Black	555,078	729,460	669,256	515,295	594,971	915,314	0.05

Sources: Author's Analysis of Population Census Data Files, DataFirst Research Unit, University of Cape Town.

Unemployment, occupational class and racial inequality

According to both the social polarization and skills mismatch/professionalization theories, we should expect to find higher unemployment rates among poorly educated workers who would otherwise have been employed in manual middle-income jobs. In the United States, the skills mismatch theory was developed to explain the high unemployment rate among poorly educated black residents of the largely black inner cities. The argument is that the decline in manual, middle-income jobs resulted in unemployment among poorly educated inner-city residents. By contrast, there was no such decline of manual middle-income jobs in the largely white edge cities. Insofar as the decline of manual middle-income jobs was restricted to the inner cities, this theory was a plausible explanation for the high rate of black unemployment, compared to the low rate of white unemployment. However, this theory does not readily translate into the context of greater Johannesburg because almost all manual middle-income jobs have been filled by black workers since the *Apartheid* period.

Nonetheless, this theory can be used to interrogate racially unequal rates of unemployment by examining the statistical relationship between race, unemployment and level of education for the whole of greater Johannesburg. If it were possible, it would also be useful to examine the statistical relationship between the race and previous occupation of unemployed workers. But this cannot be done because about two-thirds of all unemployed workers in greater Johannesburg had never been employed and therefore could not provide a previous occupation.[4]

A striking feature of the high unemployment rate in greater Johannesburg is that it varied substantially by race. When unemployment peaked in 2001, the unemployment rate among African and coloured workers was 45 and 34 per cent, respectively. By contrast, Indian and white unemployment was substantially lower at only 13 and 6 per cent, respectively (Figure 3.8). These results have something in common with those from US cities, which showed that white residents experienced much lower levels of unemployment than black residents. In the case of greater Johannesburg, the racially discriminatory education, housing and employment policies of the *Apartheid* period played an important role in improving the educational level and occupational structure of white workers over a number of generations. The result was that the numbers of white workers employed in manual jobs by the end of *Apartheid* were restricted to a small number of craft and related workers and even smaller numbers employed as machine operators. This meant that white workers were well-placed to take advantage of the growth in high-income middle-class jobs and middle-income clerical, sales and services jobs. This meant that they generally did not suffer high rates of unemployment due to the slow rate of growth in manual jobs.

The results of the statistical analysis of educational level by unemployment rate show that the unemployment rate was inversely correlated with the level of

4 Author's analysis of the Quarterly Labour Force Survey, 3rd Quarter 2011.

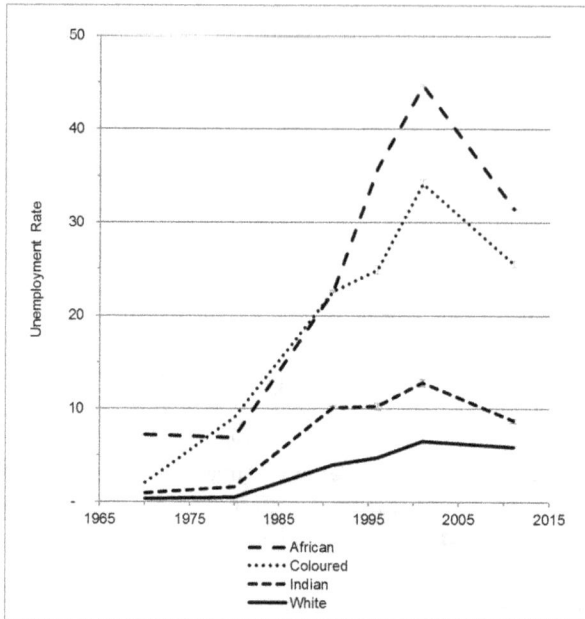

Figure 3.8 Strict Unemployment Rate by Race in Gauteng, 1970–2011
Error bars indicate the 95 per cent confidence intervals.
Sources: Author's Analysis of Population Census Data Files, DataFirst Research Unit, University of Cape Town.

education. Among all races, unemployment was highest among workers who had not completed secondary school and lowest among those who had completed a tertiary degree (Figure 3.9 to Figure 3.12). These findings are therefore consistent with the argument that the relatively slow rate of growth of low- and middle-income manual jobs, which are the occupations in which most workers do not have a completed secondary education, is one of the causes of unemployment. We can therefore conclude that the changing occupational structure, which has seen more growth among middle- and high-income non-manual jobs, has had at least some effect on the racially unequal unemployment rates.

However, not all these results are readily explained by the changing occupational structure. The unemployment rate among African workers who completed secondary school is almost the same as those who did not (Figure 3.9). This finding is not consistent with the dramatic growth of employment in middle-income clerical, service and sales jobs. Alternative explanations are therefore required to explain high unemployment among some African workers who have completed secondary school. These may include the general oversupply of workers with this low level of education in combination with the unequal schooling system that still produced many African secondary school graduates with poorer literacy and numeracy skills than other black and white secondary school graduates (Lam *et al.*, 2008: p.15). It is generally acknowledged that the most important cause of this enduring racially unequal access to education was the failure of the post-*Apartheid*

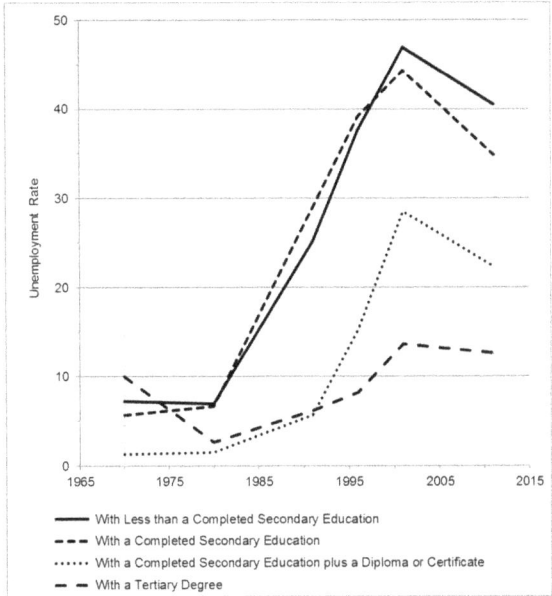

Figure 3.9 African Unemployment Rate by Level of Education in Gauteng, 1970–2011
Error bars indicate the 95 per cent confidence intervals.
Sources: Author's Analysis of Population Census Data Files, DataFirst Research Unit, University of Cape Town.

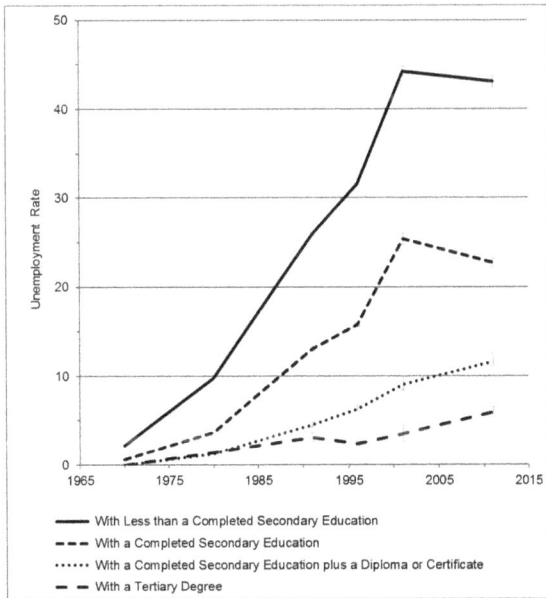

Figure 3.10 Coloured Unemployment Rate by Level of Education in Gauteng, 1970–2011
Error bars indicate the 95 per cent confidence intervals.
Sources: Author's Analysis of Population Census Data Files, DataFirst Research Unit, University of Cape Town.

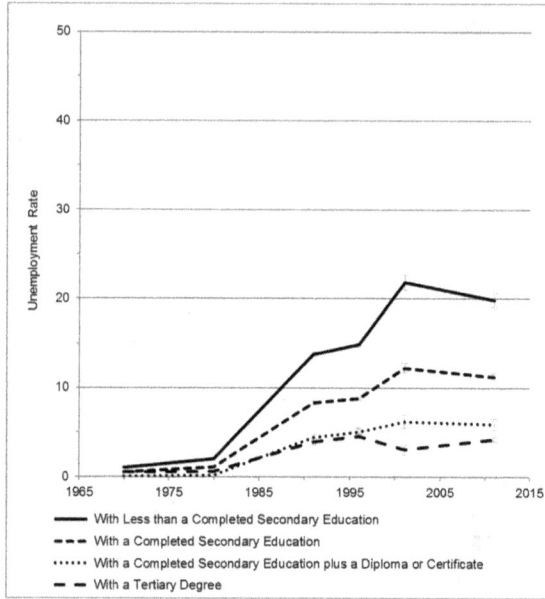

Figure 3.11 Indian Unemployment Rate by Level of Education in Gauteng, 1970–2011
Error bars indicate the 95 per cent confidence intervals.
Sources: Author's Analysis of Population Census Data Files, DataFirst Research Unit, University of Cape Town.

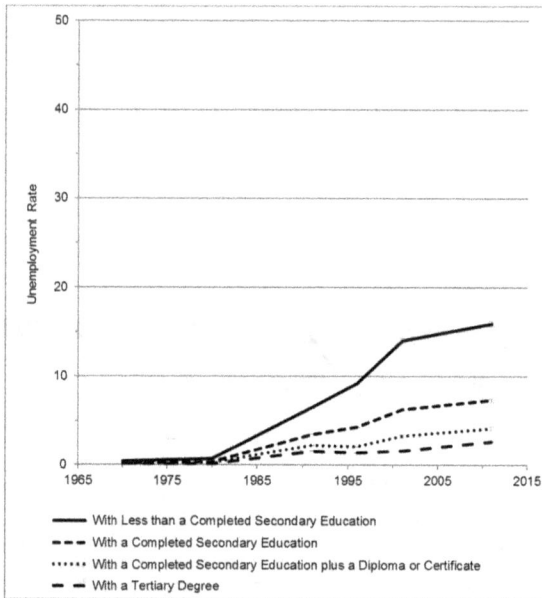

Figure 3.12 White Unemployment Rate by Level of Education in Gauteng, 1970–2011
Error bars indicate the 95 per cent confidence intervals.
Sources: Author's Analysis of Population Census Data Files, DataFirst Research Unit, University of Cape Town.

Government adequately to improve the secondary school system in poor African neighbourhoods (Spaull, 2013: pp.57–8; van der Berg, 2007: pp.862–3).

In the context of the growing demand for middle-income clerical, services and sales workers and for high-income middle-class workers, black workers with completed secondary and tertiary educations were upwardly mobile into jobs that had the most employment growth. The growing demand for these jobs and the short supply of qualified workers meant that the unemployment rate among educated black workers was much lower than the rate among poorly educated workers. By contrast, black workers who did not complete their secondary and tertiary educations were much more likely to be unemployed.

Conclusion

In this chapter, I have presented evidence to evaluate different theories of how the changing demands for and supply of different kinds of labour might explain the changing nature of racial income inequality in greater Johannesburg. I have done this by first examining the changing relationship between the occupational structure and the racial composition of employment by occupational groups. The results from the previous chapter showed that over the period from 1970 to 2011, employment opportunities for better educated workers grew substantially more than for poorly educated workers. In occupational terms, this meant that there was substantial employment growth in the non-manual and middle-income jobs of clerks, service and sales workers and in the high-income jobs of managers, professionals, technicians and associate professionals. By contrast, there was much less employment growth in manual low-income elementary occupations and the manual middle-income occupations of craft and related trades and plant and machine-operating and assembling.

To understand how this changing occupational structure has changed the pattern of racial inequality, we should consider how the effects of historical racial discrimination during the *Apartheid* period have interacted with the changing occupational structure of employment. Correspondingly, we should also consider how the abolition of racially discriminatory laws and affirmative action policy in the post-*Apartheid* period has interacted with this changing division of labour.

During the *Apartheid* period, racial discrimination in education and employment policies served to benefit white workers and to disadvantage black workers. These policies explain why black workers were largely restricted to low- and middle-income manual jobs. In the post-*Apartheid* period, the removal of racial discrimination did not dramatically change the lives of most poorly educated black residents who lived in neighbourhoods with failing schools. From the 1980s onward, these poorly educated workers were faced with the relatively slow rate of growth in the manual jobs for which they were qualified. In the context of a growing population of poorly educated workers, this meant that their unemployment rate grew dramatically from 1980 onwards.

By contrast, well-educated workers of all races benefitted from the growth of middle and high-income non-manual jobs in the post-*Apartheid* period. White workers were particularly well-placed to take advantage of this new division of labour because of their privileged access to education during *Apartheid*. The minority of black workers who secured access to a good education were also upwardly mobile into middle-income clerical, services and sales jobs and high-income managerial, professional, technical and associate professional jobs. The result was that employment in these occupations was substantially deracialized over the period from 1991 to 2011.

The strong growth of employment in middle-income clerical, services and sales jobs prevented the social polarization of the occupational structure, which would otherwise have probably concentrated most black secondary school graduates in middle- and low-income manual jobs. Although black workers already occupied about half of all non-manual middle-income jobs in 1970, these occupations were further deracialized from 1991 onwards. So the lack of social polarization of the occupational structure meant that there was upward mobility of many black workers into non-manual middle-income jobs that at least partially made up for the loss of manual middle-income jobs.

An important feature of the professionalization of the occupational structure is that it did not result in the exclusion of black workers from high-income jobs and did not solely benefit white workers. The dramatic growth of high-income jobs meant that there were not enough well-educated white workers to meet the demand for these jobs. The result was the dramatic growth of the black middle class without any substantial exclusion of white workers from these high-income jobs. By 2011, black workers made up just under two-thirds of all high-income, middle-class employment. Although by 2011, white workers were still over-represented in middle-class occupations, between 1991 and 2011 the absolute number of middle-class black workers had grown at about ten times the rate as the number of white workers.

In summary, these results suggest that the changing division of labour has benefitted well-educated workers of all races, while disadvantaging poorly educated workers. This changing occupational structure has interacted with changing patterns of racial discrimination to dramatically change the nature of racial inequality. During the early *Apartheid* period, racial inequality entailed the concentration of black workers in low- and middle-income manual jobs and the concentration of white workers in middle- and high-income non-manual jobs. Although African workers were much more unemployed than other workers, the overall unemployment rate was very low. Therefore, the early *Apartheid* pattern of racial inequality was determined largely by differences in earnings caused by the racially unequal division of labour.

By the first decade of the twenty-first century, this pattern of racial inequality had changed dramatically. By 2011, racial inequality was characterized by high unemployment among poorly educated African and coloured workers and low unemployment among Indian and white workers. Although white workers were still over-represented in high-income, middle-class occupations, there was substantial desegregation of the middle-income and high-income occupations, which were predominantly filled by white workers during the early *Apartheid* period. So whereas the black workforce was once characterized almost entirely by employment in manual jobs, by 2011 it had become highly differentiated (Table 3.7). Roughly one-third of all black workers were unemployed, one-third were employed in manual jobs, one-fifth were employed in clerical, services and sales jobs and 16 per cent were employed in middle-class occupations. In contrast to black workers, the fate of white workers had remained relatively unchanged. Their unemployment rate had increased but to only 6 per cent. By 2011, 46 per cent of white workers were still employed in middle-class jobs with only a slight decline from 50 per cent in 1970. Their relative decline in middle-income manual employment was accompanied by a slight increase in middle-income non-manual employment and in low-income manual employment. By 2011, therefore, racial earnings inequality had declined substantially due to upward occupational mobility among blacks. Although the racial division of labour was still unequal, it had been substantially eroded. However, the growth of unemployment since the late 1970s created a new form of racial inequality characterized by extremely high unemployment rates among African and coloured workers and much lower unemployment rates among Indian and white workers.

Part II

FROM A FORDIST TO A POST-FORDIST SPATIAL ORDER

Chapter 4

JOHANNESBURG'S FORDIST SPATIAL ORDER

Introduction

The most influential theory on the nature of the post-Fordist spatial order of Western cities concerns the changing geography of social inequality. According to proponents of this theory, de-industrialization led to new social differences between largely working-class, inner-city ghetto neighbourhoods and largely middle-class, suburban neighbourhoods. During the industrial, Fordist period, the inner city was distinguished by a large manufacturing sector, which employed low- and middle-income manual workers, and by its working-class residential neighbourhoods. By contrast, the suburbs were distinguished by their largely residential neighbourhoods, which were inhabited by high-income, middle-class workers (Marcuse and van Kempen, 2000: p.4).

According to the skills mismatch theory, the post-industrial, post-Fordist period was characterized by the decline of manufacturing employment, which has resulted in high levels of unemployment among less-educated, mostly black, manual workers who lived in the inner-city ghettos (Kasarda, 1989: p.34). This new development therefore transformed the racial ghetto into the 'excluded ghetto' (Marcuse, 1997: p.4). A contrasting argument, namely the social polarization theory, argues that the decline of middle-income manual jobs has led, not only to high unemployment, but also to the concentration of poorly educated inner-city residents into the growing numbers of low-income, unskilled jobs (Sassen, 2001: pp.324–5).

The residents of the suburbs, for their part, prospered in the post-Fordist period, benefitting from the growth in high-income, non-manual jobs. Simultaneously, the suburbs were transformed from largely residential neighbourhoods to satellite 'edge cities' with their own business centres and sources of employment (Marcuse and van Kempen, 2000: pp.7 and 15). Because the residents of these edge cities are largely white (Beauregard and Haila, 2000: p.29), the growing inequality between suburbs and the racial inner-city ghettos has resulted in increased racial inequality and racial residential segregation.

This debate has direct relevance to our understanding of Johannesburg's changing social geography because it provides possible explanations for the persistence of geographical racial inequality in the post-*Apartheid* period.

The argument is that during the early stage of Fordist manufacturing growth, migrants to the city experienced full employment and middle-income earnings that enabled them and their offspring to be upwardly mobile. In the cities of the United States, where such migrants were of largely European origin, their upward mobility enabled them to escape the inner-city ethnic ghettos and to assimilate into the mainstream of the urban economy. This was not the case for black migrants whose later, large-scale migration from the countryside coincided roughly with the decline of manufacturing employment. The result was that rural black migrants with low educations bore the brunt of unemployment caused by the decline of middle-income, manual jobs (Kasarda, 1989: p.27). Consequently, they were denied the upward mobility of previous generations and were restricted to the decaying inner-city ghettos where housing was cheap or sponsored by the state. This did not apply to educated, middle-class blacks. In the period after the Fair Housing Act of 1968, middle-class blacks had greater opportunities to move from these inner-city ghettos to live in the more expensive suburbs (Clark, 2007: p.295; Wilson, 2003: p.1099). The flight of the black middle class from inner-city ghettos is argued to have been an important cause of the growing concentration of unemployed and low-wage black residents in the inner-city ghetto neighbourhoods (Wilson, 1987: p.50).

These theories of the nature and causes of the racially divided spatial order are very pertinent to the study of Johannesburg's post-Fordist and post-*Apartheid* social geography because they provide us with plausible partial explanations for the persistence of the racially divided geography of Johannesburg. Specifically, this debate prompts important questions concerning the nature of the excluded ghetto in Johannesburg and its implications for Johannesburg's racially unequal geography. Is it true that Soweto, Eldorado Park and Lenasia have been transformed from a racialized ghetto into an excluded ghetto? In other words, has the decline of manual jobs for manufacturing workers resulted in the concentration of unemployment in the excluded ghetto? Alternatively, following Sassen (2001: pp.324–5), has the loss of middle-income manual jobs produced a different kind of poverty in which these black, working-class neighbourhoods are increasingly dominated by residents employed in low-income, unskilled jobs?

Has there been large-scale flight of the black middle class from the excluded ghetto to the edge city of Sandton? If so, has this resulted in the concentration of poverty in Soweto, Eldorado Park and Lenasia? Secondly, have the residents of the edge city of Sandton become increasingly middle-class? If so, has this concentration of the middle class in the northern suburbs perpetuated the racial segregation of the *Apartheid* era? Have the expensive housing estates and gated communities of the formerly whites-only northern suburbs remained racially segregated or have they undergone racial desegregation?

The social geography of Johannesburg cannot be mapped directly onto the spatial characteristics and developments that have taken place in other large world cities. There are clearly some important differences that will be discussed here. Nonetheless, my main argument is that the concepts drawn from the debate over the post-Fordist urban spatial order can facilitate an understanding of the reasons why the geography of Johannesburg's racial inequality was both reproduced and changed over the period from 1970 to 2011.

Johannesburg's Fordist spatial order

At the end of its industrial, Fordist period in the mid-1970s, Johannesburg and its satellite towns had many of the features of a typical Western city (Beall *et al.*, 2002: pp.46–51). It had a single large and prosperous downtown, or central business district (CBD). This CBD was surrounded by a residential inner-city district composed of pre-war, semi-detached and detached housing with low-rise apartment buildings and a post-war, high-rise apartment district (Figure 4.1). Further afield, in all directions, were low-density suburban residential neighbourhoods, many of them with their own local authorities. In certain other respects, however, Johannesburg was quite different.

The most important difference is that Johannesburg's inner-city residential neighbourhoods had been cleared of most low-cost housing many decades before. In the first two decades of the twentieth century, poor African and coloured residents rented rooms in the CBD and the inner city residential neighbourhoods. These rooms took the form of shacks in 'slumyards', rooms in employers' hostels, and rooms in the backyards of formal residential neighbourhoods and in sub-divided formal houses (Crankshaw, 2005: pp.371–2; Hellmann, 1948; pp.5–11; Parnell, 2003: pp.626–7).

In the 1930s, slums and many hostels in the Johannesburg CBD and Prospect Township[1] were demolished and their residents concentrated in the surrounding slum neighbourhoods of the Malay Location,[2] Sophiatown, Martindale and Albertville on the western boundary of the inner-city (Musiker and Musiker, 1999: p.107; Parnell, 1988; Parnell and Pirie, 1991: p.133) (Figure 4.2). In the 1940s and 1950s, the State, using the Slums Act, demolished much of the housing in these neighbourhoods and forcibly removed their inhabitants to racially segregated public housing estates in the southern suburbs (Lodge, 1981; Parnell and Pirie, 1991: p.134). African residents were removed to the neighbourhoods of Orlando, Meadowlands and Diepkloof in Soweto,[3] coloured residents were removed to Riverlea, Noordgesig (Moore, 2016: p.11) and Eldorado Park, and Indian residents were removed to Lenasia (Figure 4.1).

1 Prospect Township was located on the contemporary site of Prolecon.

2 The Malay Location was located on the contemporary site of Pageview.

3 Following a popular convention, I will use the term 'Soweto' to refer to what was usually named 'Greater Soweto', which, prior to 1973, included Soweto (under the authority of the Johannesburg City Council), Dobsonville (under the authority of the Roodepoort City Council) and DiepMeadow, which refers to the suburbs of Diepkloof and Meadowlands (under the authority of the Resettlement Board) (Morris, 1980: p.65).

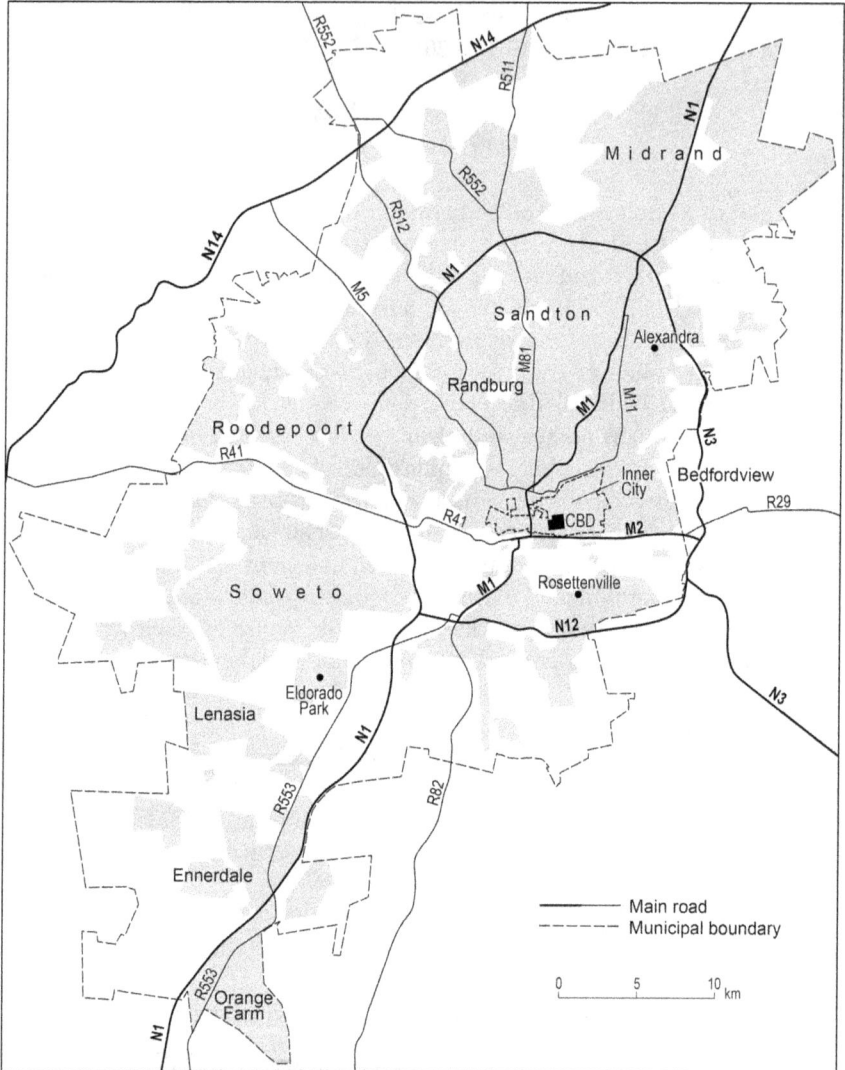

Figure 4.1 The City of Johannesburg Metropolitan Municipality
Cartography by Philip J. Stickler

So one of consequences of inner-city slum clearances and the enforcement of racial residential segregation was that low- and middle-income, working-class black residents were provided with public housing in the southern suburbs instead of being concentrated in older slum buildings and public housing in the inner city. Johannesburg's racial ghetto, unlike its New York and Chicago inner-city counterparts, was therefore displaced from the inner city to the southern suburbs. In subsequent decades, further public housing developments for black residents

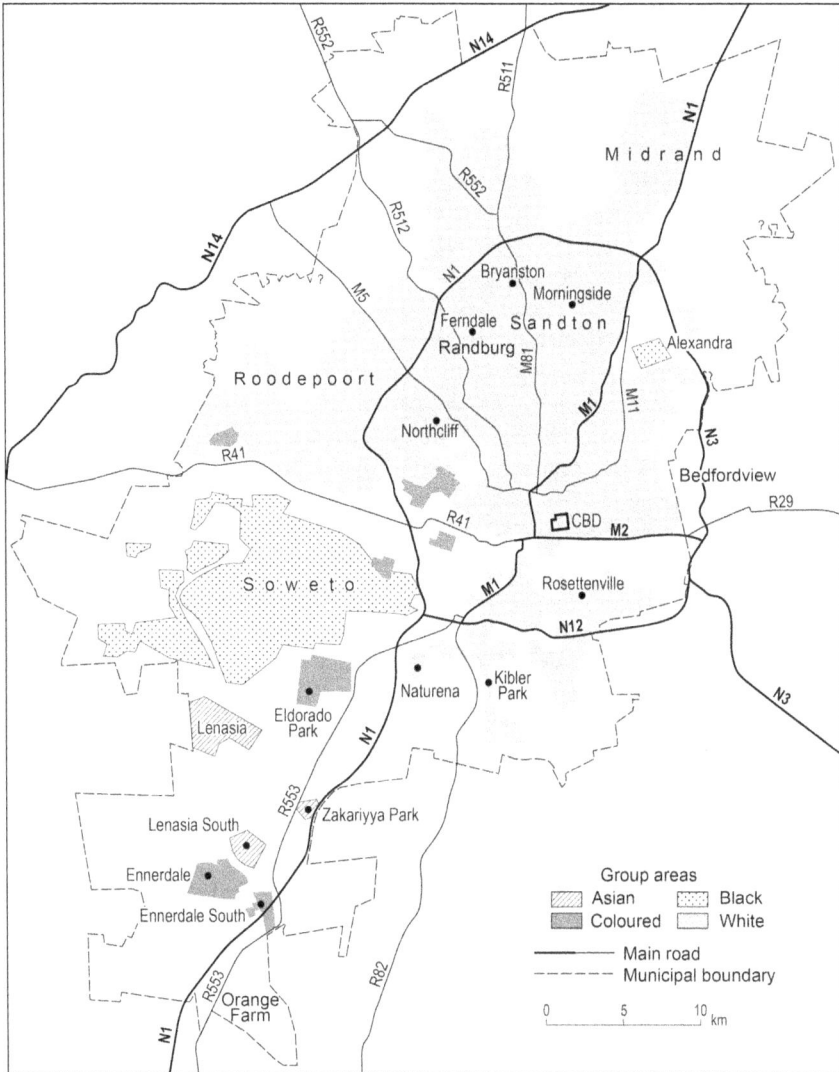

Figure 4.2 *Apartheid*-Era Racial Group Areas in Johannesburg
Cartography by Philip J. Stickler

were also built in racially segregated suburban locations. This contrasts again with post-war developments in US cities where new public housing was concentrated in the inner cities (Mabin, 2005a: p.221).

At the end of the Fordist period, in the early 1970s, Johannesburg's residential geography was segregated by both occupational class and race. Generally, the northern suburbs were home to the high-income, managerial, professional and technical middle class. By contrast, the southern suburbs had a predominantly working-class composition of non-manual clerical, sales and service workers and manual artisans machine operators, artisans and elementary (unskilled) workers (Hart and Browett, 1976). Among white residents, there was a long-standing geographical division between the working-class southern suburbs and the middle-class northern suburbs (Hart, 1968; Hart, 1975; Hart, 1976; Hart and Browett, 1976). This occupational class geography also took a racially segregated form. Among African residents, except for the northern suburb of Alexandra, *Apartheid* urban policies had concentrated them in the south-western suburbs (Figure 4.1).

The only exception to this racial geography was the neighbourhood of Alexandra in the northern suburbs, which was first established in 1912 on what was then peri-urban land (Bonner and Nieftagodien, 2008: p.17; Nauright, 1998: p.67). As in Sophiatown, Alexandra was first occupied by black landowners who were later dispossessed of their properties during the *Apartheid* period (Hooghiemstra and Cloete, 2018: p.199; Matlapeng, 2011: pp.259–63). Unlike Sophiatown, however, not all the African residents of Alexandra were forcibly removed by the State to the southern suburbs (Sarakinsky, 1984) and the East Rand (Ballard *et al.*, 2021). The result was that, by the 1970s, Alexandra was the only African ghetto in the northern suburbs.

The same could be said for coloured and Indian residents. Except for the small northern suburbs of Davidsonville, Bosmont, Westbury, Coronationville and Newclare, most coloured residents lived in the coloureds-only Group Areas of Eldorado Park and Ennerdale in the southern suburbs (Figure 4.2). Only a small number of Indian residents resisted their forced relocation from Pageview to Lenasia in the southern suburbs (Carrim, 1990) (Figure 4.3).

Commercial, financial and retail businesses were concentrated largely in the CBD with only minor suburban retail and office nodes in the suburbs (Beavon, 2004: pp.179–81). In the 1970s, Johannesburg's manufacturing sector was still one of the major employers, contributing almost one-quarter of all Johannesburg's employment (Beall *et al.*, 2002: p.33). These light manufacturing businesses were located on the south side of the CBD in a long strip of development running from east to west (Figure 4.1). The inner city of Johannesburg was therefore the focus of most economic activities and the suburbs were of a largely residential character with small shopping nodes.

Another feature of Johannesburg that distinguishes it from other world cities is that the middle class did not favour the inner city as a place of residence. Unlike New York and London, where high-income residents have carved out secure inner-city 'citadels' such as Battery Park and Mayfair, respectively, Johannesburg's middle class has preferred the northern suburbs, at least since the turn of the twentieth century.

Aims and method

In the following pages, I will present evidence concerning the long-term changes in the provision of housing and the geography of the occupation class and employment status of Johannesburg's residents. I will begin with statistical evidence that measures the occupational structure and employment status of residents in the edge city of Sandton and the excluded ghettos of Soweto, Eldorado Park and Lenasia. This will be followed with a presentation of maps to show the geography of neighbourhoods according to the occupational composition of their residents. After that, I will provide an explanation for the geography of these statistical trends by discussing the historical geography of different kinds of housing provision.

To generate and present these statistics, I have conceptualized both the edge city and the excluded ghettos in rather broad geographical terms. In doing so, my aim was to be as comprehensive as possible to avoid the criticism of presenting statistics selectively. At the same time, I did not want to do any violence to the concepts of the edge city and the excluded ghetto. As far as the edge city of Sandton is concerned, I have therefore included all neighbourhoods north of the inner-city neighbourhoods (Figure 4.3 and Figure 4.4).

I have conceptualized the excluded ghetto in the following way. First, I have included all the southern suburbs that were developed by the *Apartheid* Government to house black residents. This includes Soweto, Eldorado Park, Lenasia, Lenasia South, Zakariyya Park and Ennerdale (Figure 4.2). These neighbourhoods correspond to the concept of a racially segregated ghetto in the sense that they were used to exclude black residents from white neighbourhoods within the context of a racially oppressive society (Marcuse, 1997: p.3). Second, I have also included all post-*Apartheid* housing developments that were built within and on the periphery of these racial ghettos. These neighbourhoods include the new public housing developments in the far south of Johannesburg, namely Orange Farm, Stretford, Drie Ziek, Lakeside, Kanana Park, Vlakfontein and Unaville. Also included are the new housing developments on the western and northern flanks of Soweto, namely Bram Fischerville, Slovoville and Lufhereng (Figure 4.5).

The following employment statistics include all residents in all types of dwellings and neighbourhoods. It therefore includes the residents of residential neighbourhoods (including live-in domestic workers) and all residents living on peri-urban properties and in industrial and commercial areas.

There are several ways that descriptive statistics can be used to study the changing class geography of Johannesburg. The first entails the statistical distributions of each occupational class across the northern suburbs, the inner city and the excluded ghetto. This method shows where the different social classes are concentrated and the extent to which this geography has changed over time. The second method entails the statistical distribution of employment within each area across the occupational classes, and the extent to which this distribution has changed over time. In effect, this is a measure of the occupational class composition of each area. The third method of analysis entails the measurement of the class composition of each of the roughly 600 neighbourhoods in Johannesburg. The class composition of these neighbourhoods can then be presented in the form of maps to show the geography of neighbourhoods with specific class compositions. This method can be used to demonstrate the geography of neighbourhoods with, for example, a majority of middle-class residents.

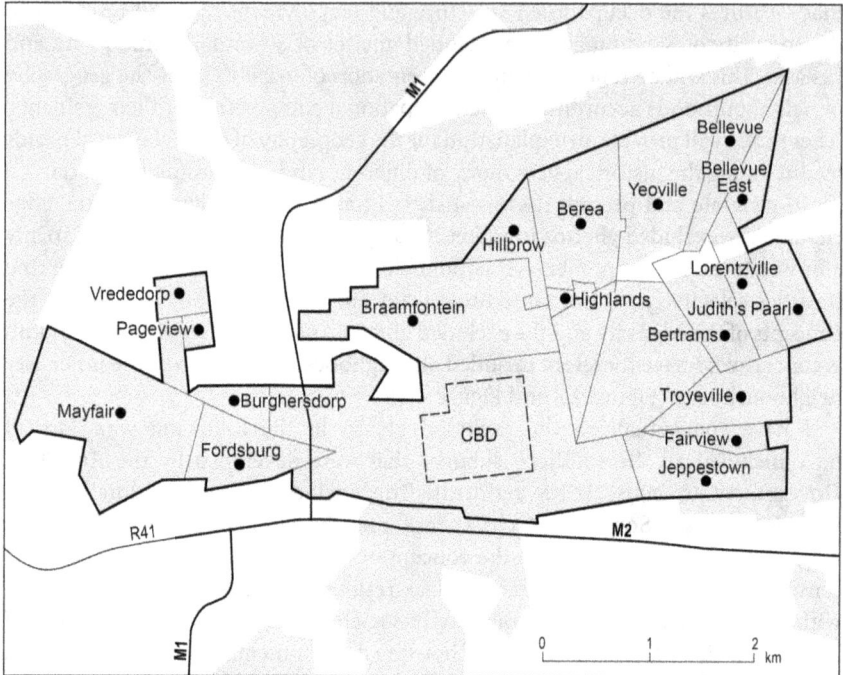

Figure 4.3 The Residential Neighbourhoods of the Inner City
Cartography by Philip J. Stickler

The following statistical analyses were possible because the results of the 1996, 2001 and 2011 Population Censuses were made available in an interactive tabular format that allows scholars to cross-tabulate statistics for small residential areas. In the language of Statistics South Africa, the State Department responsible for these population statistics, these small residential areas are known as 'Subplaces' and in most cases correspond to the sub-Municipal administrative areas that are known officially as 'townships', be they for residential, industrial or commercial use (Mabin, 2005b: p.4). As such, they are usually place names that are well-known by both residents and scholars of Johannesburg. In South Africa, scholars refer to such places as 'suburbs' and 'townships': terms that refer to racially segregated areas that were restricted under the *Apartheid* Group Areas Act for white and black residents, respectively. I have avoided this practice because it abuses the meaning of the term suburb, since many formerly whites-only inner-city residential areas are not suburban. Similarly, most black townships are suburban in nature. Furthermore, since the end of *Apartheid* many new residential areas have been developed that were not racially segregated by law and therefore cannot be described as black townships or white suburbs. Instead, I will therefore use the term 'suburb' to refer to dormitory residential areas outside the inner city and I will use the term 'neighbourhood' to refer to residential areas in general. This

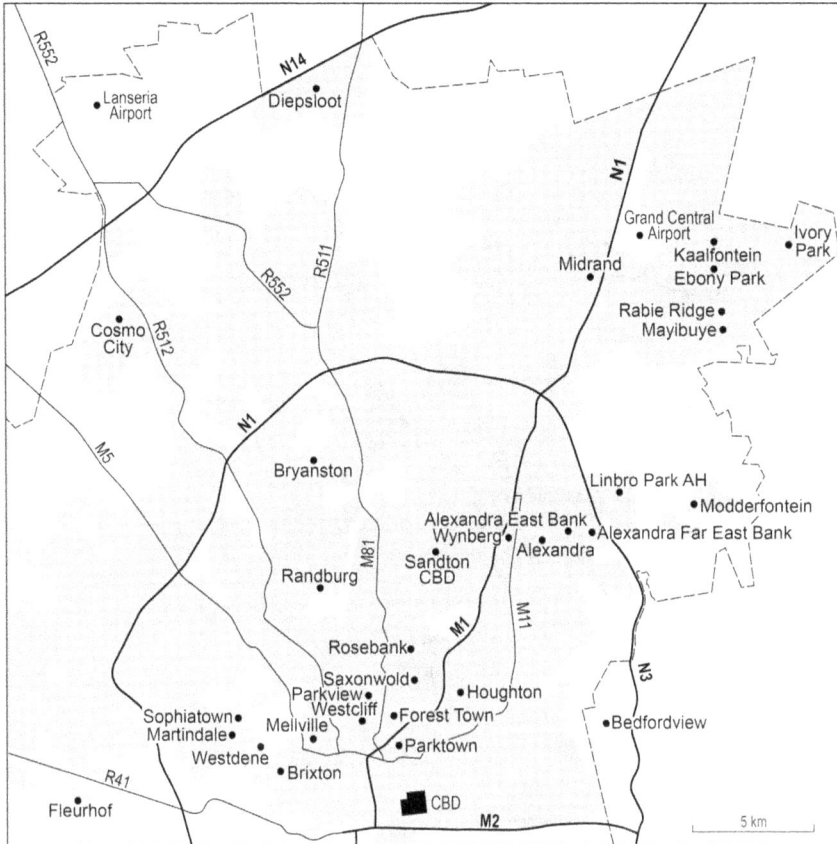

Figure 4.4 The Residential Neighbourhoods of the Northern Suburbs
Cartography by Philip J. Stickler

follows the practice of urban scholarship internationally (see also Kracker Selzer and Heller, 2010: p.200).[4]

Although the population census statistics distinguish between formal houses, apartments, backyard shacks or rooms and shacks in informal settlements, they do not distinguish between different types of formal housing. Specifically, the statistics do not distinguish between the residents of public housing, partially subsidized housing and houses built for sale at market prices. The distinction between these different kinds of houses is important for understanding how their provision has shaped the geography of inequality in Johannesburg over the last twenty years or so. These distinctions were therefore made using a combination of methods. The first

4 It is interesting that official reports press statements by the City of Johannesburg no longer refer to Soweto as a 'township', and prefer the term 'suburb' (Krige, 2012: p.22).

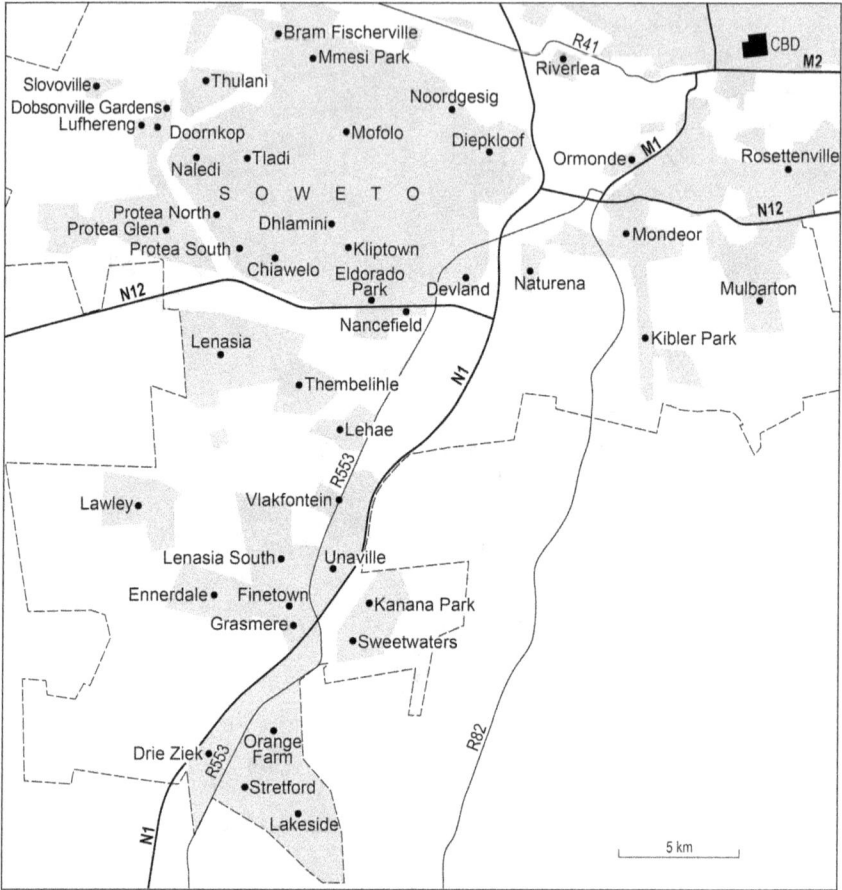

Figure 4.5 The Residential Neighbourhoods of the Southern Suburbs
Cartography by Philip J. Stickler

method entailed a study of the literature on housing provision, which deals mostly with housing for African residents. This knowledge was then consolidated and extended with observations from fieldwork that I carried out with my colleagues on a variety of research projects over roughly two decades. These research projects focused mostly on Soweto, Vlakfontein, Orange Farm and the Inner City, but also extended to city-wide surveys. More recently, this fieldwork knowledge was then supplemented with satellite and 'Street View' images provided by the software applications of Google Maps and Google Earth Pro. These images not only have the resolution to allow the detailed aerial observation of housing types in specific neighbourhoods, but also enabled me to verify aerial images with street-level views of neighbourhoods and their housing types. These images of housing types could then be reconciled with the boundaries of Census 'Subplaces' so that each neighbourhood could be classified according to its dominant housing type.[5] This was facilitated by the design of Subplace boundaries, which aim to be homogeneous with respect to housing types and land-use. In this way, I classified each of the 600 or so Census 'Subplaces' according to its housing type. This was done for the 1996, 2001 and 2011 Censuses, a task that was facilitated by the historical imagery offered by Google Earth Pro. The historical imagery prior to 2000 has a lower resolution than more recent years but was nonetheless adequate for periodizing the growth of different settlements since the mid-1990s. I also classified Subplaces according to their geographical location. With this information, I was then able to measure the population and employment trends for the following types of housing in specific locations over the period from 1996 to 2011.

1 Shacks in site-and-service schemes or unplanned settlements

Shack settlements were readily identified with satellite images because of the typical footprint of shacks, which tend to be trapezoidal rather than quadrilateral (with the sides being parallel to one another). Another feature of informal shack settlements is that their stands are not of the same size and nor does their layout follow a regular pattern or design. The same can be said for their roads, which are sometimes only narrow paths. Finally, in aerial images, the absence of shadows cast by sunlight allows one to detect that the roofs are flat rather than pitched.

Identifying these informal shack settlements is important for our understanding and measurement of geographical inequality because there are fewer financial obstacles that prevent poor people from living in these settlements. Shacks can be built at a very low cost, especially when second-hand building materials are used. For residents who do not wish to build their own shacks, rental tenure is a cheap alternative at about R450 per month in 2010 (Gunter and Massey, 2017: p.28). Research on backyard tenancy in a shack settlement in 1996 commented on the 'remarkably low' rents (Gilbert *et al.*, 1997: p.140). Furthermore, these informal settlements may have access to a water supply, but all other services are usually absent, which means that there are no service charges. These features of informal shack settlements mean that their residents are much more likely to be unemployed or to be employed in low-wage, manual jobs.

2 Fully subsidized public housing

Most fully subsidized public housing was provided for poor black residents. This means that *Apartheid*-era public housing can be identified at least partially by its geographical location which is readily established by a knowledge of the *Apartheid*-era Group Areas of Johannesburg. Furthermore, *Apartheid*-era public

---

5 The Subplace boundaries were matched with aerial images provided by Google Earth Pro using the following websites for the 2001 and 2011 Census Subplaces, respectively: https://census2001.adrianfrith.com/ and https://census2011.adrianfrith.com/.

housing largely took the form of standardized, detached housing, which were named after the prototype '51/6' model. These houses are small, with a floor area of roughly 40m², and characterized by a single-pitch roof with gables at either end (Morris, 1981: p.54). In the post-*Apartheid* period, fully subsidized public housing took a similar built form. These Reconstruction and Development Plan (RDP) houses were also 40m² detached houses with a single-pitch roof and gables on a 200m² plot of land (Palmer *et al.*, 2017: p.237). These public houses are readily identifiable from satellite images because of their size, single-pitch and gabled roof design and their simple rectangular or square footprint.

Identifying those neighbourhoods with fully subsidized housing is obviously important for our understanding and measurement of the changing geography of inequality. Wherever such housing is provided, it tends to concentrate low-income and unemployed residents who are the intended beneficiaries. In the case of the *Apartheid*-era public housing, most of this housing was aimed at low-income workers who paid a sub-economic rent to the Johannesburg City Council (Morris, 1981: p.68). In 1992, these *Apartheid*-era State-owned houses were given to the tenants at no cost (Emdon, 1993: p.7). In the post-*Apartheid* period, housing policy aimed to provide home-ownership to poor residents. These RDP houses, costing between R56,000 and R150,000, were fully subsidized for households that earned less than R3,500 per month (Rust and Steedley, 2013).[6]

3 Partially subsidized 'Gap' housing

In the post-*Apartheid* period, housing subsidies are also available to residents who earned more than R3,500 per month but who did not earn enough to buy a house. These residents, who earned between R3,500 and R15,000, were provided with a 'Gap' housing subsidy, which allowed them to buy houses that cost between R150,000 and R245,000 (Rust and Steedley, 2013). These houses were available to residents who were employed in middle-income jobs since the purchase of these Gap houses also entails the repayment of a mortgage.

Because these Gap houses are typical of the post-*Apartheid* period, their peripheral geographical location on greenfield sites was a partial clue to their identification. The literature on housing provision was also a guide to their location. These houses were often found in small clusters within fully subsidized housing developments. I further identified them by their larger size and more complex footprint, which entailed one or two wings off the main structure. Their roofs are also characterized by both gable and hipped designs. Other distinguishing characteristics include tiled roofs and face-brick walls.

---

6 From 2001, beneficiaries who earned above R1,500 per month were required to contribute R2,479 towards the purchase price of the property (Nell *et al.*, 2011: p.15). This requirement was later rescinded.

4 Non-subsidized housing

This type of housing was largely built by developers for sale at market prices with no income-tested State subsidy to the purchaser. They are therefore the most expensive type of housing and with no other sources of wealth or income, probably require at least one high-income earner in the household.

During the *Apartheid*-era most of these houses were built in areas designated by law for white residents only. As such, they could readily be identified with a knowledge of Johannesburg's white Group Areas. During the late and post-*Apartheid* period, these unsubsidized houses were also built in black Group Areas on peripheral greenfield sites. Again, the literature on housing was a guide to their location, which was confirmed by observation.

Furthermore, these houses were identified by their large size and non-standard architectural footprint. Another clue was the large plot size, which usually ranged from an eighth to half an acre. Houses of this type that were developed in the late and post-*Apartheid* period were often built as security estates or gated communities. These developments are readily identified by the common architectural style of the houses, which are often terraced. They also have a distinctive enclosed street plan that leads to a single entrance onto a main street.

Methodological considerations

This method demonstrates that my approach to measuring statistical trends in the occupational class structure of residents relied on a detailed conceptualization of the qualitatively defined character and properties of the housing market. This approach achieves two objectives. The first is that it enables the precise measurement of statistical trends in the housing market rather than using proxies for housing types, such as household income. The second is that these descriptions of the nature of the housing market allow for explanations of how the properties of the housing market, in conjunction with changes to the labour market, have shaped the geography of inequality as measured with statistics. In other words, I use statistics to establish the correlations between variables and to measure changes in the geography of inequality but not to test for causal relationships. Causal relationships are established by conceptual descriptions of the qualitatively defined nature of the housing market. This method can be contrasted with the more conventional positivist approach that places all the emphasis on statistics both to describe and to explain geographical inequality (*cf.* Fieldhouse, 1999; Geyer and Mohammed, 2016: pp.51–3).

Chapter 5

THE EDGE CITY OF SANDTON

Introduction

The post-Fordist changes in Johannesburg's economy took a geographical form that is not dissimilar to developments in US cities. The mono-centric geography was changed into a poly-centric geography with the growth of the dominant 'edge city'[1] of Sandton in the northern suburbs (Beavon and Larsen, 2014: p.382; Crankshaw, 2008: p.1698; Kracker Selzer and Heller, 2010: p.195; Larsen, 2004: pp.73–6).[2] Facilitated by the development of the 'M1' and 'N1' highways between Johannesburg and Pretoria in the 1960s and 1970s (Chipkin, 1998; Grant and Flinn, 1992: p.49; Mabin, 2013), factories, shops and offices relocated from the inner city to the northern suburbs in areas such as Sandton, Midrand and Kyalami (see Cover Image and Figure 5.1). Over the period from 1980 to 1994, hundreds of inner-city factories were closed or relocated, which amounted to a loss of roughly one-third of all inner-city factories (Rogerson and Rogerson, 1995: p.31; Rogerson and Rogerson, 1999: p.91). In the subsequent decade of the 1990s, almost half of all the remaining factories in the inner city were closed or relocated. Over the same period, roughly 500 new factories were built in the northern suburbs or were relocated there from the inner city, compared to roughly 100 new factories in the southern suburbs (Rogerson and Rogerson, 1999: p.92). This new, post-Fordist geography of factories was also reflected in the decline of manufacturing employment in the inner-city and the substantial growth of employment in the northern suburbs (Rogerson, 2000: pp.316–17).

This northward movement of manufacturing establishments was accompanied by the migration of shops and offices to the northern suburbs. Between 1982

---

1 As in the case of edge cities in the United States, Sandton was once a separate municipality before it was incorporated into the City of Johannesburg Metropolitan Municipality (Carruthers, 1993: p.62).

2 The geographical scale of Johannesburg and its edge city is not substantially different to US cities. The distance from the Johannesburg Central Business District to Midrand is roughly 35km, which is about the same distance between the Atlanta CBD and the edge city of Alpharetta, but less than the 55km from downtown Chicago to Elgin.

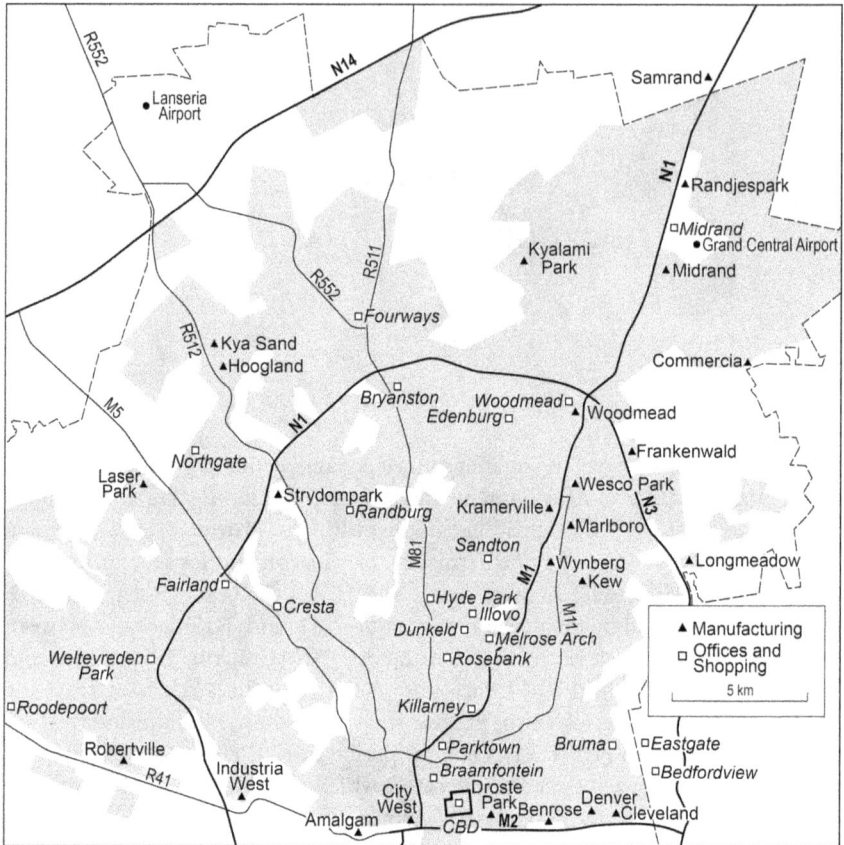

Figure 5.1 Factory, Shopping and Office Nodes in the Northern Suburbs
Cartography by Philip J. Stickler

and 1994, seventeen of the leading sixty-five corporations relocated their head offices from the CBD to business nodes in the northern suburbs. Most head offices relocated to Sandton, with the rest choosing Bedfordview, Parktown, Rosebank and Midrand (Rogerson, 1996: pp.572–3; Tomlinson, 1996: pp.182–4) (Figure 5.1). In the subsequent decades, the number of new office developments in the northern suburbs was such that by the year 2000, there was twice as much office space in the northern suburban nodes as in the CBD (Beavon, 2004: p.257). By 2011, there was almost three times as much office space (Ahmad and Pienaar, 2014: p.108). Similarly, for the retail sector, by 1999 the amount of shopping space in the large malls of the northern suburbs was almost double that of the whole CBD (Beavon, 2004: p.251). Over the subsequent decade, the number of shopping malls and centres increased dramatically (Kenny, 2019: p.45), with most of them located in the high-income northern suburbs (Khanyile and Ballard, 2018).

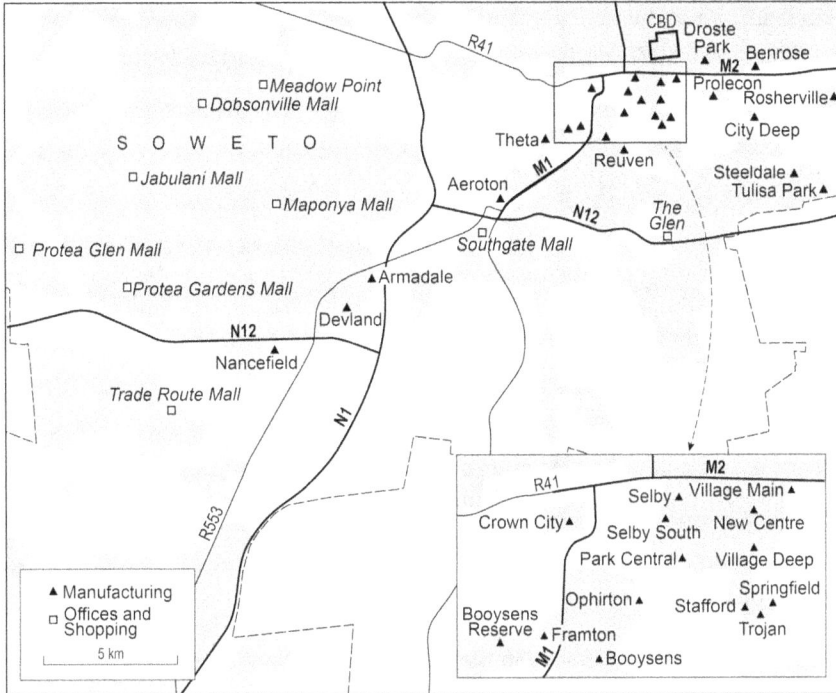

Figure 5.2 Factory, Shopping and Office Nodes in the Southern Suburbs
Cartography by Philip J. Stickler

By contrast, there was very little growth of shopping malls and office nodes in the southern suburbs. Apart from the development of the Southgate mall in Mondeor, there were no large developments in the southern suburbs (Tomlinson and Larson, 2003: p.46) (Figure 5.2). Other shopping malls, such as the new Dobsonville Shopping Centre in Soweto, were only one-sixth of the size of Sandton City in the late 1990s (Harrison and Harrison, 2014: p.308; Tomlinson and Larson, 2003: p.49). Even the development of the large Maponya Mall in Klipspruit, Soweto, in 2007 did not substantially change this unequal retail geography (CoJ, 2011: p.46; Harrison and Harrison, 2014: p.308). Similarly, the amount of decentralized office space in the southern suburbs was relatively small compared to the northern suburbs. Between 2006 and 2010, only 4 per cent of all applications for rezoning to business land use were in the southern suburbs (Harrison and Zack, 2014: p.288).

The geographical concentration of hotels also changed from the inner city to Sandton in the northern suburbs. In 1990, the largest cluster of hotels was still in the inner city. By 2010, the largest cluster was in the new CBD of Sandton (Rogerson, 2014: pp.188–90). Research on the location of new call centres in Johannesburg showed that by 2008 the largest clusters of call centres were situated in the northern suburbs of Johannesburg with only limited numbers in the old CBD and the southern suburbs. Favoured nodes were Sandton, Woodmead, Bryanston,

Randburg and Midrand (Pandy and Rogerson, 2012: p.36). By 2002, scholars could confidently state that the business node of Sandton City was the new 'commercial heart' of Johannesburg (Beavon and Larson, 2014: p.382) (Figure 5.1).

By contrast, the CBD of Johannesburg became the favoured shopping node for the mostly black working-class residents of the southern suburbs. Shops that catered for the tastes of the mostly white middle class moved from the inner city to the northern suburbs. These shops included boutique clothing and interior design shops, hobby and toy stores, jewellers and curio shops, as well as the 'high class' department stores such as Stuttafords and John Orr's (Rogerson, 1995: p.167). In general, these shops were replaced by small general dealers, fast-food outlets and street traders that catered for the needs of mostly black, working-class shoppers, (Rogerson, 1995: p.168; Tomlinson, 1996: pp.187–9).

This new post-Fordist spatial order of business locations reinforced the existing residential occupational class geography of Johannesburg by encouraging the private sector to develop even more middle-class residential areas in the northern suburbs (Murray, 2011: p.179). Evidence of applications to the Municipality by private-sector developers to build new housing for the period from 2007 to 2011 showed that about 80 per cent of all developments in Johannesburg were in the middle-class neighbourhoods of the northern suburbs (Ahmad and Pienaar, 2014).[3] During the Fordist period, the mostly white managerial and professional middle class lived in the northern suburbs but shopped and worked in the inner city. In the post-Fordist period, this commuting pattern must have changed with the development of sources of middle-class employment in the business nodes of the northern suburbs, where even manufacturing jobs were in the high-technology sector and tended to be for highly skilled, car-owning workers (Hodge, 1998: p.858). The growth of luxury shopping and entertainment facilities also made the far-northern suburbs more attractive residential areas for the high-income middle class. As a result of these mutually reinforcing forces, the housing market in the northern suburbs was the most expensive in the whole city. Ballard *et al.* (2021a: p.39) show that in 2017, the northern suburbs had substantially larger percentages of houses valued at over R1.2 million than in other areas of the city.

Over the period from 1996 to 2001, the growing white middle class became increasingly clustered in the northern suburbs as the percentage of middle-class residents in each suburb and its neighbouring suburbs increased (Kracker Selzer and Heller, 2010: p.189). Moreover, the focus of this concentration of middle-class residents was the new Sandton CBD rather than the old middle-class suburbs such as Houghton, Saxonwold, Parkview and Westcliff that were located nearer to the original Johannesburg CBD (Kracker Selzer and Heller, 2010: p.191) (Figure 4.4). A more recent study by Ballard and Hamann (2021: pp.103–5) distributed neighbourhoods into quintiles according to the absolute number of residents employed in managerial and professional occupations. Their findings show that

3 Author's own calculations from plate 20 (Ahmad and Pienaar, 2014).

the concentration of managers and professionals in the northern suburbs persisted between 2001 and 2011 and even increased in neighbourhoods north of Sandton.

The geography of Johannesburg therefore has an important feature of cities that are characterized as having a post-Fordist spatial order. The erstwhile dormitory suburb of Sandton was developed into a typical edge city or 'totalising suburb', which has its own economic, cultural and residential functions that are largely independent of the old Johannesburg CBD (Marcuse and van Kempen, 2000: p.15). Furthermore, as is the case with edge cities elsewhere, it was characterized by a largely high-income, middle-class and white residential population.

However, since the end of *Apartheid*, large public housing developments have been built in the northern suburbs. The post-*Apartheid* Government policy of subsidized housing for low-income households resulted in a large-scale house-building programme that produced 3.3 million houses over the period from 1994 to 2013 (Palmer *et al.*, 2017: p.237). State-subsidized housing provision is divided into fully subsidized and partially subsidized schemes. The fully subsidized scheme provided for households that earn less than R3,500 per month and delivered so-called RDP or BNG houses that cost about R150,000 each.[4] The partially subsidized scheme delivered so-called Gap houses for households that earn between R3,500 and R15,000 per month and who can secure loan finance for houses priced up to roughly R500,000 (Palmer *et al.*, 2017: p.235; Rust and Steedley, 2013).[5] Although most state-subsidized housing developments in Johannesburg were located in the southern suburbs, there were several large housing developments in the northern suburbs. These include the developments in the following areas (Figure 4.4):

(i)   Alexandra's East Bank and Far East Bank near Sandton (Harrison *et al.*, 2014: p.349)
(ii)   Diepsloot, located on the northern boundary of Johannesburg (Bénit, 2002; Harber, 2011)
(iii) Cosmo City,[6] which is located on the north-western boundary of Johannesburg
(iv)   Ivory Park (Huchzermeyer, *et al.*, 2014: pp.160–1; Tomlinson *et al.*, 1995), Mayibuye, Rabie Ridge and parts of Kaalfontein and Ebony Park in Midrand

In practice, the State delivery of fully subsidized houses usually entails the creation of new housing estates before beneficiaries move into the settlement. However, on some occasions housing provision is an incremental process in which

---

4 These acronyms stand for the Government's 'Reconstruction and Development Programme' and 'Breaking New Ground' housing programmes.

5 Partially subsidized 'Gap' houses are also known as 'FLISP' housing, which is an acronym for Finance Linked Subsidy Programme (Cirolia, 2016: p.626; Coetzee, 2018: p.3).

6 These are Extensions 2, 4 and 6 for fully subsidized RDP/BNG houses and Extensions 0, 8 and 10 for partially subsidized 'Gap' houses (Haferburg, 2013: p.266; Onatu, 2010: p.212; Wagner, 2014 and 2018: p.37).

beneficiaries are first provided with serviced sites, which have a water tap, a backyard toilet and an overhead electricity supply. Beneficiaries are then expected to build their own temporary homes, which usually takes for the form of corrugated-iron shacks.[7] Later, the State-subsidized standard 40m[2] house is built by private-sector builders. Alternatively, where residents are already living in unplanned or informal shack settlements, their shacks are upgraded to formal housing developments *in situ*. This means that fully subsidized housing developments sometimes have the appearance of informal settlements, but they differ from unplanned informal settlements by their road layout and property boundaries, which conform to the engineering requirements of formally planned settlements.

An important feature of the old *Apartheid*-era housing in Alexandra and the new public housing developments in Diepsloot and Ivory Park is that they are characterized, to a greater or lesser extent, by residents who rent corrugated-iron shacks and formal brick rooms in the backyards. By 2005, in the old areas of Alexandra, for example, about 70 per cent of all households lived in backyard shacks and rooms (Shapurjee and Charlton, 2013: p.656). Similarly, the post-*Apartheid* public housing developments on the Far East Bank of Alexandra (Shapurjee and Charlton, 2013: p.656) and Diepsloot (Gardner and Rubin, 2016: p.80) were also soon characterized by the proliferation of backyard shacks and rooms. Since these public housing developments and backyard accommodation provide housing for low-income and unemployed residents, the occupational class composition of these neighbourhoods is different from non-subsidized housing developments in the northern suburbs. This therefore raises the question of the extent to which these post-Apartheid public housing developments have changed the occupational class structure of residents in the edge city of Sandton.

The changing residential geography of the high-income middle class

The results of the Population Censuses demonstrate that there is a geographical concentration of the high-income, managerial, professional, associate professional and technical middle class in the northern suburbs. Roughly twice as many middle-class residents live in the northern neighbourhoods than in the southern neighbourhoods (Table 5.1). Moreover, this geographical concentration of the middle class increased slightly over the period from 1996 to 2011, during which the number of middle-class residents in the northern suburbs grew at a faster rate than the number in the southern suburbs.[8] This faster rate of growth

---

7 Examples include Thulani in Soweto and Orange Farm (Figure 4.5).

8 The number of middle-class residents in the inner city is included here only for the sake of completeness. Clearly, the number of residents in the northern and southern suburbs increased between 1996 and 2011 due to the greenfield expansion of new housing developments and some densification, both of which could not occur to nearly the same extent in the inner city because of its smaller plot sizes and high-rise apartment buildings.

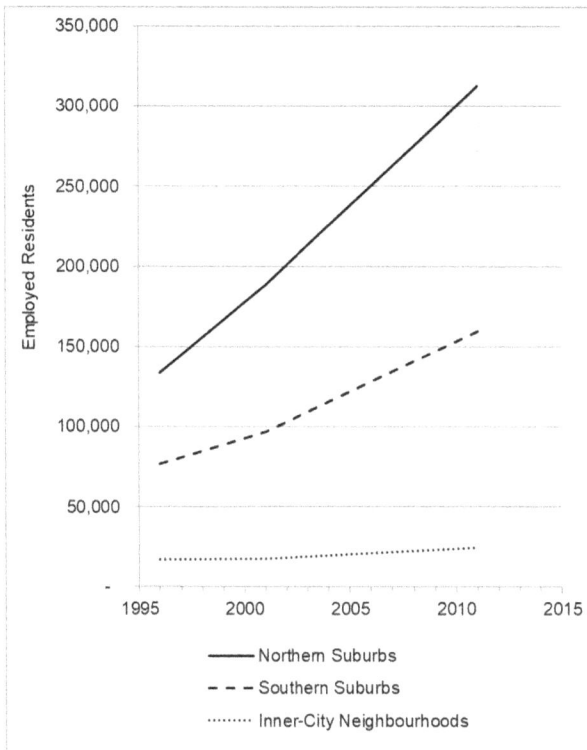

Figure 5.3 Trends in the Geographical Distribution of Residents Employed in High-
Income, Middle-Class Occupations* in Johannesburg, 1996–2011
* Managers, Professionals, Technicians and Associate Professionals
Sources: Author's Analysis of Population Census results, 1996, 2001 and 2011 (SuperCross Interactive Tables). See
       Table 5.1.

caused the concentration of middle-class residents in the northern suburbs
to increase slightly from 59 per cent of all middle-class residents in the whole
city in 1996, to 62 per cent in 2001 and 64 per cent in 2011. By comparison,
the percentage of all middle-class residents that lived in the southern suburbs
declined slightly from only 34 per cent in 1996 to 31 per cent in 2011 (Figure 5.3
and Table 5.1).

These statistics show the concentration of middle-class residents in the northern
suburbs partly because the northern suburbs have a larger employed workforce
than the southern suburbs. It therefore makes sense to control for this difference
by also measuring the occupational class composition of the northern suburbs.
The results of this analysis show that the middle-class percentage of all employed
residents in the northern neighbourhoods increased from 36 per cent in 1996 to
40 per cent in 2001 and then declined again to 34 per cent by 2011 (Table 5.1).
So although the northern neighbourhoods had a larger middle-class composition
than the inner city (20 per cent) and the southern neighbourhoods (23 per cent) in

Table 5.1 Trends in the Geographical Distribution of Residents Employed in High-Income, Middle-Class Occupations* in Johannesburg, 1996–2011[9]

	Frequency Distribution of All Middle-Class Employment			Annual Average Percentage Increase	Percentage Distribution of All Middle-Class Employment in Johannesburg		
	1996	2001	2011	1996–2011	1996	2001	2011
Northern Suburbs	133,728	188,138	312,555	6	59	62	63
Inner City	17,256	17,525	24,391	2	8	6	5
Southern Suburbs	76,882	97,000	159,658	5	34	32	32
Total	227,866	302,663	496,604	5	100	100	100

	Frequency Distribution of Employment in All Occupations			Annual Average Percentage Increase	Middle-Class Employment as a Percentage of Employment in All Occupations		
	1996	2001	2011	1996–2011	1996	2001	2011
Northern Suburbs	374,962	474,146	910,563	6	36	40	34
Inner City	72,111	87,642	120,303	4	24	20	20
Southern Suburbs	395,247	437,637	702,682	4	19	22	23
Total	842,320	999,425	1,733,548	5	27	30	29

Sources: Author's Analysis of Population Census results, 1996, 2001 and 2011 (SuperCross Interactive Tables).
* Managers, Professionals, Technicians and Associate Professionals.

2011, these results show that the development of public housing estates and shack settlements in the northern neighbourhoods has had a strong influence on the class composition of the edge city of Sandton.

This broad conceptualization of the edge city of Sandton, which includes all the northern suburbs and their many post-_Apartheid_ public housing developments, should not lead us to conclude that the residents of all the northern suburbs are homogeneously middle-class in nature. By mapping the class composition of employed residents living in each neighbourhood, the geography of class differences between neighbourhoods can be revealed.

These results show that the location of neighbourhoods with a majority of middle-class residents was concentrated in the northern suburbs and that this geographical pattern persisted over the period from 1996 to 2011 (Figure 5.4 to

9 These statistics exclude employment in a few neighbourhoods because their geography could not be established from the data for 1996 and 2011. This was due to errors in the data supplied by StatsSA. The employment numbers that were excluded amounted to only 0.1 per cent of all employment.

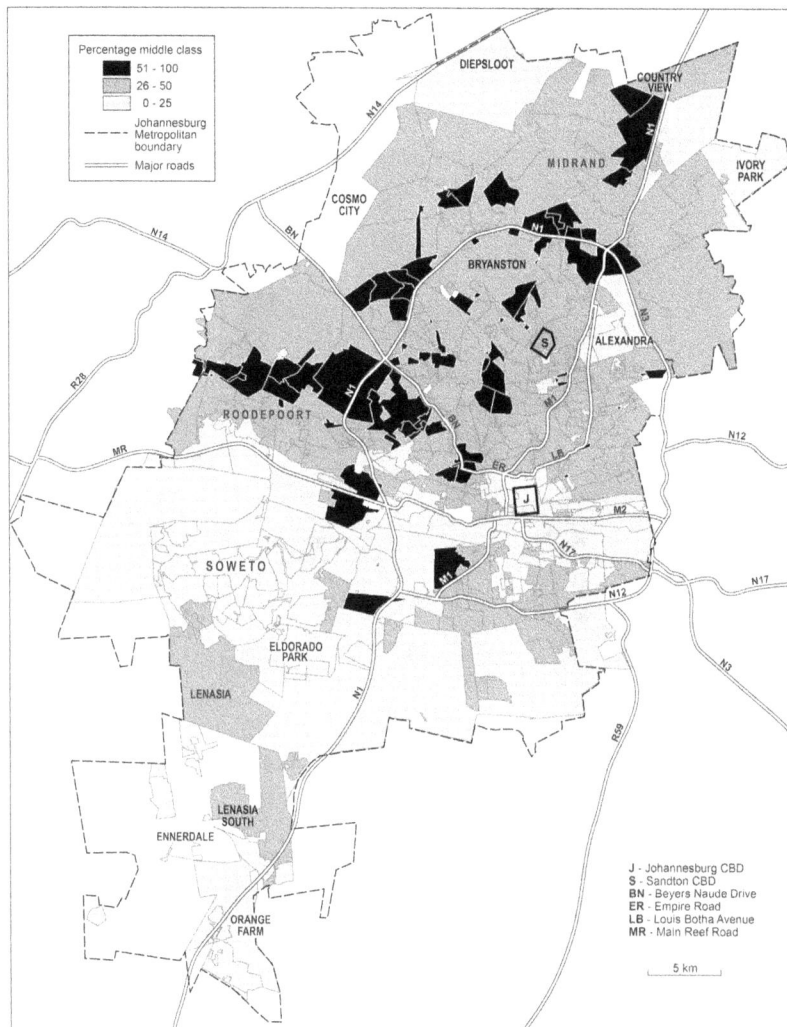

Figure 5.4 The Geography of Middle-Class Residents in Johannesburg, 1996
Sources: Author's Analysis of Population Census results (SuperCross Interactive Tables).
Measured by all employed residents living in all types of dwellings.

Figure 5.6). These results are consistent with the findings concerning the geography of managers and professionals by Kracker Selzer and Heller (2010: pp.187–9) for the period from 1996 to 2001 and by Ballard and Hamann (2021) for the period from 2001 to 2011.[10]

10 Kracker Selzer and Heller (2010: p.179) use a different definition of the middle class to the one used here. They produced separate maps for the 'upper middle class' (managers, senior officials and professionals), the 'middle middle class' (technicians and associate professionals) and the 'lower middle class' (clerical, service and sales occupations).

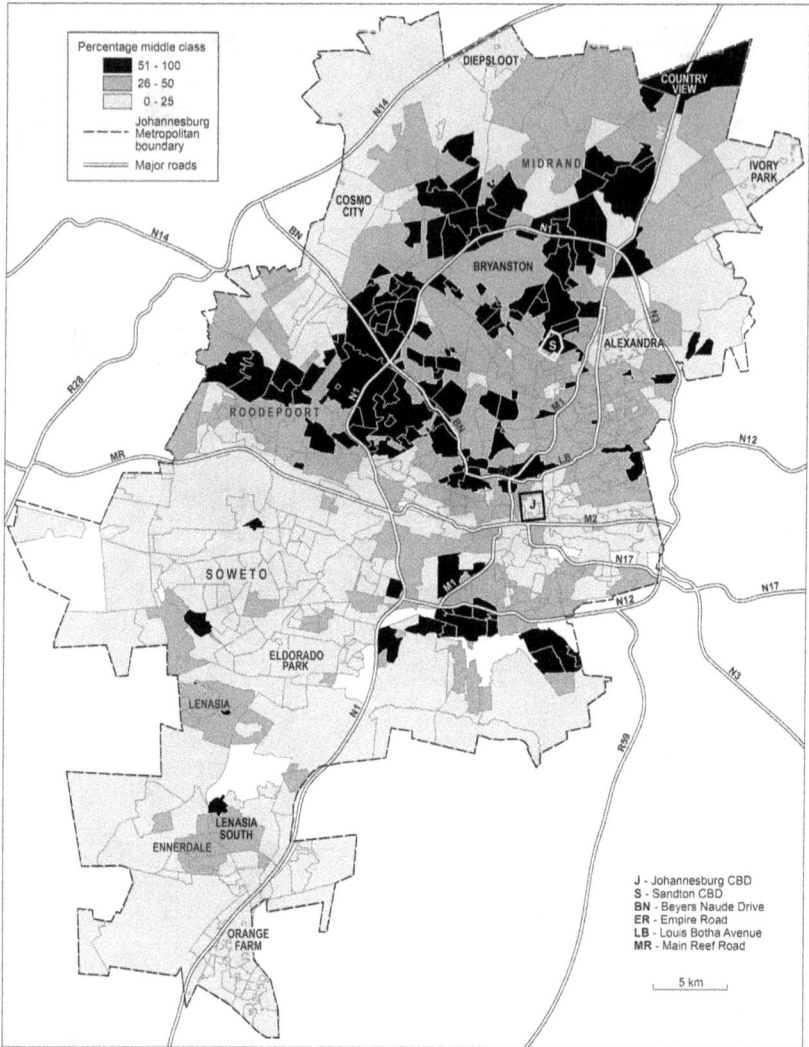

Figure 5.5 The Geography of Middle-Class Residents in Johannesburg, 2001
Sources: Author's Analysis of Population Census results (SuperCross Interactive Tables).
Measured by all employed residents living in all types of dwellings.

But these maps also reveal that there are neighbourhoods within the northern suburbs in which the percentage of middle-class residents is 25 per cent and less. If we examine the map of results of the 2011 Census only, the map shows that, apart from the *Apartheid*-era racial ghetto of Alexandra, these predominantly working-class areas are either farms, peri-urban smallholdings,

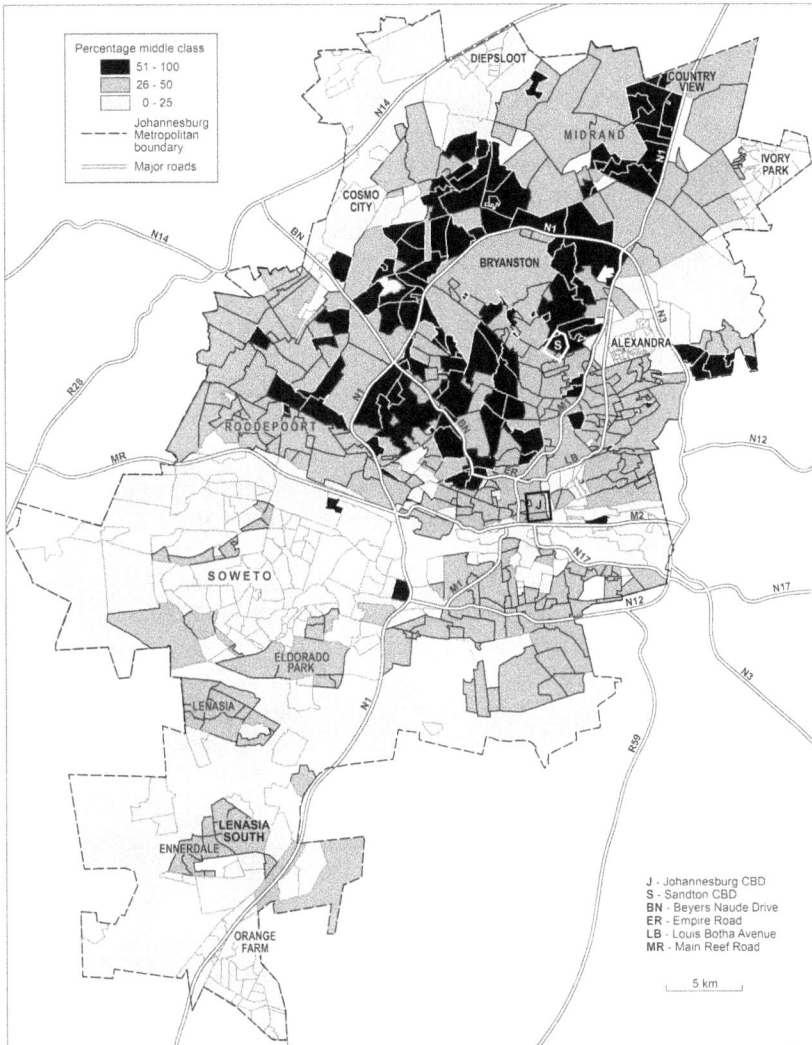

Figure 5.6 The Geography of Middle-Class Residents in Johannesburg, 2011
Sources: Author's Analysis of Population Census results (SuperCross Interactive Tables).
Measured by all employed residents living in all types of dwellings

shack settlements or post-*Apartheid* public housing developments (Figure 5.6). Although the resident property owners in peri-urban areas are likely to be middle class, they tend to employ relatively large numbers of low-paid live-in farm workers, which pushes down the overall percentage of middle-class residents on these smallholdings.

Notable farming and peri-urban areas in which the percentage of middle-class residents is 25 per cent or less are those located south of Lanseria Airport and north of Cosmo City (Figure 5.4). Other notable farms and peri-urban smallholdings are those of the farm Zevenfontein[11] and peri-urban farms to the south and east of Diepsloot (Figure 4.4). Other areas are Linbro Park Agricultural Holdings and the Modderfontein Nature Reserve on the eastern flank of Alexandra (Figure 5.4).

Other neighbourhoods where the percentage of middle-class residents is less than 25 per cent are the formerly Africans-only slum of Alexandra, the post-*Apartheid* public housing developments and informal shack settlements. The post-*Apartheid* public housing developments are those of Diepsloot, Ivory Park, Ebony Park, Kaalfontein, Rabie Ridge, Mayibuye and Alexandra's East Bank and Far East Bank (Figure 4.4). Other public housing developments are also located within the mixed development of Cosmo City, which includes unsubsidized housing in Extensions 3, 5, 7 and 9 (Wagner, 2018: p.37). Unplanned shack settlements are, among others, those of Riverbend, Itsoseng, Lion Park and Zandspruit, which are all found in the vicinity of Cosmo City (Figure 4.4).

According to the 2011 Population Census, the overall statistical differences in the occupational class composition of residents in these kinds of housing developments and shack settlements were substantial. In the formerly whites-only housing developments in the northern suburbs and their post-*Apartheid* counterparts, 40 per cent of all employed residents were middle class. By contrast, only 8 to 12 per cent of all residents in the slums of Alexandra, RDP housing and informal shack settlements were middle class. In between these two extremes were the partially subsidized Gap housing developments, where 22 per cent of the employed residents were middle class (Table 5.2).

Although the slum of old *Apartheid*-era Alexandra, shack settlements and the post-*Apartheid* public housing developments do not occupy large areas of land, they are very densely populated. So much so that, in 1996, their population contributed 59 per cent to the total population of the northern suburbs (Table 5.3). Over the next fifteen years, the population of unsubsidized housing developments, built largely for the middle class, grew at roughly twice the rate of the public housing estates and informal settlements. The result was that by 2011, the population of the largely working-class, public housing developments had declined to 38 per cent of the total population of the northern suburbs (Table 5.3). Nonetheless, this is still a sizeable percentage of the population of what is a largely middle-class edge city.

11 By 2011, the residents of the informal settlement of Zevenfontein had been moved to live in shacks and subsidized housing in Diepsloot and Cosmo City.

Table 5.2 Percentage Occupational Class Distribution of Employed Residents in the Northern Suburbs, 2011

	Unsubsidized Formal Housing	Post-Apartheid Gap Housing[1]	Apartheid-Era Alexandra Slum	Post-Apartheid RDP Housing[2]	Shack Settlements[3]
Managers, Professionals, Associate Professionals & Technicians	40	22	12	9	8
Clerical Support Workers, Sales and Service Workers	26	40	34	33	27
Craft & Related Trades Workers, Plant & Machine Operators	26	14	19	24	27
Elementary Workers, Skilled Agriculture & Fisheries Workers	8	23	35	35	39
Total Employment	100	100	100	100	100

Sources: Author's Analysis of 2011 Population Census results (SuperCross Interactive Tables).
1 Housing in Alexandra's East Bank, Ebony Park, Rabie Ridge and Kaalfontein.
2 Housing in Diepsloot and parts of Alexandra's Far East Bank, Ivory Park and Kaalfontein.
3 Sejwetla settlement (in Alexandra), Itsoseng, Riverbend and Lion Park settlements (all near Cosmo City), Malatjie and Zandspruit settlements (near Lanseria Airport) and settlements near Kya Sand and Longdale industrial areas and in parts of Diepsloot and Rabie Ridge.
* Percentages do not always add up to 100 because of rounding off.

Scholars argue that the policy of providing, not only the land and services, but also a small house, with a relatively small subsidy has forced both the State and private developers to locate public housing developments on cheap land that is typically at the urban periphery. These State-subsidized housing developments are therefore argued to be located far from places of employment and have therefore intensified occupational class and social segregation (Huchzermeyer, 2005: pp.215–17; Pieterse, 2019: p.23). This is certainly true for the large housing developments in the southern suburbs, such as Orange Farm, Lawley, Kanana Park and Lehae (Figure 5.5). However, the State-subsidized housing developments in the northern suburbs are better-placed for the employment opportunities created by the new industrial sites and commercial centres located there (Charlton, 2014: p.179). The new Government initiative to remedy this spatial mismatch is the 'Corridors of Freedom', which plans to link outlying neighbourhoods such as Ivory Park and Diepsloot to places of employment with a State-subsidized Bus Rapid Transit system (Pieterse, 2019: p.30) (Figure 4.4).

Table 5.3 The Population of the Northern Suburbs living in Informal Shack Settlements, Slums and in Public and Private Housing Developments, 1996–2011

	Frequency Distribution			Annual Average Percentage Increase	Percentage Distribution		
	1996	**2001**	**2011**	**1996–2011**	**1996**	**2001**	**2011**
Informal & Site & Service Settlements, RDP/BNG & Gap Housing	242,474	407,195	722,409	8	59	34	38
Unsubsidized Formal Housing Developments	146,608	742,166	1,132,265	15	36	62	59
Peri-Urban & Industrial Areas	19,891	39,045	28,197	2	5	3	1
Other public housing & informal settlements near the inner city	280	17,196	29,704	36	0	1	2
Total Northern Suburbs	409,253	1,205,602	1,912,575	11	100	100	100

Sources: Author's Analysis of Population Census results, 1996, 2001 and 2011 (SuperCross Interactive Tables).

Conclusion

In this chapter, I have relied on evidence from the secondary literature to argue that Johannesburg's post-Fordist spatial order has entailed the decline of the economic dominance of the Johannesburg Central Business District and the growth of the new edge city of Sandton and its suburban hinterland. This new edge city has attracted economic activity in the form of offices, shops and even manufacturing establishments. Correspondingly, there was also enormous growth in the residential population as new residential suburbs were built on greenfield sites in an arc of development north of Sandton, stretching as far as Midrand.

In North American and European cities, for which scholars first developed the theory of a post-Fordist spatial order, these edge cities were characterized by residents employed in high-income, middle-class jobs. The evidence from the Population Censuses from 1996 to 2011 shows that a greater percentage of the middle class is concentrated in the northern suburbs and that this concentration has increased slightly over this period. Furthermore, the class composition of the northern suburbs is substantially more middle-class than the inner city and the southern suburbs. In terms of its occupational class geography, Johannesburg's post-Fordist spatial order has therefore become more geographically unequal.

However, unlike many edge cities elsewhere, Government housing policy in Johannesburg has resulted in the development of large public housing estates in the northern suburbs. These new neighbourhoods are largely composed of state-sponsored housing that provides free housing for low-income and unemployed residents and partially subsidized housing for middle-income residents. Apart from the new public housing developments on the East Bank of Alexandra, an erstwhile black ghetto of the *Apartheid* era, these neighbourhoods are situated on the far periphery of the northern suburbs. In this respect, they can be said to exclude low-income and unemployed residents from easy access to the employment opportunities of the edge city and to have created a new form of occupational class segregation. However, these public housing estates are much closer to the new centre of employment and educational opportunities than their counterparts in the southern suburbs. Also, they are no further from employment opportunities than many of the middle-class suburbs that are situated in the far north of Johannesburg, such as Noordwyk and Country View. At the very least, one could argue that post-*Apartheid* housing policy has therefore slightly ameliorated the tendency of Sandton to become a homogeneously middle-class edge city.

Chapter 6

FROM RACIAL GHETTO TO EXCLUDED GHETTO: SOWETO, ELDORADO PARK AND LENASIA

Post-Fordist unemployment and the excluded ghetto

Rising unemployment is an important feature of inequality in post-Fordist Johannesburg. Statistical evidence for the Province of Gauteng shows that official or strict unemployment grew from a level of only 5 per cent in the 1970s to a peak of roughly 30 to 35 per cent by 2001 and then stabilized at about 25 per cent over the subsequent decade.[1] This high and chronic level of unemployment was not evenly distributed throughout Johannesburg. Instead, it was concentrated largely in the erstwhile black ghettos that were created during the *Apartheid* period and in the post-*Apartheid* public housing estates, site-and-service schemes and shack settlements. In this respect, Johannesburg's black ghettos are similar to those in the USA. In 1970, the strict unemployment rate among African, coloured and Indian residents was only 7, 2 and 1 per cent, respectively. By 2011, the strict unemployment rate had risen to 31, 26 and 9 per cent respectively. Following Marcuse (1997), the black ghettos of Johannesburg's Fordist period can therefore be said to have been transformed by rising unemployment into the 'excluded ghettos' of the post-Fordist period.

There are two ways that evidence concerning the geography of unemployment can be presented using the Census results for 2011. The first is to map neighbourhoods according to the strict and expanded unemployment rates of their residents (Figure 6.1 and Figure 6.2). These maps show that the neighbourhoods with the highest unemployment rates were the black ghettos of the *Apartheid* period and the public housing estates, site-and-service schemes and shack settlements of the post-*Apartheid* period. The maps also demonstrate the extent to which the excluded ghettos formed a large region of high unemployment in the

---

1 The unemployment rate is calculated by dividing the number of unemployed residents by the size of the workforce, which includes all employed and unemployed residents.

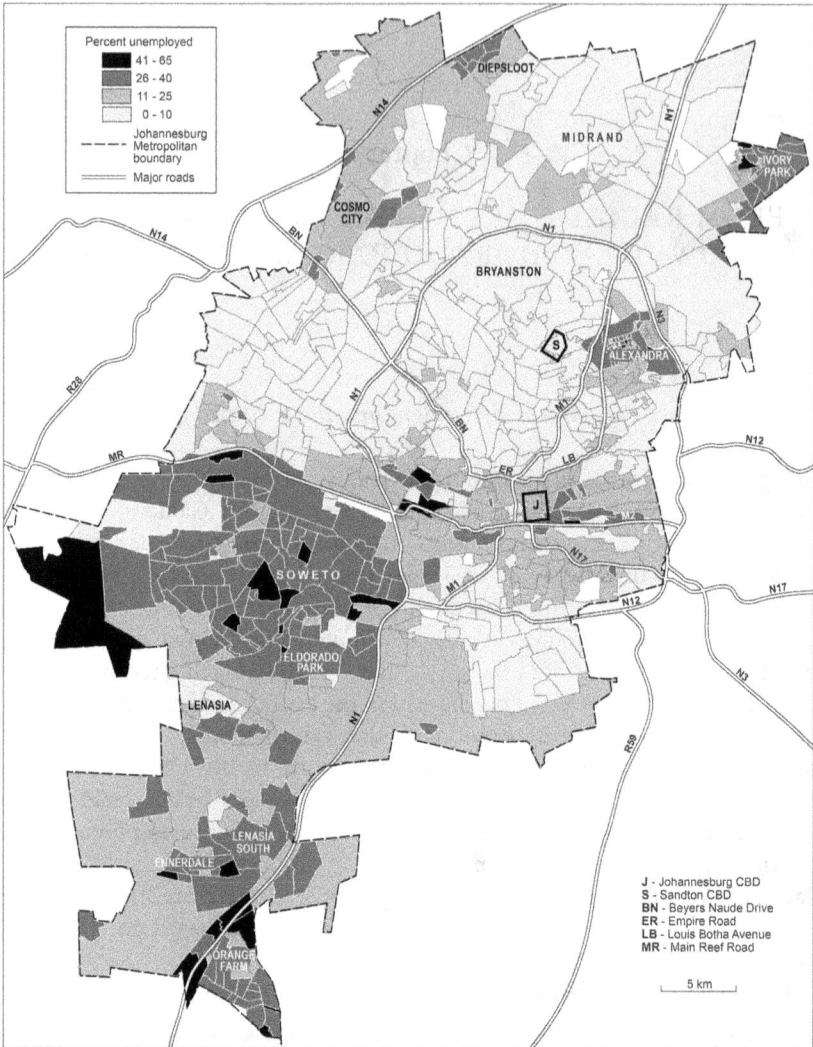

Figure 6.1 The Geography of Strict Unemployment in Johannesburg, 2011
Sources: The author's analysis of the 2011 Population Census results (SuperCross Interactive Tables).
Cartography: Philip J. Stickler

southern suburbs. Most of the suburbs of Soweto, Eldorado Park, parts of Lenasia and Lenasia South, Ennerdale and Orange Farm had strict unemployment rates above 25 per cent and expanded unemployment rates above 40 per cent (Figure 6.1 and Figure 6.2).

By contrast, the excluded ghettos of the northern suburbs covered a much smaller geographical area and are islands of high-unemployment in a large sea of neighbourhoods with low unemployment rates. Most of the

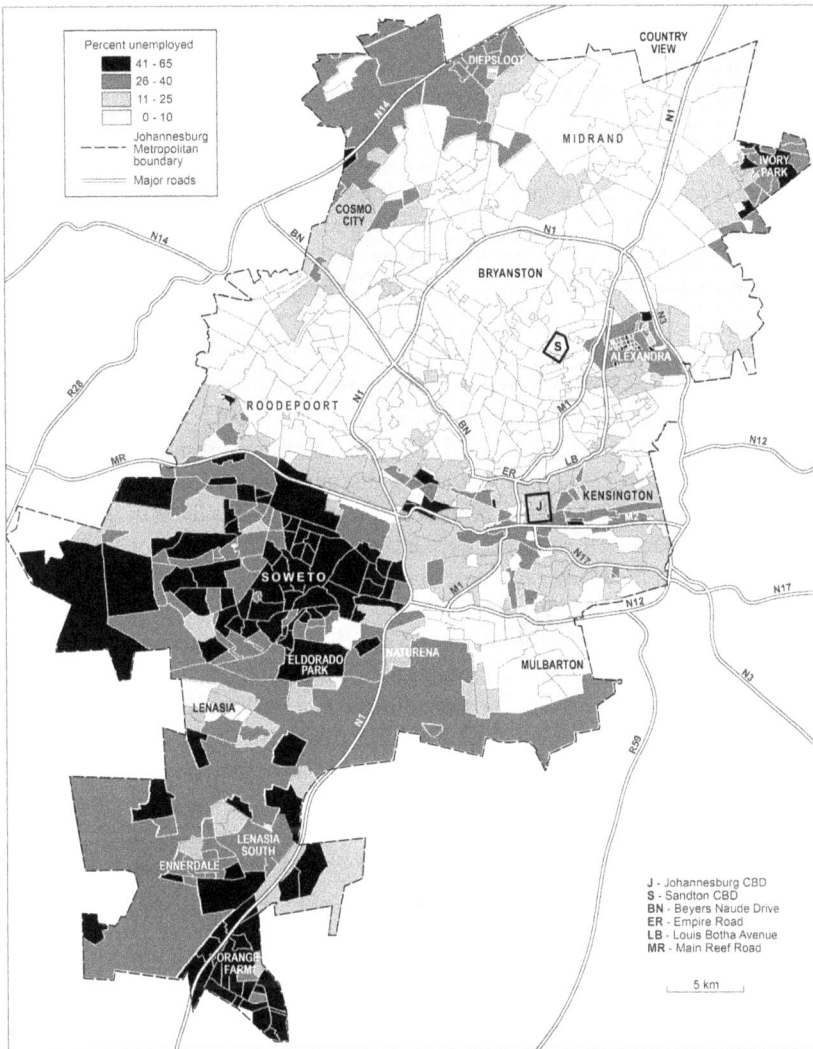

Figure 6.2 The Geography of Expanded Unemployment in Johannesburg, 2011
Sources: The author's analysis of the 2011 Population Census results (SuperCross Interactive Tables).
Cartography: Philip J. Stickler

neighbourhoods composed of expensive, unsubsidized housing developments had strict unemployment rates of 10 per cent or less. Neighbourhoods with strict unemployment rates of more than 25 per cent were found in Alexandra, Ivory Park, Zandspruit (just east of Cosmo City), Diepsloot and in the peri-urban farmlands on the north-western boundary of the city (Figure 6.1 and Figure 6.2).

Some inner-city neighbourhoods were also characterized by expanded unemployment rates of over 25 per cent. Unlike the neighbourhoods with high- and medium-rise apartment buildings, such as Hillbrow, Berea and Yeoville (where unemployment rates were less than 25 per cent), these neighbourhoods were characterized by smaller populations living in very cheap housing. In the east of the inner city, they included abandoned commercial and industrial buildings in City and Suburban, pre-War slum housing in Jeppestown, Malvern, Bertrams, Judith's Paarl and Bellevue East and the shack settlement of Thembalihle[2] in the industrial neighbourhood of Benrose. In the west, these were the erstwhile white public housing scheme of Jan Hofmeyer and the neighbourhoods of Pageview and Fordsburg.

The second method of presenting evidence on unemployment rates is to measure the statistical distribution of unemployed residents across the geography of Johannesburg and the main types of settlements in 2011. The results of this method present the percentage distribution of unemployed residents in Table 6.1. Using the expanded definition to include discouraged jobseekers, these results show that over half (59 per cent) of all unemployed residents lived in the excluded ghettos of the southern suburbs. By contrast, only 25 per cent of unemployed residents lived in the slums, shack settlements and public housing developments of the northern suburbs (Table 6.1).

Although these statistical findings are consistent with Marcuse's description of the excluded ghetto, they cannot give us insights into the reasons why unemployed residents are concentrated in the erstwhile racial ghettos. Wilson (1996: pp.27–39) has proposed several likely reasons. The first of these is the decline of manual jobs within commuting range of the ghettos in the inner city. He argued that the movement of factories and offices to the edge cities meant that inner-city workers could not afford the cost of such a long daily commute. In support of this explanation, he cites a state-initiative to rehouse unemployed inner-city workers in edge city housing, which had the result of lowering the unemployment rate of these poorly educated black workers. However, the evidence from Johannesburg suggests that this spatial mismatch is not a full explanation for unemployment among poorly educated residents. If long and expensive commutes between home and workplace were a full explanation for unemployment, then we would expect to find low unemployment in places such as Alexandra, which is situated close to many employment opportunities in and around the Sandton Central Business District (CBD). Instead, the results show that the strict unemployment rate in the old slum areas of Alexandra was as high as 32 per cent in 2011, which is almost as high as the strict unemployment rate of 34 per cent in the remote Orange Farm settlements in the southern suburbs.

2 Not to be confused with the shack settlement of Thembelihle in Lenasia.

Table 6.1 The Geography of Unemployment in Johannesburg, 2011

Area and Housing Type	Strict Unemployment Rate (%)	Expanded Unemployment Rate (%)	Percentage of All Unemployment	
			Strict	Expanded
Northern Suburbs				
Unsubsidized Housing in Formally Whites-Only Neighbourhoods[1]	7	8	7	7
Apartheid Period Subsidized Housing[2]	32	37	1	1
Post-Apartheid, Partially Subsidized Gap Housing & Unsubsidized Housing[3]	20	24	2	2
Post-Apartheid Fully Subsidized Public Housing[4]	31	36	14	14
Old Alexandra Slum	33	37	5	4
Shack Settlements[5]	29	35	4	4
All Northern Suburbs	17	20	(33)	(32)
Inner City Neighbourhoods	21	24	6	6
Southern Suburbs				
Unsubsidized Housing in Formally Whites-Only Neighbourhoods[1]	13	15	3	3
Apartheid Period, Unsubsidized Housing in Soweto[6]	24	28	1	1
Unsubsidized Housing in Lenasia, Eldorado Park & Ennerdale	20	23	2	2
Apartheid Period, Public Housing in Soweto	36	43	32	32
Post-Apartheid, Partially Subsidized Gap Housing[7]	24	28	2	2
Post-Apartheid, Fully Subsidized Public Housing[8]	36	45	16	17
Shack Settlements[9]	32	39	5	5
All Southern Suburbs	31	37	(61)	(62)
City of Johannesburg*	24	28	100	100

1 Includes neighbouring post-*Apartheid* unsubsidized suburbs.

2 Public housing for coloured residents (Westbury, Coronationville, Bosmont and Newclare) and white residents (Jan Hofmeyer and Montclare).

3 Gap housing and unsubsidized housing in parts of the East Bank of Alexandra, Cosmo City, Kaalfontein, Ebony Park and Rabie Ridge.

4 RDP housing in East Bank of Alexandra, Ivory Park, Kaalfontein, Ebony Park, Rabie Ridge and Diepsloot.

5 Sejwetla (in Alexandra), Zandspruit (near Cosmo City), Mayibuye (in Midrand), Longdale, Tanganani (in Diepsloot), Malatjie (near Lanseria Airport), Princess (in Roodepoort), Wynberg, Denver and other smaller peri-urban shack settlements.

6 Diepkloof Extension, Dobsonville Extensions, Dobsonville Gardens, Mmesi Park and Protea North.

7 Gap housing in Lufhereng, Doornkop, Protea Glen and Drie Ziek Extension 2.

8 RDP housing in Bram Fischerville, Orange Farm, Stretford, Kanana Park and Lawley.

9 Thembelihle, Tshepisong, Slovo Park (adjacent to Nancefield), Finetown (in Ennerdale), Protea South, Kanana Park, Winnie Camp (Kliptown), Eikenhof and other smaller settlements.

* Percentages do not always add up to 100 because of rounding off.

Sources: The author's analysis of the 2011 Population Census results (SuperCross Interactive Tables).

2 State-sponsored housing provision and the geography of unemployment

The second explanation offered by Wilson is that the provision of public housing for poor residents was concentrated in the inner cities rather than the suburbs. The result was that unemployed residents tended to be concentrated in the inner-city neighbourhoods instead of the suburbs (Wilson, 1996: p.48). The evidence from Johannesburg also supports this argument. The concentration of unemployed residents in the erstwhile racial ghettos in the southern suburbs can be explained largely by the geography of informal shack settlements and State-sponsored housing provision during both the *Apartheid* and post-*Apartheid* periods.

First, by their low-cost nature, these informal shack settlements and public housing developments have attracted unemployed residents who are excluded from more expensive forms of housing. As a result, unemployed residents were concentrated in these low-cost housing developments. Second, since most informal shack settlements and State-sponsored houses were located in the southern suburbs, this resulted in the concentration of unemployed residents in the southern suburbs.

Unemployed residents who have no financial support from family or friends cannot afford to pay for their own housing and are therefore excluded from even the cheapest rental accommodation in the private, unsubsidized housing market. However, because of their lack of income, unemployed residents are eligible for fully subsidized housing provided by the State. Although fully subsidized houses are in principle free to beneficiaries, in practice, bribes from R200 to R5,000 are at least sometimes paid for access to the housing, which could exclude unemployed residents (Meth and Charlton, 2017: p.111). As an alternative to RDP houses, unemployed residents can also resort to living in shack settlements with limited services where they can live rent-free if they can afford to build their own accommodation. This means that unemployed residents were concentrated in public housing estates and shack settlements. In Johannesburg, these forms of housing have been largely located in and around the erstwhile racial ghettos of the southern suburbs.

These shack settlements, site-and-service developments and fully subsidized RDP housing schemes attracted unemployed residents because they were much cheaper than partially subsidized and non-subsidized housing. In addition, the City of Johannesburg had a policy of providing all residents with a free, albeit only a limited allocation of electricity and water. So if residents used these services very sparingly, they entailed no costs. However, there is evidence that at least some households were obliged to pay for services that they could not afford and that, as a result, they chose to leave these RDP houses for cheaper accommodation elsewhere (Meth and Charlton, 2017: p.100). Furthermore, the peripheral location of many shack settlements and RDP housing meant that transport costs from these neighbourhoods were high (Howe, 2018: p.359; Howe, 2021: p.13). As far as the payment of property tax was concerned, the City of Johannesburg exempted all properties valued below R20,001. So residents of informal shack settlements and cheaper houses did not always pay property tax to the local authority (Pernegger, 2021: p.58).

Unemployed residents were attracted to these low-cost settlements for a variety of different reasons, according to their individual circumstances (Stevens and Rule, 1999: p.113). Those who were obliged to live with their parents and other relatives took the opportunity to live independent lives. Similarly, recently unemployed backyard tenants who could no longer afford their rent, seized the opportunity of rent-free accommodation, even if it entailed putting up with limited services. Lastly, the closure of peri-urban farms forced farmworkers, who had lost both their employment and their homes, to find alternative cheap accommodation in these settlements (Crankshaw, O. and Hart, T., 1990: p.67; Crankshaw *et al.*, 1992: p.137)

At the end of the Fordist period in the mid-1970s, unemployment in Soweto was kept low partly by the Influx Control Act that excluded unemployed rural-born Africans from living in Johannesburg (Bekker and Humphries, 1985: p.49; Horrell, 1982: p.72). During the early *Apartheid* period, most African residents lived in either single-sex hostels or standardized public housing (Figure 6.3 and Figure 6.4). Single-sex hostels provided accommodation for rural-born migrants with jobs but without the right to live permanently in Johannesburg. Family housing was provided for African residents with urban rights. Although the rent was partially subsidized by the State, tenants of family housing had to be employed or have other means of income to pay the sub-economic rent. The Influx Control

Figure 6.3 *Apartheid*-Era State-Sponsored Housing in Jabavu, Soweto, 1978
Source: 326:331.83, Museum Africa Photographic Library, Johannesburg.

Figure 6.4 Dube Hostel in Soweto, 1978
Source: File: 'African Housing: Soweto', Nos. 12711 and P78/2569, *The Star* Archive, Independent Newspapers, Gauteng.

Act was abolished in 1986 (SAIRR, 1987: p.339), removing legal impediments that discouraged rural-born Africans from migrating to Johannesburg. As one would expect, this change in the law was associated with an increase in the proportion of rural-born residents under the age of forty, which included residents who had migrated to Soweto during the 1980s and 1990s (Beall *et al.*, 2006: pp.239–41).

This pattern of hostels and formal family housing provision began to break down under numerous social pressures (Crankshaw and Parnell, 1999). The first of these was the *Apartheid* Government's policy of restricting the migration of rural-born Africans to Johannesburg by reducing the provision of family housing in Soweto. The *Apartheid* Government achieved this policy by removing Soweto from the authority of the Johannesburg City Council in 1973 and placing it under the government of the West Rand Administration Board (WRAB). This restructuring therefore took the control of Soweto away from the opposition United Party and placed it under the control of officials who were loyal to the ruling National Party and its *Apartheid* policies (Grinker, 2000: p.4; Morris *et al.*, 1999: p.2). Later, from 1977, Soweto was governed under a Community Council system, which had a much smaller revenue source than the Johannesburg City Council (Mandy, 1984: p.204). Both these political measures reduced the supply of state-provided family housing in Soweto from the early 1970s until the end of *Apartheid*.

The provision of state-provided houses in Soweto, which reached its peak in the late 1950s, was therefore stopped altogether by the end of

1970s (Morris, 1981: pp.63, 85 and 117). In the face of a growing population of poorly educated and low-income African residents, this policy resulted in the overcrowding of public family housing. By 1981, estimates of the extent of overcrowding ranged from seven to fourteen people per house (Morris *et al.*, 1999: p.2). The standard Council house was a 40m², four-roomed structure comprising a kitchen, living room and two bedrooms (Morris, 1980: p.142). These numbers therefore meant up to seven people per bedroom or five people per room if the living room doubled up as a bedroom.

The shortage of sub-economic housing also led residents to build their own shelter in the backyards of formal houses. These rooms were built of either bricks and mortar or corrugated iron (Figure 6.5). In Soweto, during the 1950s and 1960s, when more State-sponsored housing was being built, about one quarter of migrants first lived in backyard rooms. By the 1990s, the extent of the housing shortage meant that this percentage had almost doubled to 43 per cent (Gilbert and Crankshaw, 1999: p.2382). By 1997, about 20 per cent of Soweto's population lived in backyard accommodation, which was double the percentage of residents who lived in shack settlements (Crankshaw *et al.*, 2000: p.846).

By another measure, in 1990, 57 per cent of formal stands in Africans-only neighbourhoods in Gauteng had a backyard shack or formal room. This meant that 37 per cent of Gauteng's African population lived in backyard accommodation (Sapire and Schlemmer, 1990: pp.22 and 29). In the post-*Apartheid* period, the large-scale building of fully subsidized State housing did not meet the demand

Figure 6.5 Backyard Shack in Meadowlands Zone 3, Soweto, 1997
Source: Photograph taken by the author.

for housing. The result was that shacks and brick rooms were also built in the backyards of post-*Apartheid* public housing estates, in neighbourhoods such as Alexandra's East Bank (Shapurjee and Charlton, 2013: p.656), Diepsloot and Bram Fischerville (Gardner and Rubin, 2016: p.80; Rubin and Charlton, 2020: p.197).

The short supply of Council houses also led to the establishment of shack settlements on vacant land in and near Soweto (Figure 6.6). The location of these shack settlements in the vicinity of Soweto therefore reproduced the geography of the racial ghetto by concentrating the settlement of poorer black residents in the southern suburbs. According to official sources, by 1990, almost 90 per cent of all shacks in the free-standing, unplanned settlements of Gauteng were in or near the established public housing estates (Sapire and Schlemmer, 1990: p.28).[3] In Johannesburg, the vast majority of shack settlements were located within Soweto and in the peri-urban areas to the south. In Soweto, the largest settlements were Mshenguville and Chicken Farm. Located on the banks of the Klip River in Mofolo, these two informal settlements contained about 60 per cent of all shacks in the shack settlements of Soweto (Figure 6.5). The other, smaller, shack settlements in Soweto were built on open land in the neighbourhoods of Tladi, Kliptown, Chiawelo, Naledi, Protea South and Dhlamini (Sapire and Schlemmer,

Figure 6.6 Mandelaville Shack Settlement in Diepkloof, Soweto, 1997
Source: Photograph taken by the author.

3 At the time, this area was termed the Pretoria-Witwatersrand-Vereeniging complex, the boundaries of which corresponded roughly with those of today's Gauteng Province.

1990: pp.39–40). To the south of Soweto, shack settlements were established in Slovo Park adjacent to the industrial area of Nancefield (SERI, 2011: p.26), in Vlakfontein (Crankshaw, 1993; Crankshaw, and Hart, 1990; Crankshaw *et al.*, 1992), in Ennerdale (Adler, *et al.*, 1984) and in Weiler's Farm[4] and Lenasia[5] (Sapire, 1990: pp.21–2; Sapire, 1992: p.675; Sapire and Schlemmer, 1990: pp.39–40; SERI, 2013: p.2).

Furthermore, in the early 1990s, the post-*Apartheid* State established the new site-and-service settlement of Thulani (SAIRR, 1992: p.338) on the north-western flank of Soweto, and Orange Farm on the southern boundary of Johannesburg (SAIRR, 1993: p.220) (Figure 6.5 and Figure 6.7). By contrast, only a few shack settlements were built on empty land in the northern suburbs. These were the small settlements that were built in Alexandra and in the adjacent industrial area of Wynberg (Figure 6.4). Further north, a handful of shack settlements were established on peri-urban land in the late 1980s. These included the shack settlements on the Zevenfontein farm (Abrahams, 1992; Beall *et. al.*, 2002: pp.132–4) and in the grounds of the Wilgespruit Fellowship Centre (Black Sash, 1989: p.5). Overall, towards the end of the *Apartheid* period, 84 per cent of all free-standing

Figure 6.7 Thulani Site-and-Service Settlement in Soweto, 1997
Source: Photograph taken by the author.

4 Later known as Kanana Park.
5 The shack settlement in Lenasia was first recorded as 'Lenz Buffer' or 'Lenasia Buffer' (Sapire and Schlemmer, 1990: p.39; Sapire, 1992: p.675) and was later known as Thembelihle (Guillame, 2001: p.41; Guillaume and Houssay-Holzschuch, 2002: p.90).

Figure 6.8 State-Sponsored Post-*Apartheid* Houses in Bram Fischerville, Soweto, 2004
Source: Photograph by Per-Anders Pettersson and sourced from Getty Images.

shacks in Johannesburg were therefore established within or on the outskirts of *Apartheid's* racial ghettos, namely Soweto, Eldorado Park and Lenasia.[6]

During the post-*Apartheid* period, new subsidized housing developments in the southern suburbs were located largely on the north-western outskirts of Soweto and south of Lenasia (Figure 6.8). In Soweto, these were the large developments in Thulani, Slovoville and Bram Fischerville (Harrison and Harrison, 2014: p.299) (Figure 4.5). Also developed to the west of Soweto was the mixed housing development of Lufhereng, which included both fully subsidized houses, partially subsidized 'Gap' housing and unsubsidized houses (Charlton 2017: pp.88–9). Further south, subsidized housing developments were built in Drie Ziek, Orange Farm, Stretford, Lehae, Lawley, Kanana Park,[7] Unaville, Vlakfontein and Ennerdale (Figure 4.5). Most of these settlements were first established either as illegal shack settlements or as legal site-and-service settlements that were then at least partially upgraded to formal houses through the State housing subsidy programme.

The large-scale provision of subsidized housing by the post-*Apartheid* State was not enough to meet the demand for housing. The result was the further growth of most of the shack settlements that were first established during the late *Apartheid* period. Although many of these shack settlements were upgraded *in situ*, some were

6 Based on calculations from statistics in Sapire and Schlemmer (1990: pp.39–40).
7 Originally known as the shack settlement of Weiler's Farm.

demolished, and their residents moved to new subsidized housing developments. Well-known examples were the Soweto settlements of Mshenguville in Mofolo and Mandelaville in Diepkloof (Figure 4.5). Mandelaville was demolished in 2002 to make way for a shopping centre and its residents moved to an old mining hostel north of Bram Fischerville, which became the centre of the new Sol Plaatjie subsidized housing development (Harrison and Harrison, 2014: p.304; Ndaba, 2002; Thale, 2004). Mshenguville was demolished in 2009 for development into a public park and its residents were provided with subsidized housing in the new settlement of Lehae, on the south-eastern flank of Lenasia (Pongoma, 2009).

The overall effect of this concentration of public housing, backyard rooms and informal shack settlements within and near the racial ghettos of Soweto, Eldorado Park and Lenasia, was that it has provided unemployed residents with cheap housing opportunities on a much larger scale than elsewhere in Johannesburg. In 2011, the expanded unemployment rate among residents of these public housing developments and shack settlements ranged from 38 to 45 per cent, substantially higher than the rate of 28 per cent in the neighbourhoods with largely unsubsidized and partially subsidized houses (Table 6.1).[8] The result is that unemployed residents have been concentrated to a greater extent in the erstwhile racial ghettos of the southern suburbs. Under conditions of extremely high unemployment, these racial ghettos have therefore been transformed into ghettos of exclusion.

The concentration of public housing in the southern suburbs also partly explains the continued working-class character of residents in and around the excluded ghettos in the post-*Apartheid* period. Low- and middle-income working-class residents are usually eligible for either fully or partially subsidized housing, most of which was built in the southern suburbs. The result was that large numbers of low- and middle-income residents were provided with site-and-service shacks and formal housing within the excluded ghetto.

The changing occupational class structure of the excluded ghetto

Over the period from 1996 to 2011, the percentages of residents employed in low-wage elementary jobs and in high-income managerial, professional and technical jobs did not change substantially. In the case of the former, the percentage rose slightly from 23 to 25 per cent. In the case of the latter, the percentage grew from 18 to 19 per cent (Figure 6.9 and Table 6.2).

There was, however, an important change in the occupational composition of middle-income jobs. Between 1996 and 2011, the middle-income working class was transformed from a class composed mostly of manual workers to a

---

8 Although the rate of unemployment among the workforce living in unsubsidized and partially subsidized housing is much lower than elsewhere, it is much higher than in other similar neighbourhoods, such as the inner-city and formerly whites-only neighbourhoods.

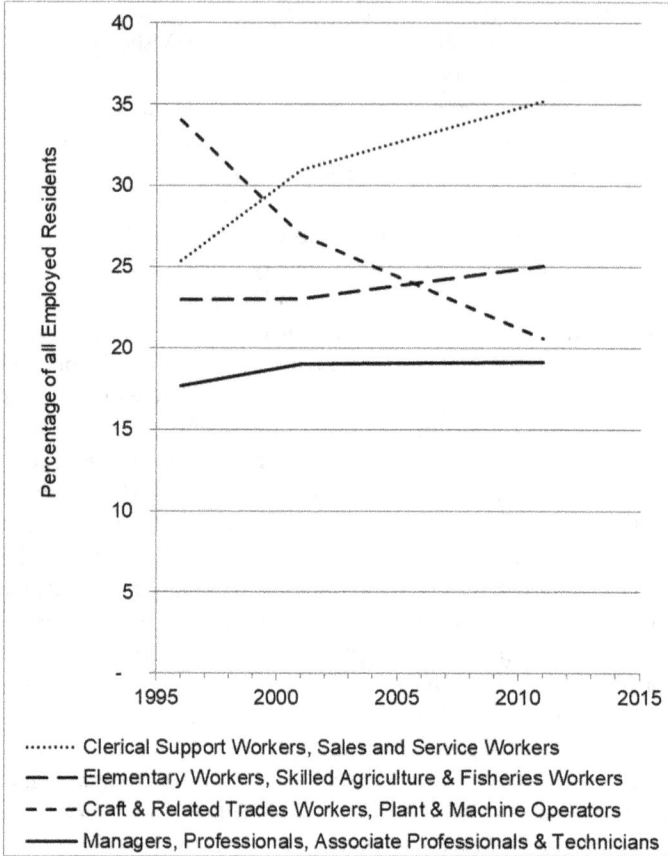

Figure 6.9 The Occupational Class Composition of Employed Residents in the Excluded Ghetto, 1996–2011

Sources: Author's Analysis of Population Census results, 1996, 2001 and 2011 (SuperCross Interactive Tables). See Table 6.2.

class mostly composed of non-manual workers. In 1996, 57 per cent of middle-income workers were employed in the manual occupations of Craft and Related Trades and Plant and Machine Operators. By 2011, 65 per cent of middle-income workers were employed as Clerical Support Workers and Sales and Service Workers. In more general terms, between 1996 and 2011, the percentage of Craft and Related Trades Workers and Plant and Machine Operators declined from 34 to 21 per cent. Correspondingly, the percentage of Clerical Support Workers and Sales and Service Workers increased from 25 to 35 per cent (Figure 6.9 and Table 6.2).

These trends in the occupational class composition of the excluded ghetto as a whole were replicated almost exactly in the suburbs of Soweto (Figure 6.10 and Table 6.3). The difference, however, is that the absolute growth of employed

Table 6.2 The Occupational Class Composition of Employed Residents in the Excluded Ghetto, 1996–2011

	Frequency Distribution			Annual Average Percentage Increase	Percentage Distribution		
	1996	2001	2011	1996–2011	1996	2001	2011
Managers, Professionals, Associate Professionals & Technicians	64,051	69,104	114,918	4.0	18	19	19
Clerical Support Workers, Sales and Service Workers	89,491	112,825	211,360	5.9	25	31	35
Craft & Related Trades Workers, Plant & Machine Operators	118,990	97,960	123,667	0.3	34	27	21
Elementary Workers, Skilled Agriculture & Fisheries Workers	79,495	83,941	150,569	4.4	23	23	25
Total Employment	352,027	363,830	600,514		100	100	100

Sources: Author's Analysis of Population Census results, 1996, 2001 and 2011 (SuperCross Interactive Tables).

residents in Soweto did not increase after 2001 probably because by then there were no further housing developments within its boundaries. A further distinction is that there was a slight decline in the absolute number of Sowetan residents employed in high-income middle class, from 83,063 in 2001 to 76,510 in 2011 (Table 6.3).

Table 6.3 The Occupational Class Composition of Employed Residents in Soweto, 1996–2011

	Frequency Distribution			Annual Average Percentage Increase	Percentage Distribution		
	1996	2001	2011	1996–2011	1996	2001	2011
Managers, Professionals, Associate Professionals & Technicians	42,503	83,063	76,510	4	17	18	18
Clerical Support Workers, Sales and Service Workers	64,837	151,478	154,666	6	25	32	37
Craft & Related Trades Workers, Plant & Machine Operators	88,702	130,565	84,823	−0.3	34	28	20
Elementary Workers, Skilled Agriculture & Fisheries Workers	61,078	108,070	102,989	4	24	23	25
Total Employment	257,120	473,176	418,988		100	100	100

Sources: Author's Analysis of Population Census results, 1996, 2001 and 2011 (SuperCross Interactive Tables).

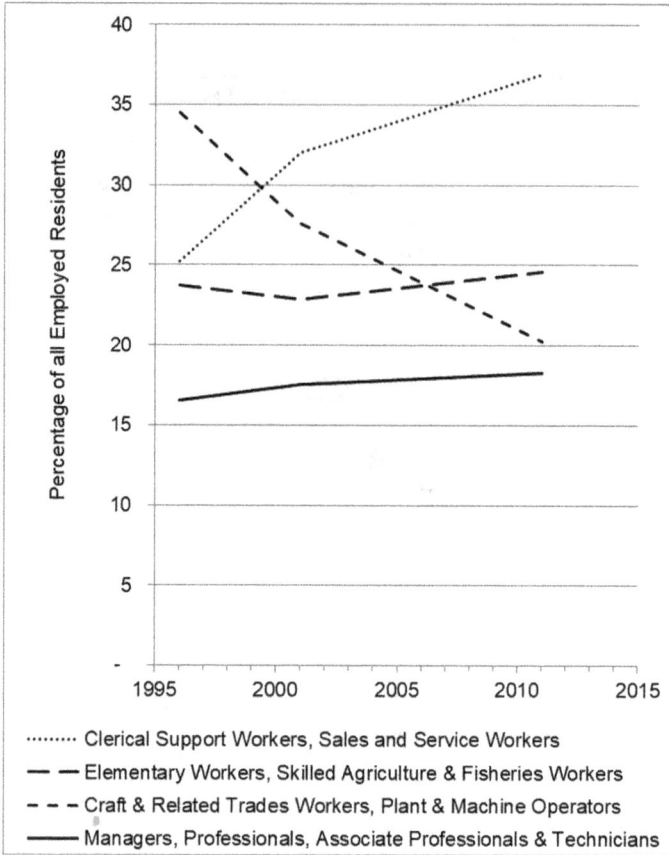

Figure 6.10 The Occupational Class Composition of Employed Residents in Soweto, 1996–2011

Sources: Author's Analysis of Population Census results, 1996, 2001 and 2011 (SuperCross Interactive Tables). See Table 6.3.

These findings have direct relevance to the debate concerning the occupational class structure of the excluded ghetto. The first is that the absolute and relative lack of growth of residents employed in middle-income manual jobs suggests that this is one of the causes of the extremely high level of unemployment among poorly educated residents. In 1996, a plurality (34 per cent) of residents was employed in middle-income manual jobs. By 2011, this percentage was reduced to only 21 per cent (Table 6.2). Although the number of residents in low-income, elementary jobs increased substantially, the overall number of residents employed in manual jobs was substantially less than it would otherwise have been. In this respect, Johannesburg's excluded ghetto has similar characteristics to the excluded ghettos of cities in the United States, where the decline of manual jobs has contributed to high levels of unemployment among its poorly educated residents (Kasarda, 1989: p.28).

However, this is where the similarity with the US ghetto ends. The decline of residents employed in middle-income manual jobs did not result in an occupational structure dominated by low-income jobs. Instead, the absolute number of middle-income workers has grown by roughly twice the number of low-skilled workers. Between 1996 and 2011, the numbers of middle-income workers grew by 126,546, compared to only 71,074 low-income workers (Table 6.4). This growth in the numbers of residents employed in middle-income jobs was due mostly to the growth of middle-income clerical, sales and service jobs, which more than made up for the almost negligible growth of middle-income workers employed in craft and machine-operating jobs (Table 6.2). This trend of growing employment in middle-income clerical, sales and service jobs is quite different from inner-city trends in the United States, where there was a decline in the number of residents employed in middle-income non-manual jobs (Kasarda, 1989: p.28).

Another distinct feature of Johannesburg's post-Fordist spatial order is that low-skilled, low-wage manual workers have not been concentrated in the excluded ghetto, as is argued to be the case in many cities of the United States and Europe. In 1996, almost two-thirds (64 per cent) of all low-wage, black Elementary Workers lived in Soweto, Eldorado Park, Lenasia and Ennerdale (Table 6.5). This

Table 6.4 Employment Change in the Occupational Class Composition of the Excluded Ghetto, 1996–2011

		Frequency Distribution				Percentage Distribution		
	Occupational Groups	1996	2001	2011	Employment Change, 1996–2011	1996	2001	2011
High-Income Workers	Managers, Professionals, Associate Professionals & Technicians	64,051	69,104	114,918	50,867	18	19	19
Middle-Income Workers	Clerical Support Workers, Sales and Service Workers, Craft & Related Trades Workers, Plant & Machine Operators	208,481	210,785	335,027	126,546	59	58	56
Low-Income Workers	Elementary Workers, Skilled Agriculture & Fisheries Workers	79,495	83,941	150,569	71,074	23	23	25
Total		352,027	363,830	600,514	248,487	100	100	100

Sources: Author's Analysis of Population Census results, 1996, 2001 and 2011 (SuperCross Interactive Tables).

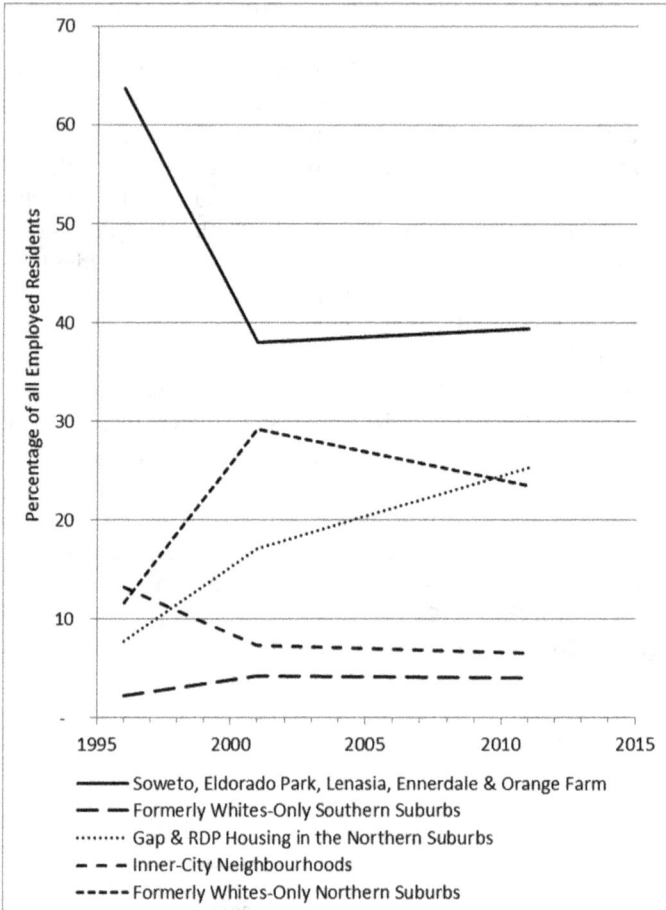

Figure 6.11 The Changing Geography of Black Residents Employed in Elementary
Occupations in Johannesburg, 1996–2011

Sources: Author's Analysis of Population Census results, 1996, 2001 and 2011 (SuperCross Interactive Tables). See
Table 6.5.

geography changed dramatically over the next fifteen years as the numbers of
black Elementary Workers living in the northern suburbs increased from only 20
per cent to as much as 48 per cent (Figure 6.11 and Table 6.5).

The one obvious explanation for the growing numbers of low-skilled, low-
wage black workers in the northern suburbs lies in the establishment and
growth of large public housing estates and informal shack settlements on the
periphery of the northern suburbs during the post-*Apartheid* period. As I have
discussed above, these are composed of three main clusters. The first cluster
includes the suburbs of Ivory Park, Rabie Ridge, Kaalfontein and Ebony Park
to the west of Midrand. The second includes the East Bank of Alexandra and

Table 6.5 The Changing Geography of Black Elementary Workers in Johannesburg, 1996–2011

	Frequency Distribution			Average Annual Percentage Increase	Percentage Distribution		
	1996	2001	2011	1996–2011	1996	2001	2011
Formerly Whites-Only Northern Suburbs[1]	9,430	64,407	89,075	16	12	29	23
Gap & RDP Housing in the Northern Suburbs	6,279	37,657	96,168	20	8	17	25
Inner-City Neighbourhoods	10,730	16,148	24,485	6	13	7	6
Formerly Whites-Only Southern Suburbs[1]	1,766	9,346	15,134	15	2	4	4
Soweto, Eldorado Park, Lenasia, Ennerdale & Orange Farm[2]	51,922	83,926	149,621	7	64	38	39
Peri-Urban & Commercial Areas	1,470	9,158	5,060	9	2	4	1
Total Employment	81,597	220,642	379,543	11	100	100	100

Sources: Author's Analysis of Population Census results, 1996, 2001 and 2011 (SuperCross Interactive Tables).
1 Including unsubsidized post-*Apartheid* suburbs.
2 Including Riverlea, Noordgesig, Lehae, Zakariyya Park, Kanana Park, Vlakfontein, Unaville, Stretford, Lakeside and Drie Ziek.

the third includes the north-western suburbs of Cosmo City, Zandspruit and Diepsloot. Although some of the formal houses in these suburbs were bought at market prices, the vast majority of them were partially or fully subsidized by the State. Other housing for low-wage workers was available in the form of the backyards of formal houses, where rooms were available for rent, and shacks in site-and-service schemes and unplanned settlements. These new housing developments and shack settlements therefore provided low-skilled, low-wage black workers with the opportunity to live in the northern suburbs where, in the past, *Apartheid* housing policies had restricted them to the racial ghettos in the southern suburbs. The number of residents in these neighbourhoods who were employed in low-skilled jobs therefore increased from about 6,000 in 1996 to nearly 100,000 in 2011 (Table 6.5). This increased the percentage of all low-skilled black residents who lived in these neighbourhoods from 8 per cent in 1996 to 25 per cent in 2011 (Table 6.5).

The growth in the numbers of low-wage black workers living in expensive non-subsidized houses in the formerly whites-only suburbs and their post-*Apartheid* counterparts can only be due to the vast growth of the housing stock in these neighbourhoods and their accompanying accommodation for live-in domestic workers.

The excluded ghetto and middle-class flight

Another distinctive feature of Johannesburg's excluded ghetto is that the high-income, middle-class residents have not completely abandoned the excluded ghetto to live in the northern suburbs. Starting in the 1980s, many middle-class black residents left the ghettos of Soweto, Eldorado Park, Lenasia and Ennerdale to live in formerly whites-only suburbs. Despite this middle-class flight from the excluded ghetto, the numbers of middle-class residents have increased in absolute terms such that their overall proportion of about one-fifth of all employment within the excluded ghetto remained roughly the same over the period from 1996 to 2011 (Table 6.3, Table 6.4 and Figure 6.10). These results therefore suggest that there has not been an increased concentration of poverty caused by the exodus of middle-class residents, as is claimed of the US ghetto (Wilson, 1996: p.42). Kracker Selzer and Heller (2010: pp.192–4) have made similar claims for the period from 1996 to 2001, which is based on the growth in the numbers of associate professionals and technicians (their 'middle middle class'). By contrast, their study showed a decline in the numbers of managers and professionals in Soweto (their 'upper middle class').[9]

The population census results can be used to measure changes in the geographical distribution of middle-class black residents of Johannesburg from 1996 to 2011. In 1996, 60 per cent of the black middle class lived in the excluded ghettos of the southern suburbs. By this time, the inner-city neighbourhoods had become substantially desegregated and about 13 per cent of the black middle class lived in these neighbourhoods. In the northern suburbs, the new housing developments in Ebony Park, Rabie Ridge and Kaalfontein included unsubsidized and partially subsidized houses where about 6 per cent of the black middle class lived. By contrast, only 16 per cent of the black middle class lived in the huge expanse of formerly whites-only neighbourhoods in the northern suburbs (Table 6.6). Over the next fifteen years, this geography of the black middle class changed dramatically in one important respect: The absolute number of middle-class black residents living in the formerly whites only northern suburbs grew dramatically, eventually exceeding the numbers in the excluded ghetto of the southern suburbs (Figure 6.12 and Table 6.6). This growth in number of black middle-class residents of the northern suburbs was supplemented by much smaller numbers living in the in new, partially subsidized housing and unsubsidized developments within the neighbourhoods of Ebony Park, Rabie Ridge and Cosmo City. The numbers of middle-class black residents living in the inner city and the formerly whites-only southern suburbs also increased, but not nearly to the same extent as those in the northern suburbs simply because of the much larger number of houses in the northern suburbs.

---

9 These statistical results are substantially lower than my own estimates. Their estimate of
   Soweto's managerial, professional, associate professional and technical middle class was
   46,904 in 1996 and 47,535 in 2001 (Kracker Selzer and Heller, 2010: p.193). My estimates
   were 42,503 for 1996 and 83,063 for 2001.

Table 6.6 The Changing Geography of the Black Middle Class, 1996–2011*

	Frequency Distribution			Average Annual Percentage Increase	Percentage Distribution		
	1996	2001	2011	1996–2011	1996	2001	2011
Soweto	44,638	45,620	75,896	4	42	30	24
Eldorado Park, Lenasia, Lenasia South, Ennerdale & Surrounds[1]	16,764	20,489	31,040	4	16	13	10
Orange Farm, Drie Ziek, Stretford & Lakeside	2,143	2,809	6,567	8	2	2	2
Sub-Total: Southern Suburbs Excluded Ghetto	*(63,545)*	*(68,918)*	*(113,503)*	*(4)*	*(60)*	*(45)*	*(36)*
Formerly Whites-Only Southern Suburbs[2]	2,877	13,673	24,164	15	3	9	8
Inner City Neighbourhoods	13,659	15,824	23,104	4	13	10	7
Formerly Whites-Only Northern Suburbs[2,3]	16,862	40,941	119,368	14	16	27	38
Gap & RDP Housing in Northern Suburbs[4]	6,259	10,620	30,045	11	6	7	10
Industrial, Commercial & Peri-Urban Areas	1,847	1,814	2,950	3	2	1	1
Grand Total	105,049	151,790	313,134	8	100	100	100

Sources: Author's Analysis of Population Census results, 1996, 2001 and 2011 (SuperCross Interactive Tables).
1 Including Riverlea, Noordgesig, Lehae, Zakariyya Park, Kanana Park, Vlakfontein, Unaville, Stretford, Lakeside and Drie Ziek.
2 Including unsubsidized post-*Apartheid* suburbs.
3 Including the formerly coloureds and Indians-only neighbourhoods of Marlboro, Newclare, Bosmont, Westbury and Coronationville.
4 Rabie Ridge, Kaalfontein, Ebony Park, Alexandra, Diepsloot, Zandspruit, Ivory Park, Cosmo City & Alexandra's East Bank & Far East Bank. These neighbourhoods are largely characterized by Gap and RDP houses, but there are some neighbourhoods with unsubsidized houses. See Wagner (2018: p.37) on Cosmo City.
* All African, coloured and Indian residents employed in Managerial, Professional, Associate Professional and Technical jobs.

In spite of this large-scale movement into the formerly whites-only northern suburbs, the number of middle-class residents of the excluded ghetto continued to grow in absolute terms. The result was that the percentage of all excluded ghetto residents who were employed in middle-class jobs remained roughly constant at 18 to 19 per cent (Table 6.2).

These striking results concerning the changing geography of black middle-class residents may surprise some readers, who will wonder if these trends were also true for middle-class African residents. It has already been shown in an earlier chapter that African, Indian and coloured residents of Johannesburg have very different occupational class profiles. Specifically, the percentage of Indian and

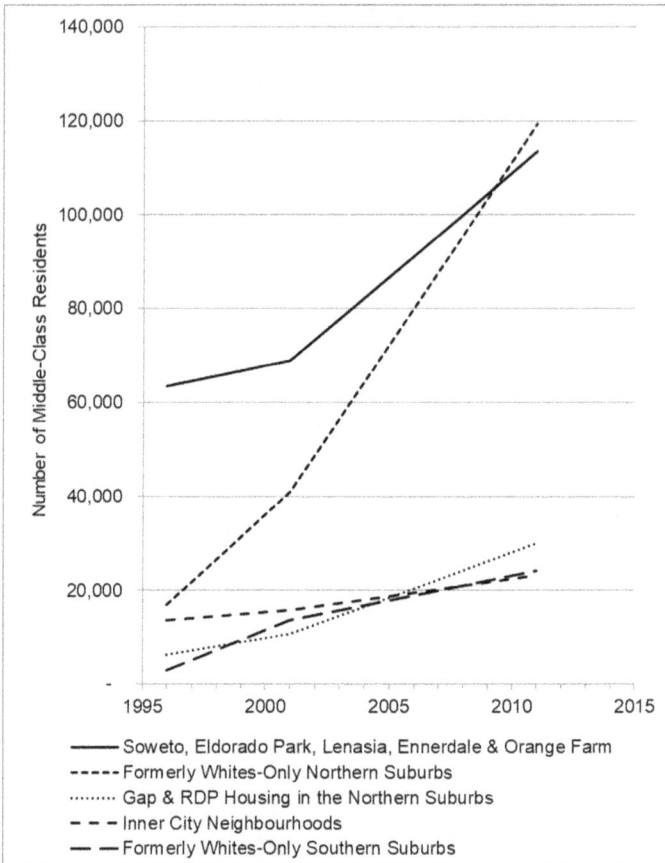

Figure 6.12 The Changing Geography of the Black Middle Class*, 1996–2011
Sources: Author's Analysis of Population Census results, 1996, 2001 and 2011 (SuperCross Interactive Tables). See
    Table 6.6.
* All African, coloured and Indian residents employed in Managerial, Professional, Associate Professional and
    Technical jobs

coloured residents who are employed in middle class jobs is much higher than
that of the African population. However, the number of African workers is so
much larger than that of Indian and coloured workers, that the trend among
middle-class African residents contributes over half of all black residents living
in the formerly whites-only northern suburbs. By 2011, there were about 120,000
middle-class black residents living in the formerly whites-only northern suburbs
and similar post-*Apartheid* suburbs. Of this number, about 70,000 (or 58 per cent)
were African residents, 16,000 (or 13 per cent) were coloured residents and 34,000
(or 29 per cent) were Indian residents (Table 6.7 to Table 6.9).

There is, however, an important difference in the middle-class geography of
African residents, on the one hand, and coloured and Indian residents, on the
other. Unlike their middle-class African counterparts, a much higher percentage

of the coloured and Indian middle class live in the more salubrious formerly whites-only northern suburbs. By 2011, whereas about one-third (31 per cent) of middle-class Africans lived in the northern suburbs, this percentage was much higher for coloured (51 per cent) and Indian residents (63 per cent) (Figure 6.13 to Figure 6.15 and Table 6.7 to Table 6.9).

A partial explanation for why the black middle-class had not completely abandoned Soweto, Eldorado Park and Lenasia lies in the nature of the housing market in the racial ghettos. Although the racial ghetto was dominated by low-cost housing and shack settlements for the poor, there was nonetheless some housing and improved infrastructure and services that satisfied the needs of a high-income middle class (Kracker Selzer and Heller, 2010: p.194).

From their inception, the coloured and Indian Group Areas were different from Soweto because there were no legal restrictions on the ownership of land

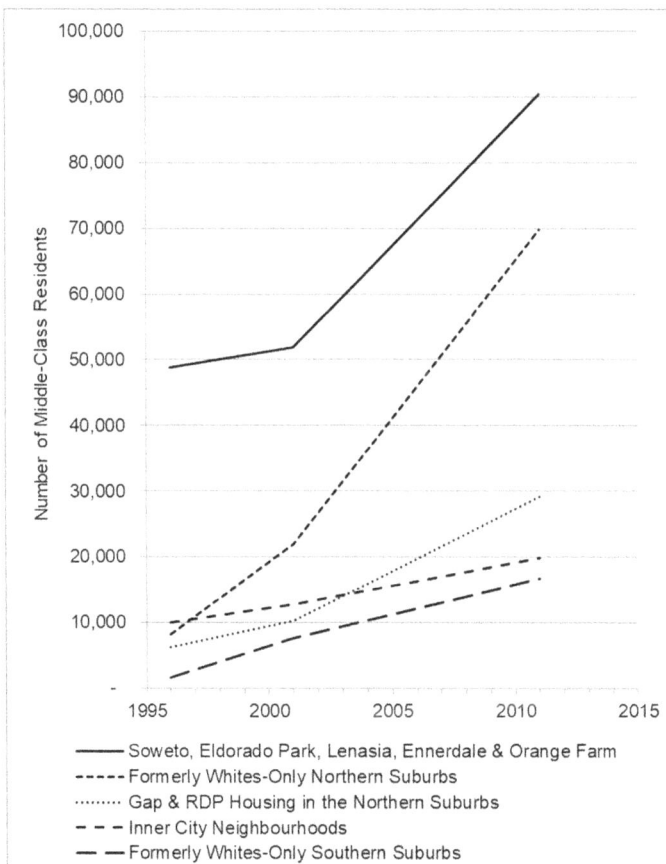

Figure 6.13 The Changing Geography of the African Middle Class*, 1996–2011
Sources: Author's Analysis of Population Census results, 1996, 2001 and 2011 (SuperCross Interactive Tables). See Table 6.7.
* All African residents employed in Managerial, Professional, Associate Professional and Technical jobs

Table 6.7 The Changing Geography of the African Middle Class, 1996–2011*

	Frequency Distribution			Average Annual Percentage Increase	Percentage Distribution		
	1996	2001	2011	1996–2011	1996	2001	2011
Soweto	44,165	44,777	74,418	4	58	42	33
Eldorado Park, Lenasia, Lenasia South & Ennerdale[1]	2,520	4,361	9,566	9	3	4	4
Orange Farm, Drie Ziek, Stretford & Lakeside	2,140	2,794	6,477	8	3	3	3
Sub-Total: Southern Suburbs Excluded Ghetto	*(48,825)*	*(51,932)*	*(90,461)*	*(4)*	*(64)*	*(49)*	*(40)*
Formerly Whites-Only Southern Suburbs[2]	1,599	7,682	16,690	17	2	7	7
Inner City Neighbourhoods	9,964	12,812	19,867	5	13	12	9
Formerly Whites-Only Northern Suburbs[2,3]	8,162	21,934	69,752	15	11	21	31
Gap & RDP Housing in Northern Suburbs[4]	6,203	10,329	29,220	11	8	10	13
Industrial, Commercial & Peri-Urban Areas	1,255	1,463	2,310	4.2	2	1	1
Total	76,008	106,152	228,300	7.6	100	100	100

Sources: Author's Analysis of Population Census results, 1996, 2001 and 2011 (SuperCross Interactive Tables).
1 Including Riverlea, Noordgesig, Lehae, Zakariyya Park, Kanana Park, Sweetwaters Vlakfontein and Unaville.
2 Including unsubsidized post-*Apartheid* suburbs.
3 Including the formerly coloureds and Indians-only neighbourhoods of Marlboro, Newclare, Bosmont, Westbury and Coronationville.
4 Rabie Ridge, Kaalfontein, Ebony Park, Alexandra, Diepsloot, Zandspruit, Ivory Park, Cosmo City & Alexandra's East Bank & Far East Bank. These neighbourhoods are largely characterized by Gap and RDP houses, but there are some neighbourhoods with unsubsidized houses. See Wagner (2018: p.37) on Cosmo City.
* All African residents employed in Managerial, Professional, Associate Professional and Technical jobs.

and houses. Although State-owned housing was provided for poorer families, those residents who could afford it were permitted to buy land and build their own houses. The coloureds-only suburbs of Eldorado Park, which were developed during the 1960s and 1970s, comprised a variety of housing types and tenures. About half of all the housing was not subsidized by the State. Most of these houses were developed by the State and sold to residents at market prices. A smaller number of plots were set aside for private development, in which homeowners purchased the land and built housing according to their own tastes and finances. The other half of the housing stock comprised State-owned houses and three-storey apartment buildings that were rented by residents at economic and sub-economic rates (Lupton, 1991: pp.15–16; 1993; Stickler, 1982: pp.53 and 56). By contrast, the coloureds-only suburb of Ennerdale, which was developed later during the 1980s, was built for homeownership by the private sector and home loans were financed by private banks (Lupton, 1991: pp.20–1; 1993).

The Indians-only suburb of Lenasia was developed from the 1950s onwards. State-owned houses, which were identical to the 'matchbox' houses in Soweto, were rented by low-income households. Larger State-owned homes, with three bedrooms, were built for tenants who could afford higher rents. Later housing developments, during the 1970s and 1980s, were built on plots as large as 750m² and were probably privately built and owned, in the same way that housing was developed in Lenasia South from the mid-1980s (SAHO, 2019).

In Africans-only suburbs, during the early *Apartheid* period, there were some exceptions to the standardized 'matchbox' houses. These exceptions were in the suburbs of Dube, Moroka, Pimville and Orlando West, in which the Government

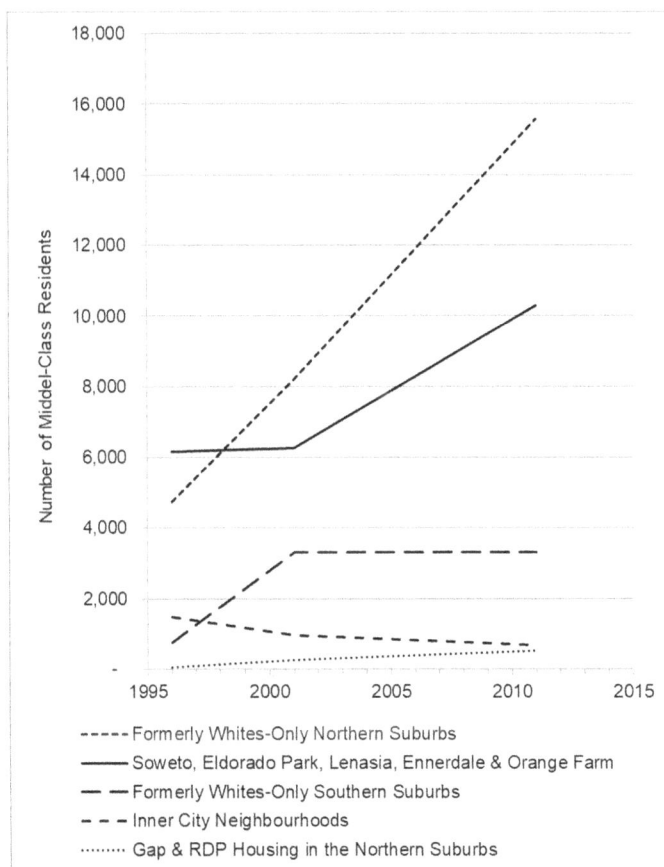

Figure 6.14 The Changing Geography of the Coloured Middle Class*, 1996–2011

Sources: Author's Analysis of Population Census results, 1996, 2001 and 2011 (SuperCross Interactive Tables).
       See Table 6.8.
* All coloured residents employed in Managerial, Professional, Associate Professional and Technical jobs

Table 6.8 The Changing Geography of the Coloured Middle Class, 1996–2011*

	Frequency Distribution			Average Annual Percentage Increase	Percentage Distribution		
	1996	2001	2011	1996–2011	1996	2001	2011
Soweto	451	816	1,146	6	3	4	4
Eldorado Park, Lenasia, Lenasia South & Ennerdale[1]	5,701	5,430	9,112	3	43	28	30
Orange Farm, Drie Ziek, Stretford & Lakeside	3	15	40	19	0	0	0
Sub-Total: Southern Suburbs Excluded Ghetto	*(6,155)*	*(6,261)*	*(10,298)*	*(4)*	*(46)*	*(33)*	*(34)*
Formerly Whites-Only Southern Suburbs[2]	759	3,306	3,320	10	6	17	11
Inner City Neighbourhoods	1,462	960	657	−5	11	5	2
Formerly Whites-Only Northern Suburbs[2,3]	4,724	8,206	15,560	8	35	43	51
Gap & RDP Housing in Northern Suburbs[4]	39	267	519	19	0	1	2
Industrial, Commercial & Peri-Urban Areas	20	165	221	0	2	1	1
Total	13,346	19,165	30,575	6	100	100	100

Sources: Author's Analysis of Population Census results, 1996, 2001 and 2011 (SuperCross Interactive Tables).
1 Including Riverlea, Noordgesig, Lehae, Zakariyya Park, Kanana Park, Sweetwaters Vlakfontein and Unaville.
2 Including unsubsidized post-*Apartheid* suburbs.
3 Including the formerly coloureds and Indians-only neighbourhoods of Marlboro, Newclare, Bosmont, Westbury and Coronationville.
4 Rabie Ridge, Kaalfontein, Ebony Park, Alexandra, Diepsloot, Zandspruit, Ivory Park, Cosmo City & Alexandra's East Bank & Far East Bank. These neighbourhoods are largely characterized by Gap and RDP houses, but there are some neighbourhoods with unsubsidized houses. See Wagner (2018: p.37) on Cosmo City.
* All Coloured residents employed in Managerial, Professional, Associate Professional and Technical jobs.

permitted the high-earning African middle class to build their own homes and to own property under the restricted terms of a thirty-year leasehold tenure (Morris, 1980: pp.54–5, 132; Parnell, 1991) (Figure 6.16). At the height of *Apartheid*, in 1968, these leasehold rights were withdrawn, but soon thereafter, in response to the growing and effective political opposition to *Apartheid*, the National Party Government introduced housing reforms in an attempt to give the African middle class a stake in a reformed *Apartheid* order (Bonner and Segal, 1998: p.104).

Reforms to African housing rights began with the restoration of thirty-year leasehold rights in 1975, and in 1978 these leasehold rights were extended to ninety-nine years (Morris, 1980: p.17). These reforms allowed large corporations to develop new home-ownership schemes for their high-earning African employees in the late 1970s. The Johannesburg City Council and IBM developed

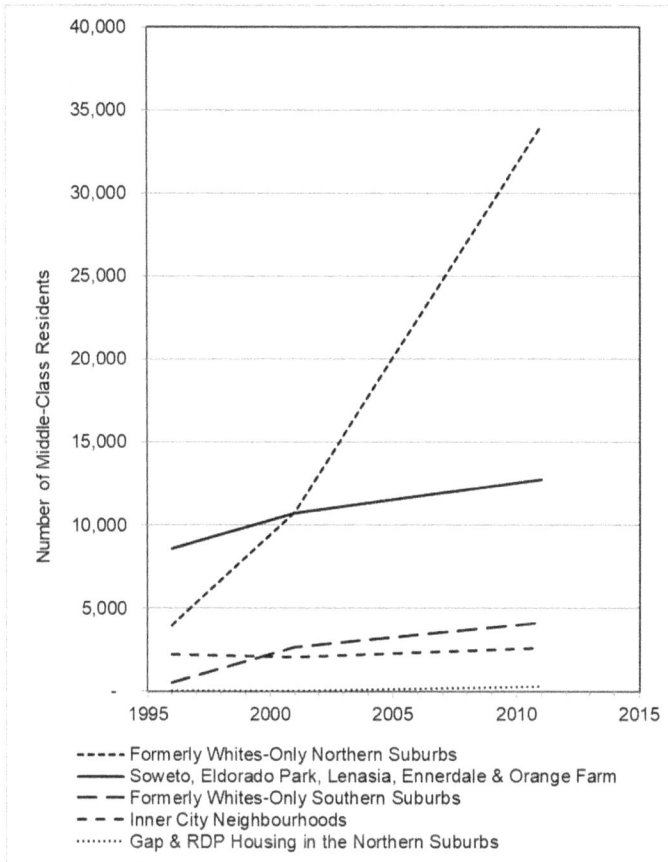

Figure 6.15 The Changing Geography of the Indian Middle Class*, 1996–2011

Sources: Author's Analysis of Population Census results, 1996, 2001 and 2011 (SuperCross Interactive Tables). See Table 6.9.

* All Indian residents employed in Managerial, Professional, Associate Professional and Technical jobs

such housing schemes in Pimville Zone 4 and in Orlando West (Nieftagodien and Gaule, 2012: pp.81–2; SAIRR, 1979: p.338). The Urban Foundation also facilitated the development of some 420 houses in Selection Park, Pimville (Morris, 1981: p.117) (Figure 6.17). A much larger housing scheme for middle-class residents was developed in the new suburb of Diepkloof Extension on the eastern flank of Diepkloof in the late 1970s and early 1980s (Bonner and Segal, 1998: p.104). Although the stands were small by white middle-class standards, this new neighbourhood comprised large houses, a few of them with a swimming pool in the backyard (Mashabela, 1988: p.57) (Figure 6.18).[10] During the 1980s and

10 Dubbed 'Prestige Park' and 'Diepkloof Expensive' by Sowetans (Bonner and Segal, 1998: p.105; Mashabela, 1988: p.57).

Table 6.9 The Changing Geography of the Indian Middle Class, 1996–2011*

	Frequency Distribution			Annual Average Percentage Increase	Percentage Distribution		
	1996	2001	2011	1996–2011	1996	2001	2011
Soweto	22	27	332	20	0	0	1
Eldorado Park, Lenasia, Lenasia South & Ennerdale[1]	8,543	10,698	12,362	3	54	40	23
Orange Farm, Drie Ziek, Stretford & Lakeside	-	-	50	Na	0	0	0
Sub-Total: Southern Suburbs Excluded Ghetto	*(8,565)*	*(10,725)*	*(12,744)*	*(3)*	*(55)*	*(41)*	*(23)*
Formerly Whites-Only Southern Suburbs[2]	519	2,685	4,154	15	3	10	8
Inner City Neighbourhoods	2,233	2,052	2,580	1	14	8	5
Formerly Whites-Only Northern Suburbs[2,3]	3,976	10,801	34,056	15	25	41	63
Gap & RDP Housing in the Northern Suburbs[4]	17	24	306	21	0	0	1
Industrial, Commercial & Peri-Urban Areas	385	186	419	1	2	1	1
Total	15,695	26,473	54,259	9	100	100	100

Sources: Author's Analysis of Population Census results, 1996, 2001 and 2011 (SuperCross Interactive Tables).
1 Including Riverlea, Noordgesig, Lehae, Zakariyya Park, Kanana Park, Sweetwaters Vlakfontein and Unaville.
2 Including unsubsidized post-*Apartheid* suburbs.
3 Including the formerly coloureds and Indians-only neighbourhoods of Marlboro, Newclare, Bosmont, Westbury and Coronationville.
4 Rabie Ridge, Kaalfontein, Ebony Park, Alexandra, Diepsloot, Zandspruit, Ivory Park, Cosmo City & Alexandra's East Bank & Far East Bank. These neighbourhoods are largely characterized by Gap and RDP houses, but there are some neighbourhoods with unsubsidized houses. See Wagner (2018: p.37) on Cosmo City.
* All Indian residents employed in Managerial, Professional, Associate Professional and Technical jobs.

early 1990s, other large housing developments for homeowners were built on the north-western and western boundaries of Soweto. These were the new suburbs of Dobsonville Gardens (Mashabela, 1988: p.63), Protea North and Protea Glen (Ceruti, 2013: p.56; Harrison and Harrison, 2014: p.309). Although these new houses were available for purchase by households, they were also bought by large companies who were eager to improve the housing conditions of their clerical and managerial staff. These middle- and high-income staff either rented such a house from their employer or bought it using a loan secured against their pension contributions (Mather and Parnell, 1990: pp.246–7).

In 1983, the Government introduced another major reform that allowed tenants of State-owned houses to buy both their houses (and the land on which

Figure 6.16 An Unsubsidized House in Dube, Soweto
Source: 326:331.83 Museum Afrika Photographic Library, Johannesburg.

Figure 6.17 Unsubsidized Houses in Pimville, Soweto, 1997
Source: Photograph by the author.

Figure 6.18 An Unsubsidized House in Diepkloof Extension, Soweto, 1997
Source: Photograph by the author.

they stood) in terms of ninety-nine-year leasehold ownership (SAIRR, 1984: pp.230–1). In 1986, new legislation allowed State tenants and residents who held thirty-year and ninety-nine-year leaseholds to buy their houses and land under freehold tenure (SAIRR, 1987: p.369). The change from being tenants of the local State to freeholders incentivized residents to enlarge and generally upgrade their rudimentary housing (Mather and Parnell, 1990: p.246). As a result, many of the residents of original 'matchbox' houses were able to obtain mortgages to finance substantial renovations to their homes (FM, 1983: p.17). Home renovations included features such as new fences, additional rooms, inside toilets, exterior plastering and garages for motor vehicles (Krige, 2012: p.36) (Figure 6.20). These major renovations stand in contrast to the minor improvements that tenants undertook prior to the introduction homeownership reforms. Such minor improvements entailed plastering internal walls, laying concrete floors and installing ceilings and interior doors (Ginsberg, 1996: pp.130–4).

Although this reform provided security of tenure and improved housing to those who could afford to buy and renovate their homes, it did not create new, homogeneously middle-class neighbourhoods since it applied to already-existing State-sponsored houses in largely working-class neighbourhoods.

In the post-*Apartheid* period, private developers saw the opportunity to build housing for higher-income residents on the periphery of Soweto. Butcher (2020: p.345) argues that the relatively low price of land and the demand for housing by upwardly mobile Sowetan residents made these housing developments profitable. As a manager of one of these development companies put it, 'Sowetans are born

Figure 6.19 Unsubsidized Houses in 'Beverley Hills', Orlando West, Soweto, 1989
Source: File: 'African Housing: Soweto', No.83662, *The Star* Archive, Independent Newspapers, Johannesburg.

Figure 6.20 A Renovated *Apartheid*-era 51/6 House in Dube, Soweto, 1997
Source: Photograph by the author.

in Soweto they don't want to leave Soweto ... So we are [providing houses] there'
(Butcher, 2020: p.345). These housing developments were aimed at residents who
earned between R10,000 and R15,000 per month, which meant that they did not
qualify for fully subsidized housing but did benefit from the once-off 'Gap' housing
subsidy. These 'Gap' housing developments were built in neighbourhoods such as
Protea Glen (Butcher, 2016: p.190) (Figure 4.5).

During the post-*Apartheid* period, Government policy aimed to upgrade the
level of services and infrastructure in the formerly blacks-only neighbourhoods,
which had been severely underfunded during the *Apartheid* period. Because of its
important political constituency, Soweto was the main beneficiary of such State-
led investment (Harrison and Harrison, 2014: p.302). Many of these developments
would have been important to middle-class residents and therefore may have
played a role in making Soweto their residential choice. These developments
included major changes to the infrastructure of Soweto, such as the upgrading
of gravel roads by installing kerbstones, tarred surfaces and stormwater drainage.
Other improvements included pedestrian walkways, cycle paths and new public
parks (CoJ, 2011: p.20; Harrison and Harrison, 2014: p.303). Another important
kind of development that may have attracted middle-class residents entailed the
building of new shopping malls. Prominent among these was the Jabulani Mall,
which included housing, business premises and recreational facilities (Harrison
and Harrison, 2014: p.304). Yet another was the building of new sports facilities,
which even included '[s]porting activities generally associated with more affluent
areas, such as tennis and equestrian sports' (CoJ, 2011: p.6).

The occupational class composition of residents in these more expensive
housing developments in Soweto can be partially measured by first identifying these
housing developments and then using neighbourhood-level statistics to measure
the occupational composition of these neighbourhoods. This identification of
partially and unsubsidized housing developments was done by studying the
literature on housing provision in Soweto, and by making observations during
fieldwork and of aerial images provided through the software applications of
Google Maps and Google Earth Pro.

There are three difficulties in making a complete measurement of the
occupational class composition of residents in the unsubsidized homes for high-
income earners. The first is that the boundaries of the Census 'Subplaces' or
neighbourhoods do not always coincide with these new housing developments for
higher-income residents. The result is that the neighbourhood boundaries include
both the more expensive unsubsidized houses and erstwhile public houses, making
it impossible to distinguish the occupational class composition of the former.
Second, houses that have been upgraded from the original 'matchbox' houses to
the standards of high-income, middle-class residents are scattered throughout
the early *Apartheid* public housing developments of Soweto. The result is that the
statistics for any Subplace in these areas contains a mixture of residents who lived
in original 'matchbox' houses and upgraded houses. Finally, it is also difficult to
visually distinguish unsubsidized housing from partially subsidized Gap housing
developments. It is a straightforward matter to identify the 'matchbox' public

houses of the early *Apartheid* era and the RDP/BNG houses of the post-*Apartheid* period. Both these types are obviously smaller than other houses, at only 40m². This also means that they have a simple rectangular footprint with a pitched single-ridge roof with gables at each end. This stands in contrast with the larger Gap and unsubsidized houses, which are both larger and have non-standard footprints, often with wings off the main structure. The pitched roof is also not standardized and can be a gabled roof or a hipped roof with four sloped sides. So it is the non-standard designs of Gap and unsubsidized housing that make them difficult to distinguish these two types visually. This problem is compounded by the similar types of building material used in Gap and unsubsidized housing. Both types usually have tiled roofs and very often have walls built of fired clay face bricks instead of walls built with stock bricks that are finished with plaster.

These problems notwithstanding, statistical evidence from the latest census concerning the occupational class distribution of residents in these unsubsidized housing developments shows a substantially higher percentage of middle-class Managers, Professionals, Technicians and Associate Professionals than in other types of housing. In 2011, 43 per cent of employed residents in the unsubsidized housing developments of Diepkloof Extension, Dobsonville Extensions 1 and 3, Protea North and Mmesi Park were middle class (Table 6.10). In Diepkloof

Table 6.10 Occupational Class Differentiation of Employed Residents by Housing Types in Soweto, 2011 (Percentage Distribution)

Major Occupational Groups	Unsubsidized Housing[1] (Apartheid Era)	Unsubsidized & Gap Housing[2] (Post-Apartheid Era)	Public Housing (Apartheid Era)	RDP Housing[3] (Post-Apartheid Era)	Shack Settlements
Managers, Professionals, Associate Professionals & Technicians	43	29	18	11	11
Clerical Support Workers, Sales and Service Workers	35	41	39	32	28
Craft & Related Trades Workers, Plant & Machine Operators	11	14	19	25	27
Elementary Workers, Skilled Agriculture & Fisheries Workers	12	16	24	31	34
Total Employed	100	100	100	100	100

1 Diepkloof Extension, Dobsonville Extensions 1 and 3, Protea North and Mmesi Park.
2 Dobsonville Gardens, Protea Glen, Dobsonville Extensions 4, 5 and 7.
3 Thulani, Bram Fischerville, Slovoville, Sol Plaatjie, Leratong Village, Devland, Freedom Park (Devland) and Matholesville (north of Bram Fischerville).
4 Chris Hani (Kliptown), Freedom Charter Square (Kliptown), Motsoaledi (Diepkloof), Thulani, Mandela View (Eldorado Park), Winnie Camp (Kliptown), Protea South and Slovo Park (Nancefield).
Source: Author's analysis of the 2011 Population Census Results (SuperCross Interactive Tables).

Extension, as much as 50 per cent of employed residents were middle class, a percentage that was as high as many of the northern suburbs.[11] In the newer, post-*Apartheid* unsubsidized and partially subsidized Gap developments, the percentage was lower, at 29 per cent. By contrast, only 18 per cent of all residents in the *Apartheid*-era public housing developments were middle-class, and in the fully subsidized RDP housing developments and in shack settlements it was as low as 11 per cent (Table 6.10).

Conclusion

In this chapter, I have argued that the nature of poverty in the racial ghettos of Johannesburg changed substantially during the post-Fordist period. Prior to the mid-1970s, poverty was caused mainly by low wages since unemployment was low. By contrast, after the mid-1970s, poverty was increasingly also caused by high levels of unemployment, largely among poorly educated workers who did not complete high school. So, in a manner that is strikingly similar to the racial ghettos of US cities, the ghettos of Johannesburg's southern suburbs were transformed into ghettos of exclusion, where poverty was increasing caused by unemployment rather than solely by low wages.

I have argued in an earlier chapter that an important cause of the rise in unemployment was the relatively slow growth of employment in low- and middle-income manual jobs in the face of the growth in the numbers of poorly educated residents. In this chapter, I have argued that unemployed residents were concentrated in the southern suburbs because of the geography of cheap housing. During both the *Apartheid* and post-*Apartheid* periods, the provision of State-subsidized housing for the poor was concentrated in the southern suburbs. In addition, informal shack settlements tended to be established in and around these State-sponsored housing developments.

An important consequence of the concentration of poorly educated residents in the southern suburbs is that it has increased the scale of the labour market spatial mismatch. The growth of the edge city of Sandton shifted the geography of employment opportunities further north of the Johannesburg CBD and therefore even further away from residents in the excluded ghetto. In addition, many of the State-sponsored housing developments, such as Orange Farm, are located on the southern periphery of Johannesburg, some 40km from the original Johannesburg CBD and roughly 60km from the new Sandton CBD. In this respect therefore, Johannesburg's excluded ghetto shares the geographical features of many other cities, most notably those of the northern USA.

Another theory that was developed from research on US cities is that an important cause of the concentration of unemployment in the racial ghetto was

---

11 A similar estimate was produced by Rule's 1990 survey of households in Diepkloof Extension (Rule, 1993: p.11).

the out-migration of employed middle-class and working-class black residents from the inner-city ghettos to the edge cities (Wilson, 1987: p.49). The reasoning here was that the out-migration of better-educated employed residents resulted in the concentration of less-educated unemployed residents in the excluded ghetto. The findings from Johannesburg demonstrate that the percentage of middle-class residents in the excluded ghetto of the southern suburbs has remained constant. Furthermore, the relative decline in the number of residents employed in middle-income manual jobs was compensated for by the relative rise in the number of middle-income, white-collar workers. In absolute terms, there was almost twice as much growth in middle-income, manual and non-manual jobs as there was in low-income jobs. The absolute number of high-income, middle-class jobs also grew over this period. Finally, an analysis of the city-wide distribution of residents employed in low-income elementary jobs showed that they have not become increasing concentrated in the excluded ghetto of the southern suburbs. These results suggest that the excluded ghetto of Johannesburg has retained a heterogeneous occupational mixture among employed residents and has not seen a decline of its middle class.

So extremely high unemployment in the excluded ghetto has gone together with a change in the occupational structure of the employed workforce. These labour market trends have been accompanied by the growth of partially subsidized 'Gap' housing estates and unsubsidized houses sold at relatively low prices due to their location in and near the erstwhile racial ghettos. In addition, there was widespread improvement and enlargement of the existing *Apartheid*-era State-sponsored 'matchbox' houses. The location of these more expensive and larger housing types within the excluded ghetto probably acts both as a reason why better-paid residents remain in the excluded ghetto and as a cause of their commitment to living there. The result is that Johannesburg's excluded ghetto has some similarities with excluded ghettos elsewhere in the world: There are extremely high numbers of unemployed workers who are concentrated in State-sponsored housing and shack settlements. However, unlike the US ghetto, it is also home to a substantial high-income managerial, professional and technical middle class and a middle-income clerical, services and sales class. Although these higher-earning occupational classes are segregated from low-income elementary workers and unemployed workers by housing types, they are nonetheless neighbours in the erstwhile racial ghetto.

Methodological comment

The reader will have noted that I have used an unconventional approach in the use of evidence for establishing causal relationships. The conventional positivist approach to using statistics would have proposed that the housing and labour markets are causally related and then tested this hypothesis by cross-tabulating the statistical distribution of housing type by the statistical distributions of occupation and employment status. Statistical correlations between these variables would then be interpreted as evidence for a causal relationship. By contrast, my approach was to identify and describe the qualitative nature of both the housing and labour markets to explain how their interaction segregated the population geographically by housing type and occupational class. The evidence of the causal mechanism is therefore provided by the descriptions of the properties of the housing and labour markets. The statistical evidence demonstrates the extent of the operation of this causal mechanism, rather than providing proof of its existence.

Chapter 7

RACIAL RESIDENTIAL DESEGREGATION IN WHITES-ONLY NEIGHBOURHOODS

Introduction

The Debate over racial residential desegregation in South African cities

Scholars are deeply divided in their assessment of the extent of racial desegregation in the formerly whites-only neighbourhoods of South African cities. Some scholars have argued that racial segregation in South African cities has remained largely unchanged, even ten years after the end of *Apartheid* (Beavon, 2004; Christopher, 2005: p.274). More recently, some studies have made the same kind of claim. While arguing that the post-*Apartheid* city has been transformed by the provision of housing and services to poor black residents, Heller argues that 'despite concerted efforts to "de-racialise" the city through spatial planning and investment priorities, South African cities remain as segregated as ever' with only a 'slight decline in racial segregation' (Heller, 2017: p.41). In their study of eThekwini, Schensul and Heller reach similar conclusions. Examining trends over the period from 1985 to 2001, they concluded that 'If one looks only at aggregate measures such as the index of dissimilarity, the answer is that there has been little change beyond perhaps a slow and small erosion of the inherited spatial form' (Schensul and Heller, 2011: p.103). Similarly, Parry and van Eeden (2015: p.31) have argued that, although the level of racial residential segregation in Johannesburg had declined between 1991 and 2011, it was still 'highly segregated' in racial terms.

Journalists reporting on South African cities have made similar assessments. Commenting on post-*Apartheid* South Africa, John Pilger (2006) argued that 'Apartheid Did Not Die' (cited in Seekings, 2011: p.536). Much more recently, Justice Malala argued, 'The rich of Johannesburg still live in the sumptuous northern suburbs, where the food at some restaurants is Michelin-star quality and house prices are eye-watering … Even with the explosive rise of the black middle class in the mid-2000s, the presence of black people in formerly white suburbs across Johannesburg remains low' (Malala, 2019).

By contrast, other scholars have argued that there was substantial racial residential desegregation in many cities.[1] These include studies of inner-

1 For a detailed review of these studies, see Crankshaw (2017).

city neighbourhoods, which were characterized by considerable racial desegregation in Johannesburg (Crankshaw and White, 1992 and 1995; Fick *et al.*, 1988; Gnad *et al.*, 2002; Jürgens *et al.*, 2002 and 2003a; Morris, 1994a and 1999; Rule, 1988 and 1989), eThekwini (Maharaj and Mpungose, 1994; Morris and Hindson, 1997), East London (Ownhouse and Nel, 1993), Tshwane (Donaldson *et al.*, 2003) and Bloemfontein (Hoogendoorn and Visser, 2007; Jürgens *et al.*, 2003b).

Other studies argued that there was substantial racial residential desegregation in at least some formerly whites-only suburbs in Johannesburg (Crankshaw, 2008; Jürgens *et al.*, 2003a; Rule, 2002 and 2006), Tshwane (Horn and Ngcobo, 2003), eThekwini (Schensul and Heller, 2011), Cape Town (Crankshaw, 2012; Lemanski, 2006; Myburgh, 1996; Saff, 1998), Msunduzi (Wood, 2000), Margate (Lemon and Clifford, 2005) and Polokwane (Donaldson and Kotze, 2006; Donaldson and van der Merwe, 1999a and 1999b).

Much of this disagreement about the extent of racial residential desegregation lies in the different methods that were used to measure desegregation. Specifically, most of the evidence for the persistence of racial segregation is derived from studies that use the dissimilarity index to measure segregation. Conversely, scholars who argue that substantial racial desegregation has taken place have based their claims on the use of statistics that describe the racial composition of neighbourhoods. This chapter will therefore explore this methodological problem and provide evidence to resolve it.

Whites-only neighbourhoods and edge-city development

One of the central theories of the post-Fordist geography of deindustrializing cities concerns the development of edge cities and their implications for racial and class segregation. Edge cities are understood to be a new form of urban settlement that is based on the growth of high-income, middle-class jobs in service sector activities. In the case of US cities, edge cities are usually described as predominantly white suburban neighbourhoods. As such, it is argued that the development of edge cities has probably increased racial residential segregation. This was certainly Beavon's view of Johannesburg's northern suburbs. He argued that this new post-Fordist geography of Johannesburg took the form of a 'neo-apartheid city' (Beavon, 2004: p.278). By 'neo-apartheid', Beavon meant that although the racial geography of Johannesburg was no longer governed by the Group Areas Act, by 2001 the middle-class enclave of the northern suburbs edge city had an 'almost exclusively white residential population' (Beavon, 2004: p.279).

In this chapter, I will therefore examine the changing racial composition of the residents of the formerly whites-only neighbourhoods of Johannesburg, but with an approach that is sensitive to post-Fordist theories. Specifically, I will relate the changes in the racial desegregation of formerly whites-only neighbourhoods to the geography of the different housing markets and class character of the residents.

Method

What is the appropriate method for measuring the extent of racial desegregation in the formerly whites-only neighbourhoods of Johannesburg? To answer this question, we need first to clarify precisely what social feature is being measured. Then we need to establish the appropriate statistical method to measure this social feature. On the face of it, this might seem unnecessary, so I will demonstrate its relevance by first describing my approach and then by reviewing and comparing its results to those of other studies of racial residential desegregation.

My aim in studying racial desegregation of the formerly whites-only neighbourhoods is to measure the extent to which upward occupational mobility among black residents has enabled them to buy or rent houses that were occupied by white residents in formerly whites-only neighbourhoods. This is therefore a specific process that requires a specific method of measurement. For example, it would not be appropriate for me to include in such a measurement those black residents who were live-in domestic workers in formerly whites-only neighbourhoods. Fortunately, the Population Censuses collected statistics on a variety of features that allow us to fine-tune our measurement. The first feature that is recorded by the censuses concerns the nature of each neighbourhood. The variable of 'Enumerator Area Type' allows researchers to distinguish between places that are peri-urban farms, or characterized by formal houses, shack settlements, hostels or industrial and commercial buildings. Furthermore, these census data are also linked to spatial boundary data that allows researchers both to map the boundaries of each neighbourhood and to link these maps to satellite images and street-level photographs using the Google Earth software application.

Using this information, I was therefore able to identify and list those neighbourhoods that were formerly whites-only residential neighbourhoods. One task was to distinguish the formerly whites-only residential neighbourhoods from African-, coloureds-, and Indians-only neighbourhoods. This task was facilitated by the unique domestic architecture of public and private housing in Johannesburg and by the rich literature on *Apartheid* housing policy and practice. Other tasks entailed identifying peri-urban farmland falling within the boundaries of Johannesburg and excluding it from the analysis. The reason for this is that these areas house large numbers of African farmworkers that would exaggerate the levels of racial residential desegregation. Peri-urban farmland was readily identified using aerial images because of their large individual stands with agricultural fields, their peripheral geography and information from the population censuses. Informal shack settlements, employer's hostels and industrial and commercial areas were also excluded using aerial images to identify the different types of buildings, which were then cross-checked with information from the population censuses.

Another feature that is enumerated in the census data concerns the type of housing occupied by residents. This variable of 'Type of Main Dwelling' allows researchers to distinguish between residents living in domestic servants' quarters, backyard rooms, backyard shacks, shacks in informal settlements, formal brick houses and apartments. These descriptions of the dwelling types occupied by residents therefore allowed me to exclude from the measurement of racial desegregation those types of housing that are not appropriate to the research question. I did this by including in the measurement of racial desegregation only those residents who lived in the 'Main Dwelling' that was either a formal brick house or an apartment.[2] All other kinds of housing, most notably 'caravans', 'rooms', 'flatlets', 'domestic servant quarters' and 'granny flats' that are found in addition to the main house on the property, were excluded from the measurement of racial desegregation. One aim of this method was to exclude black domestic workers from being included in the measurement of racial desegregation, since many properties were built with backyard rooms for domestic servants (Ginsberg, 2000). Furthermore, it had the added benefit of excluding tenants who lived in converted domestic quarters (Falkof, 2016). Another aim was to provide a refined measure of the extent to which racial desegregation had taken place only in accommodation that blacks were excluded from by law. The result was a measurement of racial residential desegregation that includes only the residents of the main formal house on each residential property and the residents of apartments in apartment buildings.

During the process of data checking and analysis, I noticed that a substantial number of domestic workers were recorded in the censuses as living in the main house on the property instead of in the domestic servants' rooms. I have assumed that this was due to census enumerators who erroneously recorded domestic workers as belonging to their employer's household. I therefore excluded all black residents in formerly whites-only neighbourhoods who were employed as domestic workers. This required me to include only employed residents in the measurement of racial residential desegregation.

Statistical trends in the racial desegregation of the formerly whites-only neighbourhoods

The results of this analysis showed that the percentage of white residents living in all formerly whites-only neighbourhoods declined from 61 per cent in 1996 to 44 per cent in 2011. Correspondingly, the percentage of African residents increased from 30 per cent in 1996 to 39 per cent in 2011. The percentage of coloured residents increased from 4 to 6 per cent and Indian residents from 4 to 10 per cent (Figure 7.1 and Table 7.1). This overall trend of racial desegregation is substantial, and the rate of desegregation accelerated in the decade from 2001 to 2011. By projecting the absolute numbers of employed residents based on the growth rates for the period from 2001 to 2011, I estimate that the percentage of white residents would have been the same as that of African residents by 2014.

2 In specific terms, this included the following types of main dwelling: (a) 'House or brick/ concrete block structure on a separate stand or yard or on a farm', (b) 'Flat or apartment in a block of flats', (c) 'Cluster house in complex', (d) 'Townhouse (semi-detached house in a complex)' and (e) 'Semi-detached house'.

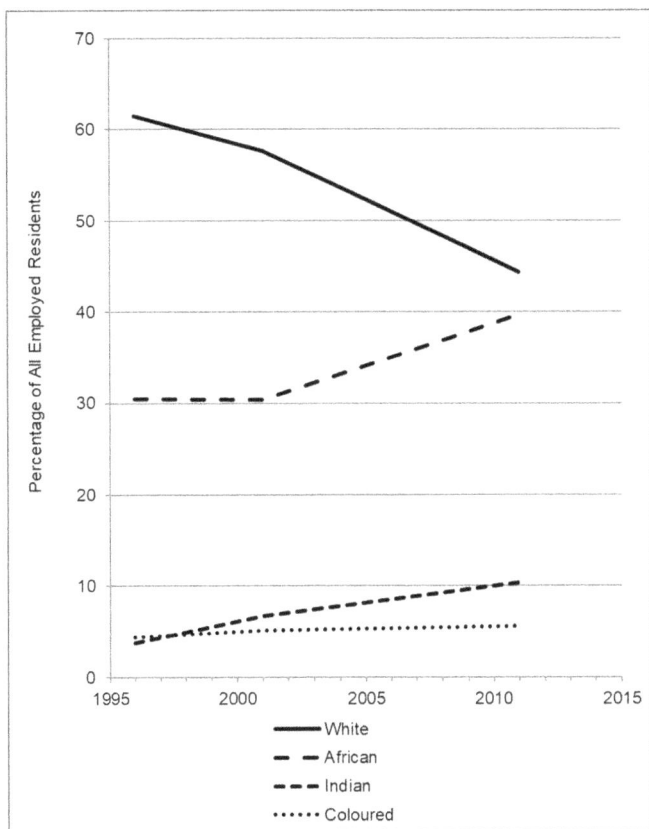

Figure 7.1 The Changing Percentage Racial Composition of the Formerly Whites-Only
Residential Neighbourhoods of Johannesburg, 1996 to 2011

Sources: Author's Analysis of Population Census results, 1996, 2001 and 2011 (SuperCross Interactive Tables).
Measured by the number of employed residents living in the main house or apartment and excluding black
domestic workers living on the property

Table 7.1 The Racial Composition of the Formerly Whites-Only Residential
Neighbourhoods of Johannesburg, 1996 – 2011

	Frequency Distribution			Percentage Distribution		
	1996	2001	2011	1996	2001	2011
African	96,515	124,088	249,016	30	30	40
Coloured	13,883	21,078	35,111	4	5	6
Indian	11,808	27,571	65,381	4	7	10
White	194,814	235,552	276,114	61	58	44
All Races	317,020	408,289	627,622	100	100	100

Sources: Author's Analysis of Population Census results, 1996, 2001 and 2011 (SuperCross Interactive Tables).
Measured by the number of employed residents living in the main house or apartment and excluding black
domestic workers living on the property.

Furthermore, this overall decline in the level of racial segregation took place while the number of employed residents of all races in these neighbourhoods increased in absolute terms (Figure 7.2). These results therefore demonstrate that this extensive racial desegregation was not caused by high levels of white flight from Johannesburg. To the contrary, the trend towards racial desegregation took place in the context of population growth of all races and the expansion of housing stock in the formerly whites-only neighbourhoods and their adjacent, similarly priced post-*Apartheid* housing developments.

These results, even for the 2001 Population Census, stand in contrast to the conclusions of studies that relied on the dissimilarity index to measure the extent

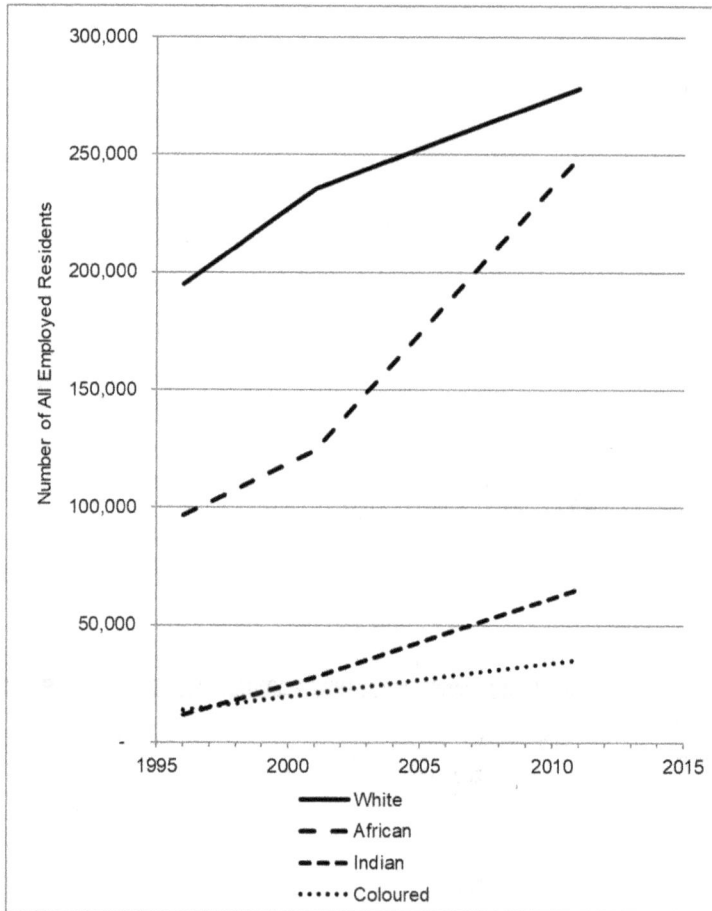

Figure 7.2 The Absolute Racial Composition of the Formerly Whites-Only Residential Neighbourhoods of Johannesburg, 1996 – 2011

Sources: Author's Analysis of Population Census results, 1996, 2001 and 2011 (SuperCross Interactive Tables).
Measured by the number of employed residents living in the main house or apartment and excluding black domestic workers living on the property

of racial residential desegregation in Johannesburg. Using the dissimilarity index, many scholars have presented evidence that racial residential segregation in South Africa's towns and cities has remained extremely high in the post-*Apartheid* period with very little sign of change. For example, Christopher (2001, p.453) calculated that the white index of segregation for Johannesburg declined only slightly from 96 to 86 over the period from 1985 to 2001. His studies of all urban areas produced similar indices of segregation, leading him to conclude that 'Desegregation is taking place in South African cities, but it is progressing at a very slow pace' (Christopher, 2005: p.274). A recent study by Parry and van Eeden (2015: p.41) showed that the African-white dissimilarity index for Johannesburg had decline only slightly from 89 in 1991 to 87 in 2011.

On the face of it, these results produced by the dissimilarity index seem to underestimate the extent of racial residential desegregation as reported by measures of the racial composition of formerly whites-only neighbourhoods. Specifically, the evidence up to 2001 based on the racial composition of the formerly whites-only neighbourhoods showed that there was substantial residential desegregation of the inner city (Crankshaw and White, 1995; Fick *et al.*, 1988; Jürgens *et al.*, 2002, 2003a; Morris, 1999) and the southern suburbs (Crankshaw, 2008). And yet the segregation index had decreased only slightly by 2001. The evidence from 2011 census shows the same apparent contradiction. Parry and van Eeden's (2015: p.41) calculation of a dissimilarity index showed a decline of only 2 percentage points over the period from 1991 to 2011, whereas this study shows that white residents comprised only 44 per cent of the population of formerly whites-only neighbourhoods (Table 7.1).

The reason for these contradictory findings can be understood once we know precisely what the dissimilarity index is designed to measure. The index for the segregation of a racial group within a city's population is calculated by measuring the proportions of a race in each neighbourhood and comparing their sum with the overall proportion of that race within the total population. The index is therefore a measure of the percentage of residents who would have to change neighbourhoods in order to achieve perfect desegregation.

A close examination of exactly how the dissimilarity index is calculated provides some understanding of why it has produced such low estimates of racial desegregation in Johannesburg. This entails an examination of the mathematical properties of its formula. Duncan and Duncan (1955: p.217) were the first to observe that the statistic calculated by the dissimilarity index is partly due to the data and partly due to the mathematical properties of the formula itself. They argued that the formula works in such a way that the proportion of each race in the total population affects the size of the dissimilarity index. Cortese *et al.* (1976: p.632) demonstrated the validity of this argument by applying the formula to a number of data sets, each with a randomly distributed black and white population, but which differed in respect of the proportion that the black race contributed to the whole population.[3] Their results showed that the size of the dissimilarity index

3 See also Gorard (2009: p.644) for the same argument.

is affected by the relative size of the black population in a city. The pattern is such that if the proportion of black residents increases from a low percentage to 50 per cent, the calculated value of the dissimilarity index decreases. Once the percentage of black residents exceeds 50 per cent, the value of the dissimilarity index increases. To apply their reasoning to Johannesburg, if the percentage of black residents in the city is above 50 per cent and increases in each successive census, then the dissimilarity index will increase, even if there is no change in the level of segregation. To put this in simple terms, estimates of racial residential segregation produced by the dissimilarity index can be artefacts of the mathematical properties of the formula and may not reflect real rates of racial segregation.

This argument is readily understood if we examine the properties of the formula for the dissimilarity index. The index for the segregation of a racial group within a city's population is calculated by measuring the proportions of a race group in each neighbourhood and comparing their sum with the overall proportion of that race group in the total population. The comparison is achieved by calculating a ratio with the denominator being 1 minus the overall proportion of the race group in the whole population (see the denominator in the formula below). The greater the proportion that the race group 'X' contributes to the total population, the larger the denominator '1-X/Z' will be. It therefore follows that the larger the proportion of the race group, the larger will be the index of dissimilarity, since it is being divided by an increasingly smaller denominator. So, all things being equal, in this case the actual proportions of the race group in each neighbourhood, a larger proportion of a majority race will produce a higher index of dissimilarity.

$$\text{Dissimilarity Index} = \frac{1}{2} * \frac{\sum |x_i - z_i|}{1 - X/Z}$$

Where:

x_i represents the percentage of the X sub-group or race in ith Subplace
z_i represents the percentage of the total population in ith Subplace
X represents the absolute size of the X sub-group in the whole city
Z represents the absolute size of the total population of the city
(Christopher, 2001: p.464)

This means that in a context where the racial composition of neighbourhoods is being measured over time, and the relative total size of the majority race increases over time, the formula will produce an increase in the dissimilarity index even when there is no actual increase in racial segregation. We can therefore conclude that the dissimilarity index should never be used to compare segregation levels using data for cities with different total racial proportions. Nor should the index be used to compare segregation levels in the same city if the total racial proportions of the population change over time.

Scholars are interested in measuring the extent of racial residential desegregation because it is a measure of racial inequality. The main feature of

Apartheid's Group Areas Act was not only that it excluded blacks from living in whites-only neighbourhoods. It was also that these whites-only neighbourhoods received better public services, better-funded schools and were better-located with respect to places of work, shopping and leisure (Beavon, 2004). So the exclusion of black residents from these neighbourhoods created an unequal racial geography. In this context, scholars who studied racial residential desegregation were not really interested in the extent to which white residents moved to live in formerly Africans-only neighbourhoods. Nor are they particularly interested in the movement of African residents into formerly coloureds-only and Indians-only neighbourhoods. To the contrary, the focus of attention was always on the exclusion of blacks from the formerly whites-only neighbourhoods precisely because these neighbourhoods have better facilities and locations. To quote Schensul and Heller (2011, p.81), 'We are thus interested not only in racial mixing, but also in the extent to which such mixing is associated with proximity to services, public facilities and economic opportunities, particularly for the city's poor African residents.'

If the aim of measuring residential desegregation is therefore to measure the extent to which black residents enjoy access to the better-serviced, formerly whites-only neighbourhoods of the city, then the dissimilarity index is not the best method for the task. This is because the dissimilarity index measures, implicitly, the results of two different social processes rather than only one social process. These two processes are:

(i)   The movement of residents from racially homogenous neighbourhoods into racially mixed neighbourhoods. This means that the index measures the extent to which formerly blacks-only neighbourhoods have become desegregated, as well the extent to which formerly whites-only neighbourhoods have become desegregated.
(ii) The increasing relative size of the African population in racially homogeneous formerly Africans-only neighbourhoods.

Consider the specific nature of racial residential segregation in Johannesburg. The vast majority of the city's population is composed of African residents, most of whom live in formerly Africans-only neighbourhoods that have not become racially desegregated. The African population of these formerly Africans-only neighbourhoods has grown much more than the populations of minority coloured, Indian and white races. The African population more than doubled in size, growing from roughly 1.5 million in 1996 to 3.4 million by 2011, which amounts to a percentage increase of 116 per cent. By contrast, the white population increased from 477,382 in 1996 to 543,228 in 2011, which is an absolute increase of only 65,846 and a percentage increase of only 14 per cent (Figure 7.3 and Table 7.2).

Logically therefore, even if many African residents moved to live in formerly whites-only neighbourhoods, in order for their number to lower the dissimilarity index, it would have to exceed the number of new African residents who migrated to or were born in neighbourhoods with few or no white residents. So the larger

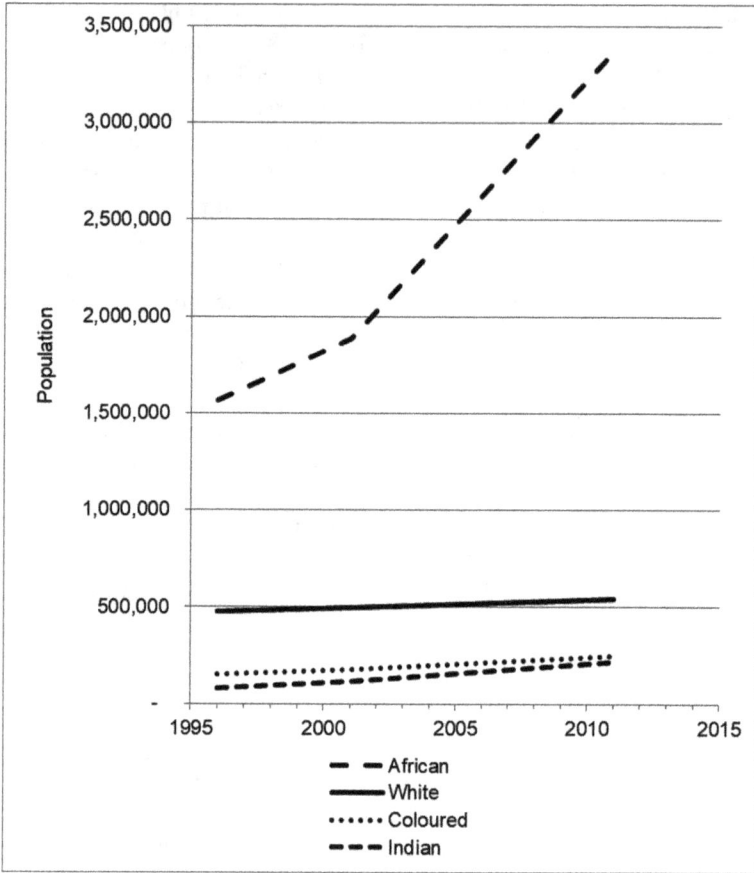

Figure 7.3 The Population of the City of Johannesburg by Race, 1996–2011
Sources: Author's Analysis of Population Census results, 1996, 2001 and 2011 (SuperCross Interactive Tables).

Table 7.2 The Population of the City of Johannesburg by Race, 1996–2011

	1996	2001	2011	Absolute Distribution of Increase from 1996–2011	Percentage Distribution of Increase from 1996–2011
African	1,565,979	1,885,142	3,382,008	1,816,029	85
Coloured	149,905	174,075	246,127	96,222	5
Indian	79,389	114,201	215,847	136,458	6
White	477,382	499,306	543,228	65,846	3
Unspecified	22,376	-	38,495	16,119	1
All Races	2,295,031	2,672,724	4,425,706	2,130,674	100

Sources: Author's Analysis of Population Census results, 1996, 2001 and 2011 (SuperCross Interactive Tables).

growth of the African population and its concentration in racially homogenous African neighbourhoods is one reason why the dissimilarity index remains high. As such, it is not a measure solely of the racial desegregation of the formerly whites-only neighbourhoods.

My response to these limiting features of the dissimilarity index was to focus instead on the measurement of the outcome of a single process: namely the movement of black residents into accommodation in residential neighbourhoods that were once reserved for white residents only. The appropriate statistics for this measurement are the absolute and relative trends in the number of black residents living in the main houses and the apartments of the formerly whites-only neighbourhoods.

Another way of summarizing these changing geographical patterns of racial desegregation in statistical terms is to measure the changes in the numbers of neighbourhoods with different levels of racial segregation. This was done by distributing the Population Census Subplaces, which I have called 'neighbourhoods', according to their level of segregation for each Census. The results of this method show that the percentage of all neighbourhoods in which black residents made up at least 26 per cent of the population increased steadily from 29 per cent of all neighbourhoods in 1996 to 76 per cent of all neighbourhoods by 2011. Correspondingly, the percentage of neighbourhoods in which black residents comprised less than 26 per cent of all residents declined from 71 per cent in 1996 to 19 per cent in 2011 (Figure 7.4 and Table 7.3). So these statistics demonstrate that by 2011 only a small minority of formerly whites-only neighbourhoods were still at least 76 per cent white. This result shows that the racial desegregation of formerly whites-only neighbourhoods was widespread rather than being concentrated in relatively few neighbourhoods.

The geography of racial desegregation in the formerly whites-only neighbourhoods

The racial residential desegregation of formerly whites-only neighbourhoods took a particular geographical form. The first neighbourhoods to desegregate were those in the inner city of Johannesburg (Figure 7.5 and Figure 7.6). These inner-city neighbourhoods can be divided into those with high-rise apartment buildings, most of which were built during the 1950s and 1960s, and those with a mixture of detached and semi-detached housing with some low-rise apartment buildings that were built before the Second World War. The high-rise neighbourhoods are the residential areas in the Central Business District (CBD), Braamfontein, Hillbrow, Joubert Park and Berea (Figure 4.3). As early as 1985, black residents already comprised a substantial minority of the residents living in these high-rise apartment neighbourhoods and this trend continued into the 1990s (Crankshaw and White, 1995; De Coning *et al.*, 1986; Morris, 1994; Morris, 1999). The inner-city neighbourhoods with houses and low-rise apartment buildings were the next

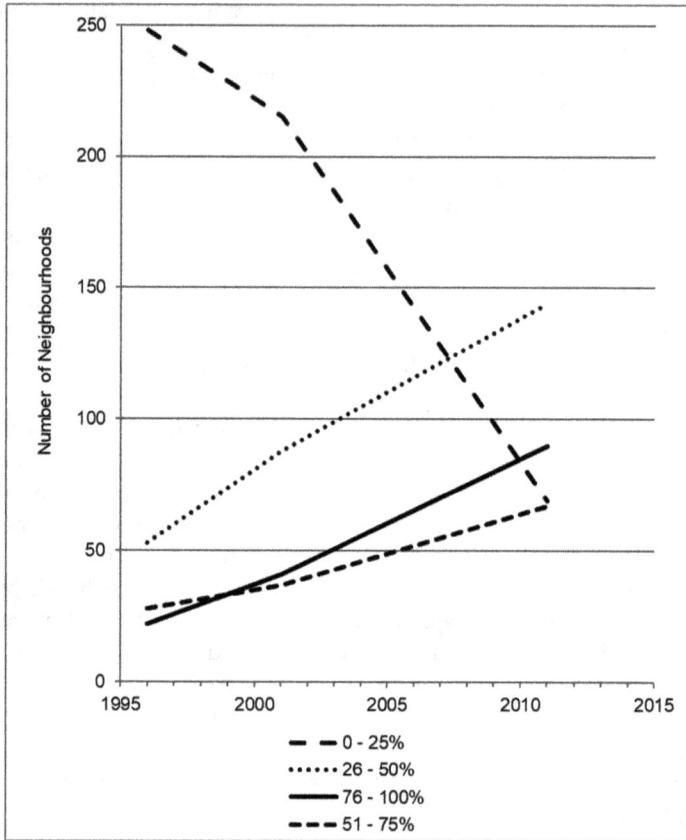

Figure 7.4 The Distribution of Johannesburg's Formerly Whites-Only Neighbourhoods by Their Percentage of Black Residents, 1996–2011
Sources: The author's analysis of Population Census results for 1996, 2001 and 2011 (SuperCross Interactive Tables).

Table 7.3 The Distribution of Johannesburg's Formerly Whites-Only Neighbourhoods by Their Percentage of Black Residents, 1996–2011

Percentage Black	Frequency Distribution			Percentage Distribution		
	1996	2001	2011	1996	2001	2011
0–25%	248	215	69	71	56	19
26–50%	53	88	144	15	23	39
51–75%	28	37	67	8	10	18
76–100%	22	41	90	6	11	24
Total	351	381	370	100	100	100

Sources: The author's analysis of Population Census results for 1996, 2001 and 2011 (SuperCross Interactive Tables).
Measured by the number of employed residents living in the main house or apartment and excluding black domestic workers.

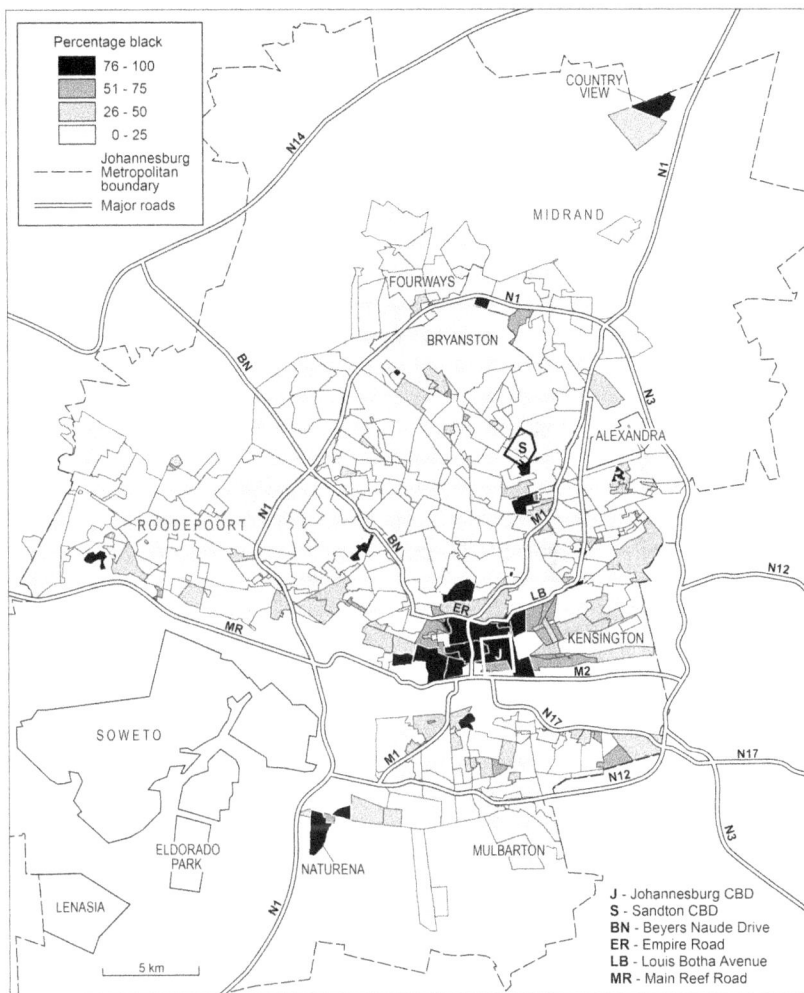

Figure 7.5 The Geography of Black Residents in the Formerly Whites-Only
              Neighbourhoods of Johannesburg, 1996

Sources: The author's analysis of the 1996 Population Census results (SuperCross Interactive Tables). Measured by the
       number of employed residents living in the main house or apartment and excluding black domestic workers
       living on the property.
Cartography: Philip J. Stickler

to become substantially desegregated (Crankshaw and White, 1992; Fick *et al.*,
1988; Gnad *et al.*, 2002; Jürgens *et al.*, 2002 and 2003a; Rule, 1988; Rule, 1989).
These were the neighbourhoods of Yeoville, Bellevue, Bellevue East, Highlands,
Bertrams, Judith's Paarl, Lorentzville, Troyeville, Jeppestown, Fairview, Mayfair
and Vrededorp (Figure 4.3).

By the time of the 2001 Population Census, there were three more areas of
substantial desegregation in which at least 26 per cent of residents were black.

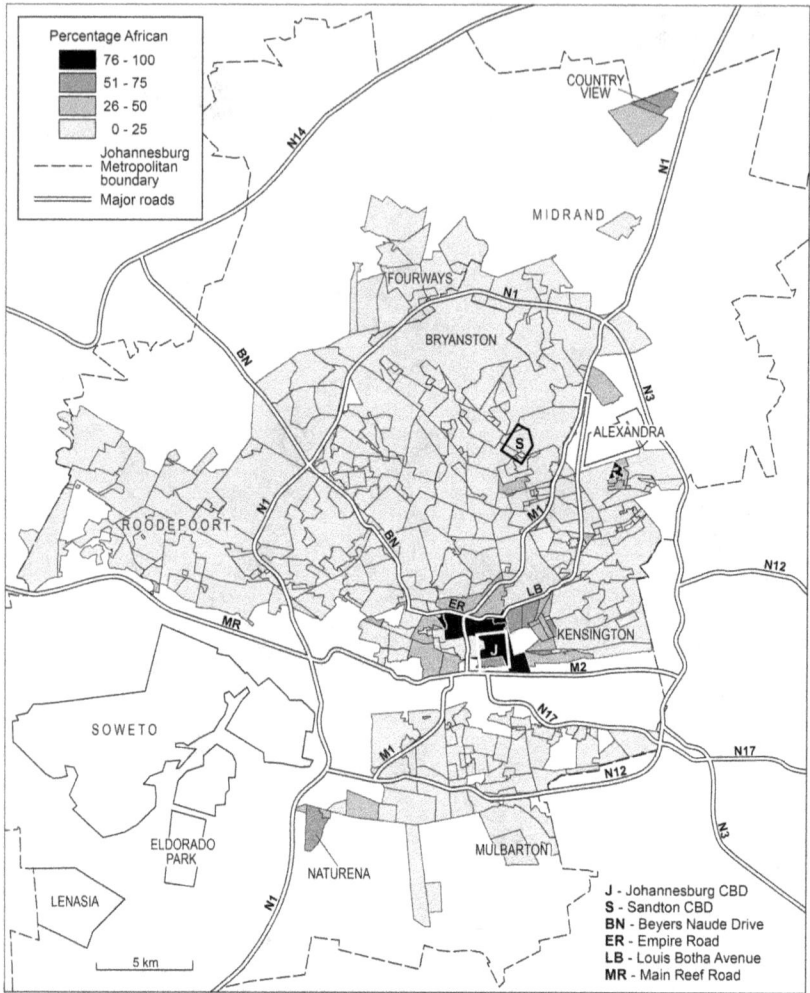

Figure 7.6 The Geography of African Residents in the Formerly Whites-Only
Neighbourhoods of Johannesburg, 1996

Sources: The author's analysis of the 1996 Population Census results (SuperCross Interactive Tables). Measured by the
number of employed residents living in the main house or apartment and excluding black domestic workers
living on the property.
Cartography: Philip J. Stickler

The first of these was the southern suburbs, the majority of which had undergone
substantial desegregation. The second area was the strip of pre-War suburbs along
the north flank of Main Reef Road and the 'M2' Highway, to the East and West of
the inner city. The third area was the ribbon of northern suburbs in Midrand on
either side of the 'N1' Highway, with a conglomeration surrounding the formerly
Africans-only suburb of Alexandra (Figure 7.7 and Figure 7.8).

By 2011, the geographical extent of substantial racial desegregation had expanded into most of the northern suburbs, with only small pockets of neighbourhoods in which the percentage of black residents was 25 per cent or less (Figure 7.9). The percentage of black residents in other areas increased substantially between 2001 and 2011: In the southern suburbs and the western suburbs along Main Reef Road there was an increase in the number of neighbourhoods in which at least

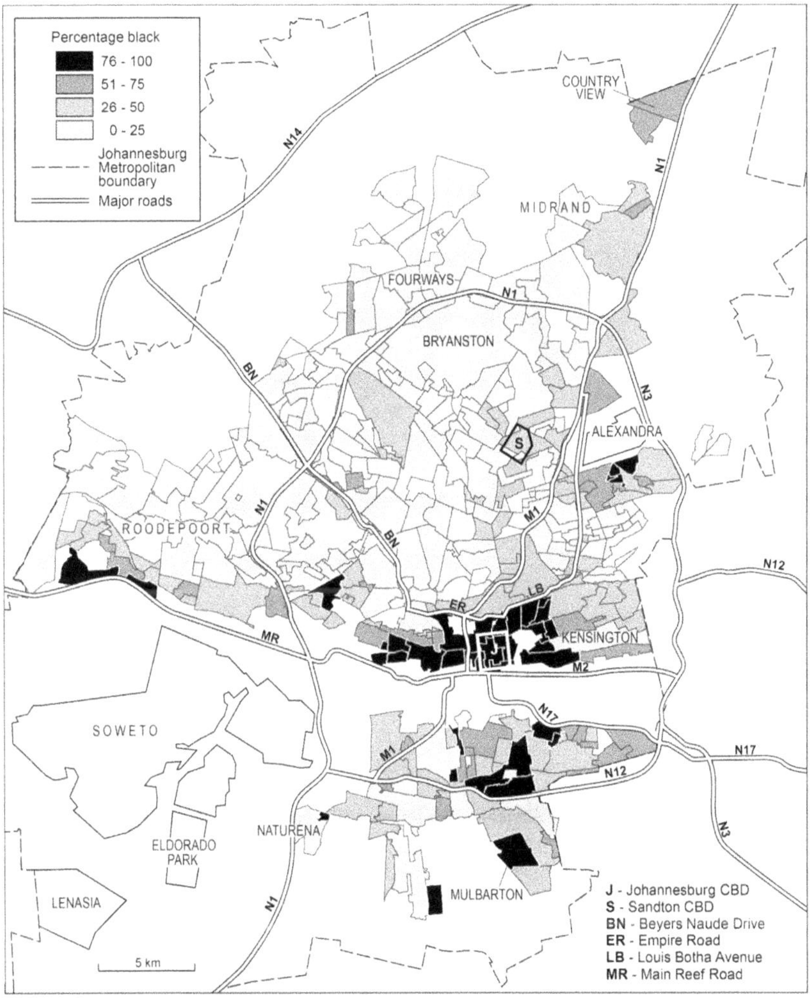

Figure 7.7 The Geography of Black Residents in the Formerly Whites-Only Neighbourhoods of Johannesburg, 2001

Sources: The author's analysis of the 2001 Population Census results (SuperCross Interactive Tables). Measured by the number of employed residents living in the main house or apartment and excluding black domestic workers living on the property.

Cartography: Philip J. Stickler

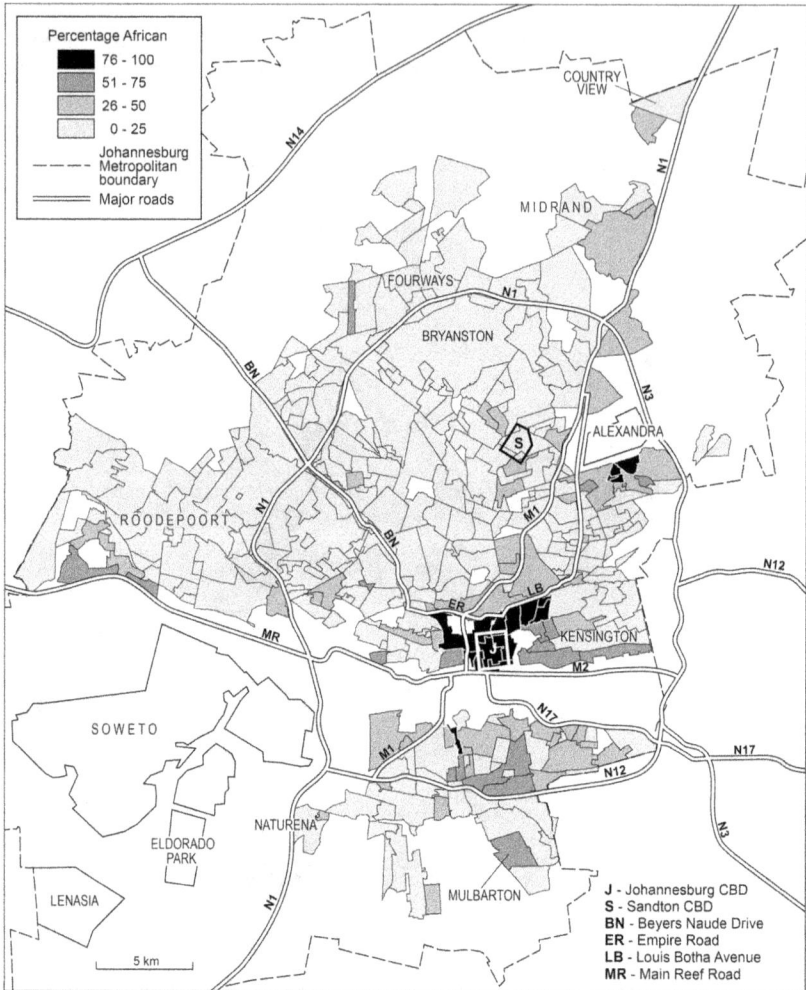

Figure 7.8 The Geography of African Residents in the Formerly Whites-Only
Neighbourhoods of Johannesburg, 2001

Sources: The author's analysis of the 2001 Population Census results (SuperCross Interactive Tables). Measured by the
number of employed residents living in the main house or apartment and excluding black domestic workers
living on the property.

Cartography: Philip J. Stickler

75 per cent of employed residents were black. The same can be said for the strip
of northern suburbs along the 'M1' North Highway and the Midrand suburbs
along the 'N1' Highway (Figure 7.9). The distribution of northern suburbs with a
substantial percentage of African residents also followed this geographical pattern,
except that the rate of desegregation was obviously lower (Figure 7.10).

These results therefore show that the racial desegregation of formerly whites-
only neighbourhoods began before the abolition of the Group Areas Act in 1991,

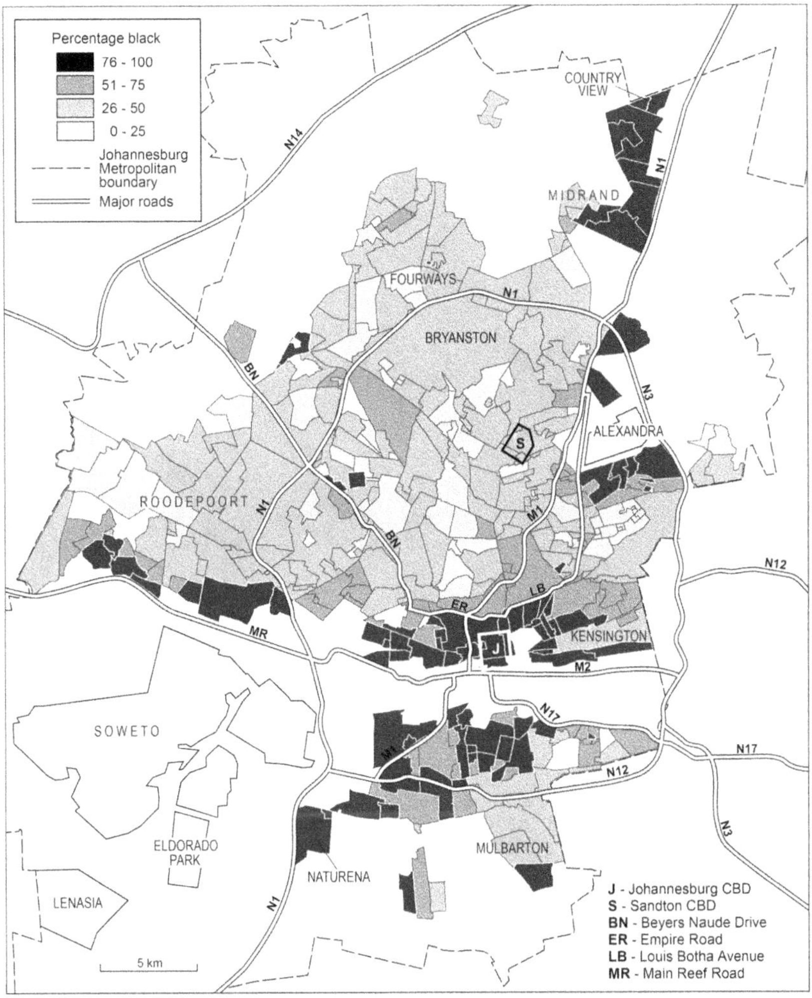

Figure 7.9 The Geography of Black Residents in the Formerly Whites-Only
           Neighbourhoods of Johannesburg, 2011
Sources: The author's analysis of the 2011 Population Census results (SuperCross Interactive Tables). Measured by the
        number of employed residents living in the main house or apartment and excluding black domestic workers
        living on the property.
Cartography: Philip J. Stickler

starting in the inner-city neighbourhoods during the 1980s, and then spreading
out first to the southern suburbs and Main Reef Road suburbs and finally into the
more expensive northern suburbs.

These findings provide new evidence concerning the geographical nature of
the extent of racial desegregation over a fifteen-year period. These changes can be

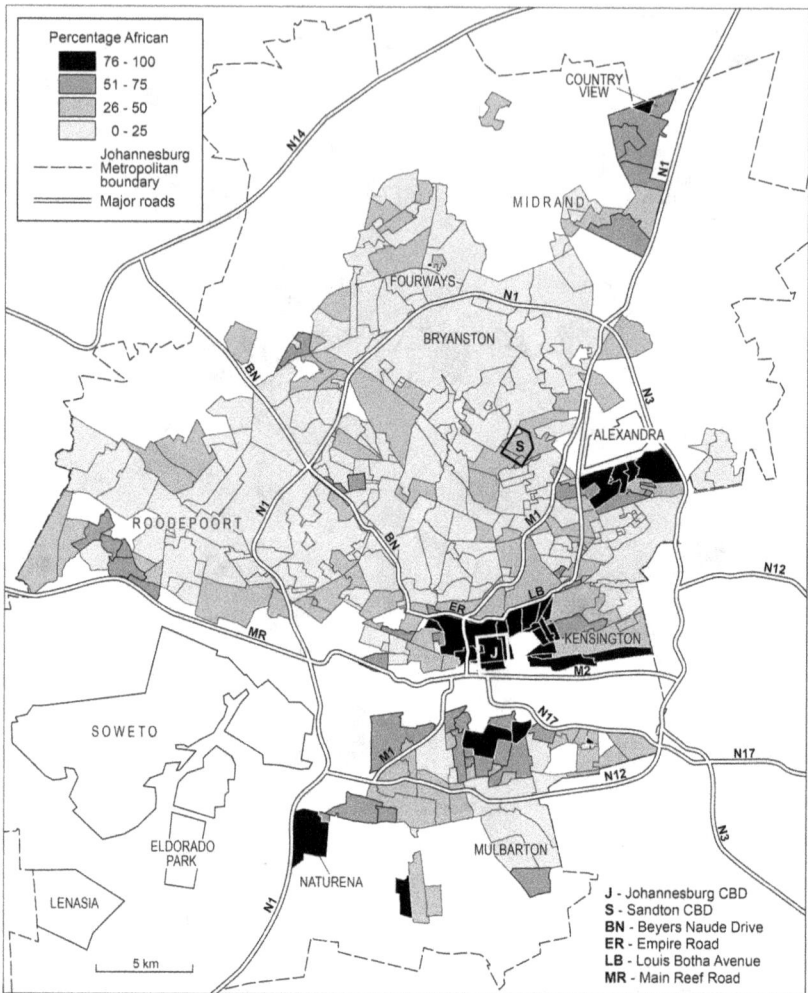

Figure 7.10 The Geography of African Residents in the Formerly Whites-Only
Neighbourhoods of Johannesburg, 2011
Sources: The author's analysis of the 2011 Population Census results (SuperCross Interactive Tables). Measured by the
    number of employed residents living in the main house or apartment and excluding black domestic workers
    living on the property.
Cartography: Philip J. Stickler

measured precisely by examining the changing racial composition of the inner-city, the southern suburbs and the northern suburbs.

The inner-city neighbourhoods

The residential desegregation of the inner-city neighbourhoods began well before the abolition of the Group Areas Act in 1991. In as early as 1977, there were newspaper reports of coloured and Indian residents moving into inner-city neighbourhoods (Morris, 1994: p.821; Pickard-Cambridge, 1988: p.2). By 1985, the percentage of black residents in the inner-city neighbourhoods was 30 per cent. This trend continued and by 2011, the percentage of black households had risen to 98 per cent (Figure 7.11 and Table 7.4).

The southern suburbs

In the southern suburbs, the percentage of white residents declined from 70 per cent in 1996 to 28 per cent in 2011 (Figure 7.12 and Table 7.5). Correspondingly, the percentage of black residents doubled over this period. The percentage of

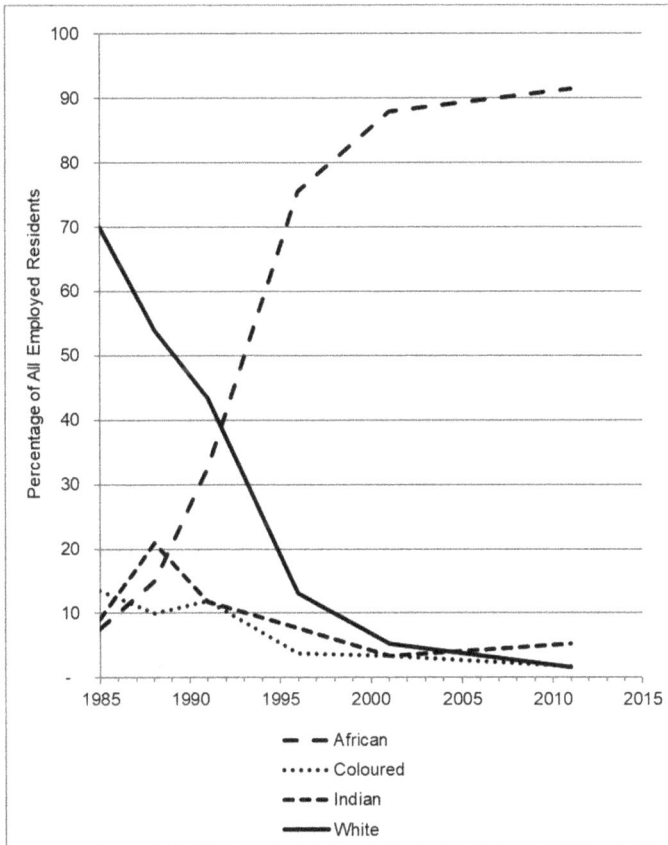

Figure 7.11 The Changing Percentage Racial Composition of the Formerly Whites-Only Inner-City Neighbourhoods of Johannesburg, 1985–2011

Sources: Crankshaw and White (1995: p.628) and the author's analysis of Population Census results for 1996, 2001 and 2011 (SuperCross Interactive Tables).

Table 7.4 Percentage Racial Composition of the Inner-City Neighbourhoods of
Johannesburg, 1985–2011

	1985	1988	1991	1996	2001	2011
African	8	15	33	75	88	91
Coloured	14	10	12	4	3	2
Indian	9	21	12	8	3	5
White	70	54	43	13	5	2
All Races	100	100	100	100	100	100
All Blacks	30	46	56	87	95	98

Sources: Crankshaw and White (1995: p.628) and the author's analysis of Population Census results for 1996, 2001 and
2011 (SuperCross Interactive Tables).[4]

African residents increased from 20 per cent in 1996 to 49 per cent in 2001. The
percentage of coloureds and Indians increased from 10 per cent in 1996 to 23 per
cent in 2011. In absolute terms, the numbers of white residents increased from
1996 to 2001 and then declined again to just below its 1996 level.

The northern suburbs

In the northern suburbs, the pace and extent of racial desegregation has been
slower and less than elsewhere (Rule, 2002 and 2006). Nonetheless, the percentage
of black residents had already reached 27 per cent by 1996. Over the next fifteen
years, this percentage increased steadily, reaching 44 per cent in 2011 (Figure 7.13
and Table 7.6). Correspondingly, the percentage of white residents fell to 56 per
cent. So, even in the expensive northern suburbs, by 2011 white residents were
very close to a minority race in these formerly whites-only suburbs.

Causes of racial residential desegregation

The main causes of the racial desegregation of the formerly whites-only
neighbourhoods probably lie in the changing racial demography of the city's
population and the general shortage of black housing, even for middle-class black
residents. As far as the changing racial demography is concerned, almost all the

---

4 The estimates for 1985 to 1991 are based on sample surveys of all household heads living
in the high-rise apartment neighbourhoods only. The estimates for 1996 to 2011 are
based on the population census results for all the inner-city neighbourhoods and are
measured by the number of employed residents living in the main house or apartment
and excluding black domestic workers living on the property.

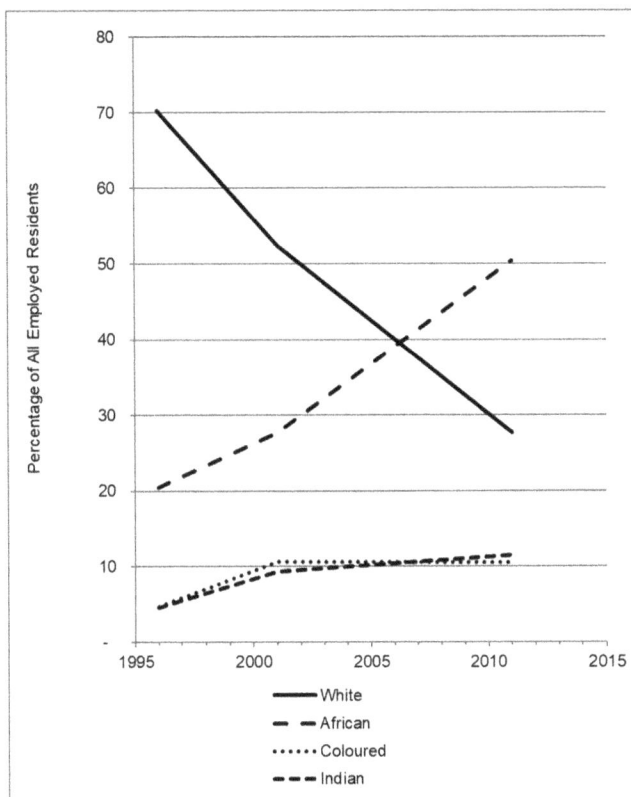

Figure 7.12 The Changing Percentage Racial Composition of the Formerly Whites-Only
Southern Suburbs of Johannesburg, 1996–2011
Sources: The author's analysis of Population Census results for 1996, 2001 and 2011 (SuperCross Interactive Tables).
Measured by the number of employed residents living in the main house or apartment and excluding black
domestic workers living on the property.

Table 7.5 The Racial Composition of the Southern Suburbs of Johannesburg, 1996–2011

	Frequency Distribution			Percentage Distribution		
	1996	2001	2011	1996	2001	2011
African	7,334	17,525	41,456	20	28	50
Coloured	1,691	6,719	8,631	5	11	10
Indian	1,638	5,898	9,415	5	9	11
White	25,202	33,157	22,781	70	52	28
All Races	35,865	63,299	82,283	100	100	100
All Blacks	10,663	34,661	59,502	30	50	72

Sources: The author's analysis of Population Census results for 1996, 2001 and 2011 (SuperCross Interactive Tables).
Measured by the number of employed residents living in the main house or apartment and excluding black
domestic workers living on the property.

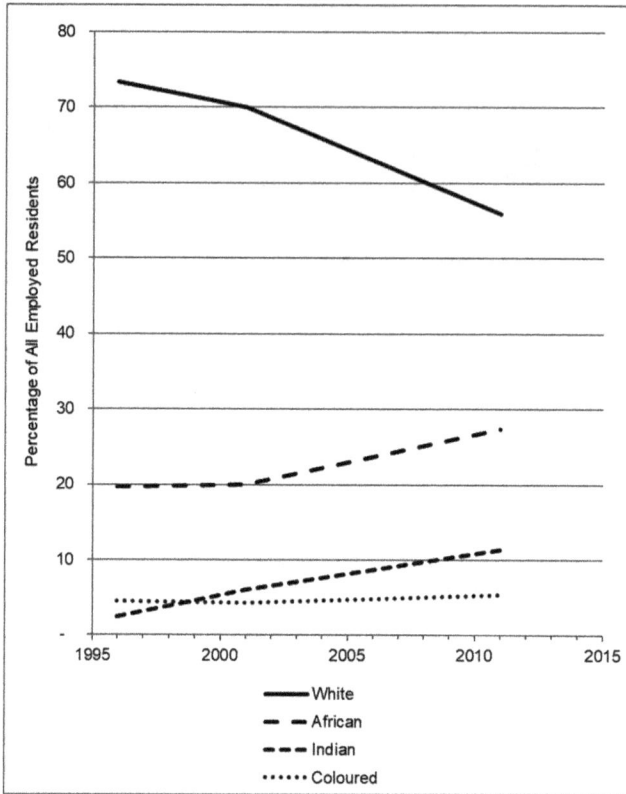

Figure 7.13 The Changing Percentage Racial Composition of the Northern Suburbs of
Johannesburg, 1996–2011

Sources: The author's analysis of Population Census results for 1996, 2001 and 2011 (SuperCross Interactive Tables).
Measured by the number of employed residents living in the main house or apartment and excluding black
domestic workers living on the property.

Table 7.6 The Racial Composition of the Northern Suburbs of Johannesburg, 1996–2011

	Frequency Distribution			Percentage Distribution		
	1996	**2001**	**2011**	**1996**	**2001**	**2011**
African	43,357	60,276	124,436	20	20	27
Coloured	9,901	13,146	24,665	4	4	5
Indian	5,527	17,937	51,329	3	6	11
White	161,633	213,140	253,741	73	70	56
All Races	220,418	304,499	454,171	100	100	100
All Blacks	58,785	91,359	200,430	27	30	44

Sources: The author's analysis of Population Census results for 1996, 2001 and 2011 (SuperCross Interactive Tables).
Measured by the number of employed residents living in the main house or apartment and excluding black
domestic workers living on the property.

increase (97 per cent) in the size of the city's population between 1996 and 2011 was due to the growth of the black population (Table 7.2). As I have shown in an earlier chapter, a sizeable proportion of this growth in the black population was among middle- and high-income residents. Because of the shortage of housing in the blacks-only suburbs (De Vos, 1986: p.4; Morris, 1994: p.828; Morris, 1998: p.65), these better-off black residents had a good reason to look for housing in the formerly whites-only neighbourhoods. Consistent with this shortage of housing in blacks-only neighbourhoods, a household survey undertaken in 1987 found that the main reason that black residents chose to live in the inner city was the shortage of accommodation in black Group Areas (Schlemmer and Stack, 1990: p.100).

Furthermore, there was only limited opposition from white residents and the *Apartheid* Government to racial desegregation. During the late 1970s and early 1980s, opposition by white residents in Hillbrow was organized by the National Front, which was formed by British immigrants (Morris, 1998: pp.66–73; Morris, 1999: p.25; Pickard-Cambridge, 1988: pp.5 and 15). Complaints by white residents to the police led to charges being laid against hundreds of black residents in the late 1970s. Morris argues that the State then withdrew charges against these transgressions of the Group Areas Act, which suggests that the Government itself had intervened to prevent further prosecutions This was followed by the landmark court case of *State versus Govender* in 1982, which stopped the State from evicting black residents from their homes in white Group Areas (Morris, 1998: p.60). The *Apartheid* Government could have redrafted this legislation to side-step the judicial ruling but instead chose not to do so. Scholars have argued that this was because the Government did not wish to threaten its relationship with coloured and Indian political leaders whose support it needed to legitimate the new Tricameral Parliament that gave limited political rights to coloured and Indian residents (Morris, 1998: p.64; Pickard-Cambridge, 1988: pp.8 and 19).

An indication of the weak opposition to racial desegregation by white residents in the inner city was demonstrated by their lack of support for the right-wing Conservative Party, which broke away from the ruling National Party: in the 1987 General Election, only a quarter of white residents in the Hillbrow constituency voted for the Conservative Party (Pickard-Cambridge, 1988: p.25). The *de-facto* desegregation of white inner-city neighbourhoods was legally formalized a decade later. With the end of *Apartheid* now an inevitable outcome, the National Party Government abolished the Group Areas Act in 1991.

Much of the explanation for the geographical pattern of racial desegregation probably lies in the nature of the housing stock and its location with respect to the formerly blacks-only neighbourhoods (Figure 7.14). Although the high-rise apartment districts of the inner city first began to desegregate because landlords could not find white tenants to rent their apartments (Pickard-Cambridge, 1988: p.3), the nature of the housing stock also facilitated rapid desegregation. First, almost all (80 per cent) apartments in the high-rise neighbourhoods of

Figure 7.14 High-Rise Apartment Buildings in Hillbrow
Source: Photograph by Fred Mlangeni of EyeEm and sourced from Getty Images.

the inner city were either bedsits or one-bedroomed apartments, making them the cheapest accommodation in the formerly whites-only neighbourhoods (Crankshaw and White, 1995: p.626). Second, according to a household survey conducted in 1991, almost all (92 per cent) apartments in the high-rise neighbourhoods were let by landlords, which meant that the financial barriers of entry into this housing market were much cheaper than in other formerly whites-only neighbourhoods where homeownership was the norm.[5] This is demonstrated by the finding that 70 per cent of the tenants reported that they rented an apartment because they could not afford to buy either an apartment or a house.[6]

The reason for the rapid racial desegregation of the inner-city neighbourhoods characterized by houses and low-rise apartment buildings was that they were composed of old housing stock, built before the Second World War. Most of the accommodation was composed of apartments in low-rise, walk-up, buildings

---

5 This estimate has a 95 per cent confidence interval of 4 per cent. These high-rise apartment neighbourhoods were Hillbrow, Berea, Joubert Park, the CBD and Braamfontein. Source: Johannesburg Inner City Survey, 1992, Human Sciences Research Council. Survey conducted by the author.

6 This estimate has a 95 per cent confidence interval of 7 per cent. Source as above.

(72 per cent) and detached houses on small properties (22 per cent).[7] The remaining stock was composed of semi-detached and terraced houses. As such, these were relatively cheap houses that were more readily affordable to first-time black homeowners.

After the inner city, the formerly whites-only neighbourhoods next to undergo racial desegregation were the southern suburbs and the neighbourhoods with pre-War housing to the east and west of the inner city. One probable reason for this was that most of the houses in these suburbs were relatively cheaper than their counterparts in the northern suburbs. Historically, the older parts of these suburbs were occupied by middle-income manual workers. The houses were built as detached and semi-detached units on small properties, with some terraced housing and small low-rise apartment buildings (Harrison and Zack, 2014: p.271). Although the housing stock in the older suburbs is solidly built, it is old-fashioned and lacking in modern amenities. Another probable reason is that these southern suburbs are near Soweto, Lenasia and Eldorado Park, making it a more attractive option for black residents who wished to live near to their families and to make use of healthcare and entertainment facilities in Soweto (Butcher, 2021: p.193).

The formerly whites-only northern suburbs were the last to undergo substantial desegregation. One reason for this may have been the high property prices in these suburbs, which probably required a period of saving and residential movement up the housing ladder, even for high-income black residents. As shown in the previous chapter, the formerly whites-only northern suburbs and the unsubsidized post-*Apartheid* housing developments have a largely middle-class population. The high prices and high rents in these suburbs effectively exclude residents who do not earn high incomes. The result is that the occupational class distribution of black residents in these suburbs almost exactly matches that of the white residents. In 2011, 60 per cent of all employed white residents living in the main house were middle class. For Indian residents it was also 60 per cent, for African residents it was 51 per cent and for coloured residents it was 49 per cent (Table 7.7).

The middle-class character of desegregation in the northern suburbs has been replicated in the other metropolitan cities of South Africa. In eThekwini, the main geographical pattern of residential desegregation has been the racial desegregation of middle-class, formerly Indians-only and whites-only, neighbourhoods. Specifically, these were the formerly whites-only neighbourhood of Berea and the formerly Indians-only neighbourhoods south of Chatsworth (Schensul and Heller, 2011: pp.96 and 100). In Cape Town, the formerly whites-only middle-class suburbs that are located to the south-west and northern areas have also undergone partial racial desegregation (Crankshaw, 2012; Myburgh, 1996; Saff, 1998;

---

7 These estimates both have a 95 per cent confidence interval of 7 per cent. These are the neighbourhoods of Bellevue, Bellevue East, Highlands, Rand View, Yeoville, the low-rise part of northern Berea, Bertrams, Lorentzville, Judith's Paarl, Troyeville, Fairview, Jeppestown, Pageview, Vrededorp, Burghersdorp and Fordsburg. Source as above.

Table 7.7 The Occupational Class Composition by Race of Employed Residents in the Formerly Whites-Only Northern Suburbs, 2011 (Percentage Distributions)

	Africans	Coloureds	Indians	Whites	All Races	All Blacks
Managers	18	17	25	26	23	20
Professionals	21	19	26	22	22	22
Technicians & Associate Professionals	11	14	10	12	12	11
Clerical Support Workers	16	25	19	18	18	18
Services & Sales Workers	19	13	14	15	16	17
Skilled Agricultural, Forestry & Fishery Workers	1	0	0	1	1	0
Craft & Related Trades Workers	10	9	5	5	7	8
Plant & Machine Operators & Assemblers	3	3	2	1	2	2
Elementary Occupations	1	1	1	0	1	1
Total	100	100	100	100	100	100
All Middle-Class Occupations	51	49	60	60	57	53

Sources: The author's analysis of Population Census results for 2011 (SuperCross Interactive Tables). Measured by the number of employed residents living in the main house or apartment and excluding black domestic workers.

Solomon, 2019). Similarly, many formerly coloureds-only middle-class suburbs of Cape Town have also undergone some racial desegregation (Solomon, 2019).

Security estates and racial desegregation in the northern suburbs

One of the striking features of Johannesburg's northern suburbs in the post-Fordist period was the growth of a new type of housing, namely the 'security estate'. Also known as a type of 'gated community', these security estates are characterized primarily by high walls or fences that surround the entire estate, including its streets, parks and communal leisure facilities. Access to these estates is usually through a gate that is guarded day and night, with strict rules applying to who may enter the property (Landman and Badenhorst, 2012: p.14). Security estates are usually very large, some occupying up to 350 hectares (Jürgens and Landman, 2006: p.11), and are therefore more suited to greenfield development where large tracts of land can be purchased by property developers (Lemanski *et al.*, 2008: p.147). In the northern suburbs, these security estates were therefore developed on the peri-urban periphery of the city on agricultural holdings such as Kyalami, Glenferness, Bridle Park and Broadacres north of the N1 Highway (Landman and Badenhorst, 2012: pp.17, 27) (Figure 4.4).

Scholars have disagreed about the relationship between racial segregation and the development of these security estates. Some argue that security estates were developed precisely to exclude blacks from the formerly whites-only neighbourhoods. Writing in 2001, Christopher argued that 'Resistance to integration is still in evidence as witnessed by the development of exclusionary "gated" White suburbs' (Christopher, 2001: pp.455–7). Others argue that the expensive nature of security estates has excluded black residents but not white residents. Lemanski *et al.* (2008: p.150) argued that 'Whilst accurate that gated communities do not differentiate between black or White property purchasers, they do differentiate between wealthy and poor residents (only the former would be able to purchase property in a gated community), they are overwhelmingly populated by White families'. Similarly, Hook and Vrdoljak (2002: pp.204–5) argued that although the residents of security estates were segregated 'increasingly along economic rather than merely racial lines … [n]onetheless, these divisions defer largely to the structural socio-historical opportunities left behind by apartheid, and serve to reify inequality in the old terms of a privileged white minority and a dispossessed black majority'.

This view was disputed by Jürgens and Landman (2006, p.120) who argued that 'Gated communities are not only restricted to white higher-income areas, but also occur in middle-income areas and have mixed-race groups living inside. They are indeed a new form of segregation, but it is a social and economic segregation rather than a new form of racial segregation.'

All these studies referred to above are case studies of particular security estates and are therefore not able to make general statistical claims about the extent of racial residential desegregation in all security estates. However, such general statistical claims can be made using the 2011 Population Census results. Although the Census does not have a variable that distinguishes households living in security estates from those living outside of them, it is nonetheless possible to make this distinction using aerial images of neighbourhoods. This is because houses in security estates are required to conform to a specific architectural design (Hook and Vrdoljak, 2002: p.202). The result is an architectural uniformity that can readily be observed in aerial images and makes it possible to distinguish the boundaries between different security estates and between security estates and other kinds of developments. These observations can be checked with a closer look using the 'Street View' function of the Google Earth software application. Using this method, I classified Census 'Subplaces' in the northern suburbs according to the prevalence of security estates within their boundaries and calculated their racial composition. I did this by matching the boundaries of 2011 Census Subplaces with aerial images using a GIS software application and the website provided by Adrian Frith.[8]

8 The Subplace boundaries were matched with aerial images provided by Google Earth Pro using the following website for 2011 Census Subplaces: https://census2011.adrianfrith. com/.

Table 7.8 The Percentage Racial Distribution of Residents in Security Estates in the Northern Suburbs, 2011

	African	Coloured	Indian	White	All Races	All Blacks
Neighbourhoods composed only of Security Estates	28	3	14	55	100	45
Neighbourhoods with at least 50% of housing in Security Estates	26	3	13	58	100	42
Neighbourhoods with less than 50% of housing in Security Estates	22	5	7	65	100	35
Neighbourhoods with No Security Estates	28	7	11	54	100	46
All Northern Suburbs	27	6	11	56	100	44

Sources: The author's analysis of Population Census results for 2011 (SuperCross Interactive Tables). Measured by the number of employed residents living in the main house or apartment and excluding black domestic workers.

The results show that, in 2011, the extent of racial desegregation in security estates was about the same as the extent of desegregation in neighbourhoods with no security estates (Table 7.8). In neighbourhoods (Census Subplaces) that were composed solely of security estates, 45 per cent of residents were black. In neighbourhoods with no security estates, 46 per cent of residents were black (Table 7.8).

These results might seem counter-intuitive since houses in security estates are understood to be the most luxurious and therefore the most expensive of all housing. Any mention of security estates is bound to evoke the names of luxury estates such as Dainfern, Eagle Canyon Golf Estate and Steyn City (Ballard *et al.*, 2021b). However, security estates take a variety of forms, many of which are affordable to most middle-class managers, professionals and technicians. Landman and Badenhorst (2012, pp.13–18) distinguish between the more expensive 'Golf Estates',[9] 'Country Estates', 'Nature Estates' and 'Lifestyle Estates', on the one hand, and the less-expensive 'Secure Townhouse Complexes', on the other. One of the arguments made by real estate agents is that, all things being equal, houses in these secure townhouse complexes are less expensive than houses on large freehold properties with their own private facilities such as a swimming pool or tennis court (Chipkin, 2013: p.233). This is because less-expensive security estates are developed on the model of small individual properties with shared communal facilities such as parks, swimming pools and tennis courts (Chipkin, 2013: p.233; Jürgens and Gnad, 2002: p.340). Houses in these security estates often take the form of terraces[10] to maximize the amount of land for communal facilities. In

9 For a case study of a golf estate in the northern suburbs, see Duca (2013).

10 Terraced housing is usually characterized by two-storey houses that are built in rows, with shared adjoining walls.

these compact estates, the floor area of houses can be relatively small by middle-class standards, ranging from roughly 50 to 150m^2 on properties of only 500 to 600m^2 (Jürgens and Gnad, 2002: p.345). To put this in perspective, typical middle-class houses in the northern suburbs are built on properties roughly twice this size, that range from 1,000 to 2,000m^2.

This research on the racial composition of the residents of security estates therefore concludes that black residents have not been excluded from these purpose-built security estates in the northern suburbs. These results therefore directly contradict the claims made by Lemanski *et al.* (2008: p.150) and Hook and Vrdoljak (2002: pp.204–5). Their argument is that although these security estates exclude residents based on their low earnings rather than by racial discrimination, they nonetheless exclude black residents because black residents are generally poorer than white residents. Consequently, they argue that security estates 'are overwhelmingly populated by White families' (Lemanski *et al.*, 2008: p.150). This argument assumes that because a smaller percentage of black and African residents are middle class, the sizes of the black and more especially, the African middle class will therefore be much smaller than the white middle class. Consequently, the argument is that white residents will predominate in these expensive housing estates because the percentage of white residents who are middle class is much larger than the percentage of black residents who are middle class.

As I have shown in an earlier chapter, although the percentage of all blacks and Africans who are middle class is much smaller than the percentage of all whites who are middle class, the much larger size of the black population means that the absolute size of the black middle class in 2011 was nonetheless almost twice the size of the white middle class. So although it is certainly true to argue that only a small percentage of all blacks live in the security estates of the northern suburbs and that a larger percentage of all whites live in these security estates, this does not mean that the residents of security estates are overwhelmingly white. This is the error that lies at the heart of the hypothesis that racial desegregation cannot take place until there are equal proportions of the middle-class among both black-and-white workers. As I have shown above, the much larger absolute size of the black middle class relative to the white middle class is an important cause of the racial desegregation of the middle-class northern suburbs.

Conclusion

This study of the changing racial composition of the formerly whites-only neighbourhoods of Johannesburg has shown that, by 2011, there was much more racial desegregation than is generally acknowledged by other studies. These results differ from earlier studies because they are not based on the dissimilarity index. Instead, these results use statistics that calculate the percentage racial composition of each of the formerly whites-only neighbourhoods. I argue that the use of the dissimilarity index produces misleading results that underestimate the extent of racial residential desegregation in formerly whites-only neighbourhoods. This is because the dissimilarity index is a measure, not only of the extent of desegregation of formerly whites-only neighbourhoods, but also of the large number of black residents living in exclusively-black neighbourhoods. This limitation of the dissimilarity index is exacerbated when the results of different population censuses are compared over time. In this case, the growing relative size of the black population living outside of the formerly whites-only neighbourhoods has the effect of increasing the estimate of racial segregation even if the percentage of blacks living in formerly whites-only neighbourhoods remains constant.

These results have also shown how the different kinds of housing markets in the formerly whites-only neighbourhoods have interacted with the class composition of black residents. Generally, the neighbourhoods with cheaper house prices and with properties that are available to rent rather than to buy are those that have become much more racially desegregated. Correspondingly, neighbourhoods with more expensive houses and characterized largely by homeownership are somewhat less desegregated.

These differences notwithstanding, the overriding characteristic of black residents that have moved to live in the formerly whites-only neighbourhoods is that a relatively high percentage of them are employed in high-earning middle-class occupations. The relatively much larger size of the black population has meant that even though the black middle class forms a relatively small percentage of all black workers, it is nonetheless much larger than the white middle class. This large growth of the black middle class in the context of a shortage of middle-class housing in formerly blacks-only neighbourhoods is therefore the main reason for the extent of racial residential desegregation in Johannesburg. This is especially the case in the far northern suburbs that have become the new edge city of Sandton. Unlike cities in the United States, where black and Latino residents are still mostly a minority, the edge city of Sandton has become substantially desegregated because white residents form a very small minority of the total population. This study has therefor established that the rise of the edge city of Sandton has not increased levels of racial segregation in Johannesburg as a whole.

Chapter 8

CONCLUSION: URBAN INEQUALITY

The results of this study have implications for at least two scholarly and policy debates. The first of these is the social polarization debate, which is an international debate about the changing nature of inequality in both global cities and de-industrializing cities more generally. Unlike many scholarly debates that have their origin in the West, the social polarization debate has been taken up by scholars in the non-Western world, which makes this a truly international debate. So it is my hope that this study of greater Johannesburg will be a contribution to our understanding of urban inequality, not only in cities of the developing 'south' but also in cities of the more developed 'north'.

The second area of scholarship is the debate over racial inequality in South African cities. This scholarship has tended to be insular in the sense that it has not drawn upon concepts and theories from other countries. The consequence of this insularity is that racial inequality in South African cities has been conceptualized largely in terms of State policy. Specifically, the causes of racial inequality are mostly limited to the racially discriminatory policies of the *Apartheid* period and the extent to which *Apartheid* patterns of racial inequality have been eroded or not by post-*Apartheid* State policies. There was also a focus on the theory of neo-liberal state policies, with a debate over whether the privatization of public services has produced new urban inequalities (Seekings, 2011: p.542). The debates over social polarization and the post-Fordist spatial order therefore offer a range of possible explanations for the changing patterns of urban inequality in post-*Apartheid* Johannesburg. These lines of enquiry include the topics of de-industrialization, migration, the changing division of labour and the changing geography of housing and labour markets.

The international social polarization debate

This study of employment trends in greater Johannesburg has provided an important comparative test of the competing theories in the social polarization debate. The reason for this is that labour market trends in greater Johannesburg have shown occupational and earnings professionalization among employed workers, which was one of the causes of the rising unemployment rate. There was no trend towards growing employment in both low and high-income occupations, with less growth in middle-income occupations. Instead, there was much more employment growth in non-manual middle-income occupations and in high-income occupations than there was in low- and middle-income manual jobs.

This is a surprising finding because, according to the contributions to the social polarization debate, one would have expected to find a trend of occupational and earnings polarization. This is because greater Johannesburg meets three of the conditions that are thought to be crucial for social polarization to occur. The first condition is that the labour market was deindustrialized. The second condition is that there was an adequate supply of low-skilled labour, and the third condition is that there were no substantial unemployment benefits for unemployed workers.

In respect of de-industrialization, Sassen (2000) argued that the service sector was more polarized than the manufacturing sector in terms of its occupational and earnings structure. Therefore, she concluded that declining manufacturing employment and growing service-sector employment would lead to growing social polarization as the occupational structure of the service sector increasingly dominated the labour market. In respect of the adequate supply of low-skilled workers, Hamnett (1996) has argued that social polarization occurs only under conditions of large-scale in-migration of low-skilled workers to deindustrializing cities. In other words, Hamnett argued that the increasing employment of workers in low-income jobs could be due to employers responding to the new supply of cheap, low-skilled workers. This is argued to be the reason why the labour markets of Western European cities such as London and Randstad have experienced professionalization, whereas US cities such as New York are claimed to have experienced social polarization (Hamnett, 1994). Finally, Hamnett (1996: p.1428) argued that the absence of long-term and generous unemployment benefits is an important reason for the growth of employment in low-income jobs. His reasoning is that generous unemployment benefits can offer low-income workers a greater incentive to opt for unemployment instead of working for a low income. In the absence of these benefits, poorly educated workers have no choice but to accept low-income jobs. So instead of growth in low-income employment, there is growth in unemployment among poorly educated workers.

This study has provided an ideal test of the competing theories in this debate because the labour market in greater Johannesburg (i) has undergone substantial de-industrialization, (ii) has also seen the dramatic growth in the numbers of poorly educated, low-skilled workers by both natural population increase and in-migration and (iii) does not provide comprehensive social welfare for unemployed workers. So under these conditions we would expect to see strong employment growth in low-income jobs. The finding that the strong employment growth in high-income occupations was not matched by employment growth in low-income occupations therefore demonstrates that there are serious limitations to these explanations of social polarization.

Sassen's argument that de-industrialization causes social polarization would hold true only if the occupational structure of the service sector was polarized and that each individual economic sector remains unchanged. If the occupational structures of the manufacturing and service sector changed over time, then these intra-sectoral changes could ameliorate and even over-ride the polarizing effect of inter-sectoral employment change. As it turned out, research showed that the occupational structure of the service sector in greater Johannesburg was not polarized (Crankshaw and Borel-Saladin, 2014). Furthermore, research by Borel-Saladin (2013) revealed that the professionalization of the occupational structure was not caused mostly by de-industrialization. Although de-industrialization was an important reason for the decline of manual middle-income employment, it was not a major cause of the lack of growth of low-income jobs and nor was it a major cause of the growth of high-income jobs. Instead, the main cause of the professionalization of the occupational structure was found in the changes to the occupational structures within each economic sector. So these studies of greater Johannesburg have contributed to the debate on social polarization by showing, not only that the occupational structure is becoming more professionalized rather than polarized, but that de-industrialization is not necessarily the main cause of changes in the occupational structure. Instead, these changes can also be due to intra-sectoral changes in occupational structure.

These results have important implications for labour market policies. Restoring the competitiveness of South Africa's manufacturing sector will not provide a full solution to unemployment because even the manufacturing sector has exhibited a professionalizing employment trend. If the employment trends of the past persist in a revived manufacturing sector, then this would lead to some growth in middle-income manual jobs, but it would also result in more employment in high-income non-manual jobs and very little growth in low-income manual jobs. Instead, policymakers will need to encourage much more labour-intensive kinds of manufacturing activities if unemployment is to be reduced among poorly educated workers (Black, 2016; Nattrass and Seekings, 2019). Furthermore, since all economic sectors have exhibited a professionalizing trend, economy-wide policies are needed to promote employment growth in manual occupations in all economic sectors. On the supply side of the labour market, these results also support the policy argument that the State needs urgently to improve the performance of secondary schools in poor neighbourhoods (Spaull, 2013) so that young workers are adequately prepared for employment in non-manual jobs.

Racial and class inequality in greater Johannesburg

By drawing upon the theories in the social polarization and post-Fordist spatial order debates, I hope to have introduced helpful insights into the study of racial inequality in greater Johannesburg. In particular, I hope that my engagement with these debates has provided some answers to the question of how and why the post-*Apartheid* period has been characterized by increasing black poverty, on the one hand, and the growth of the high-income, black middle class, on the other.

Framing urban inequality in terms of these theories focused my attention on just how much the labour market and the economic geography of Johannesburg have changed over the forty-year period of this study. One of the claims that many commentators make of post-*Apartheid* Johannesburg is that there has been very little social change. However, the results of this study show that there were dramatic changes to the labour market and economic geography of the city. In the 1970s, unemployment was very low, and most workers were employed in manual jobs, either as unskilled labourers or as machine operators and assembly-line workers. Forty years later, unemployment was extremely high, and most workers were employed in non-manual jobs, as clerks, sales workers, service workers, technicians, associate professionals, professionals and managers. This changing labour market, which benefitted better-educated workers and severely disadvantaged poorly educated workers, had an enormous impact on the pattern of racial inequality.

For white workers, who received the lion's share of State expenditure on education during *Apartheid*, this resulted in their continued prosperity, which took the form of a low unemployment rate and employment in middle and high-income non-manual jobs. The growth of middle-class jobs far exceeded the growth of the white workforce and therefore provided middle-class employment opportunities for many well-educated black workers. The same was true for the growth of middle-income clerical, sales and service jobs. The result was upward occupational mobility for some black workers. However, this changing division of labour severely disadvantaged a great many poorly educated black workers who were left jobless. The combined effects of racially unequal schooling during the *Apartheid* period, generally low employment growth and the changing occupational structure meant that it was poorly educated coloured and African workers who bore the brunt of unemployment.

The economic geography of Johannesburg has also been transformed by the decline of manufacturing activities in the inner city and the growth of the edge city of Sandton. This new post-Fordist spatial order has deepened the *Apartheid* geography by concentrating the middle class in the northern suburbs and concentrating unemployed workers in the now excluded ghettos in the southern suburbs. Although this post-Fordist spatial geography has some resemblance to the geography of *Apartheid* Johannesburg, there are nonetheless substantial differences. The social composition of the old racial ghettos of Soweto, Eldorado Park and Lenasia has been substantially changed by extremely high levels of unemployment and by the replacement of middle-income manual workers with middle-income non-manual workers. The middle-class edge city, for its part, was dramatically transformed by substantial racial desegregation due to the large numbers of middle-class black residents who chose to live there. The middle-class edge city was also transformed by the large-scale development of State-sponsored housing for poor residents.

Johannesburg's post-Fordist spatial order is therefore characterized by an edge city with a racially mixed middle-class population, on the one hand, and an excluded ghetto with high levels of unemployment alongside an employed workforce of largely middle-income workers, on the other.

The scholarly focus on racial categories as a crude proxy for inequality has tended to underplay the extent to which racial income inequality has changed over the past forty years. This approach was exemplified by Thabo Mbeki's 1998 speech to Parliament, in which he described South Africa as a country of two nations: the 'prosperous' white nation and 'poor' black nation (Nattrass and Seekings, 2001: p.45). Although this would have been an accurate description of racial inequality at the height of the *Apartheid* period, it was certainly not an accurate description in 1998, and was even less accurate by 2011.

As I have shown, the occupational profile of black workers has changed substantially over the period from 1970 to 2011. In 1970, almost all black workers were employed in low-income and middle-income manual jobs. By 2011, this percentage had decreased to just less than 50 per cent. The remaining black workers were employed in high-income middle-class and middle-income non-manual occupations. This transformation resulted in the racial desegregation of employment in middle-class and white-collar occupations that were once predominantly filled by white workers. In 1970, at the height of the *Apartheid period*, about 90 per cent of all middle-class jobs were held by white workers. Forty years later, this percentage had been reduced to only one-third. By 2011, therefore, it was no longer sensible to describe Johannesburg's black population as uniformly poor. Correspondingly, the concept of race is no longer a useful proxy for describing social inequality in greater Johannesburg.

My approach to the study of racial inequality was enriched by the social polarization debate because of its emphasis on the growth of the high-income middle class. In the context of Johannesburg, the extraordinary growth of middle-class employment opportunities was the basis for the upward mobility of black workers into middle-class occupations. This growth in the size of the black middle-class was one of the important causes of the residential desegregation of the formerly whites-only neighbourhoods in Johannesburg. Contrary to the claims of other research on Johannesburg, this study has shown that the formerly whites-only neighbourhoods were substantially desegregated by the time of the most recent Population Census in 2011. At the last count, white residents were a minority of the population in these neighbourhoods. Even the very expensive northern suburbs were substantially desegregated, with white residents making up just over half the population.

The second contribution that this study makes to the debate on urban inequality in South Africa is that the changing occupational structure of employment was an important reason for the perpetuation of black poverty in the post-*Apartheid* period. It is well known that high unemployment rates among black, particularly African workers, is a major cause of racial inequality. This study has shown that the professionalization of the occupational structure resulted in a high demand for well-educated workers and little demand for poorly educated workers who were qualified only for employment in manual jobs. In this way, the changes in the occupational structure contributed to high unemployment among poorly educated black workers. This research result came directly from my engagement with the theories and concepts in the social polarization debate.

The third contribution of this study concerns the changing occupational class geography of Johannesburg's residents. Most studies of South African cities have focused on the racial characteristics of the population to the neglect of other features. One consequence of this is that the racial ghettos are seen to be composed of homogeneously poor neighbourhoods. This study has shown that examining changes in the housing and labour markets can provide new insights into the social character of the erstwhile racial ghettos of Johannesburg. The results show that although the racial ghetto of the *Apartheid*-period was transformed into an excluded ghetto with extremely high unemployment, this change was accompanied by growing diversity in the housing and labour markets. So whereas the expansion of shack settlements and State-subsidized housing provided homes for low-wage and unemployed workers, there was also some growth in partially subsidized Gap housing and expensive unsubsidized housing that provided homes for middle-income and high-income workers. The result was the absolute growth in the numbers of middle-income non-manual and high-income middle-class black workers in the excluded ghettos. Consequently, the occupational structure of the excluded ghetto became much more diverse. Again, this finding was a direct result of an engagement with the theories and concepts in the literature on the post-Fordist spatial order.

Methodology, evidence and theory

This study has also engaged in methodological debates that are relevant to research on urban inequality. I have argued that a central flaw in much of the quantitative research on the occupational structure and residential segregation is that scholars have a cavalier approach to the use of statistics. This approach is characterized by a lack of attention to how the qualitative nature of phenomena and social processes are first conceptualized before they are measured. The result is that the statistical evidence produced by some research is not a valid measure of the phenomenon being studied.

Many studies of social polarization have made the mistake of using concepts in a metaphorical and rhetorical manner, instead of using them to provide precise descriptions of phenomena. The result of such an approach is that the statistical evidence it produces does not directly test the hypothetical claims. I have shown that the failure to accurately conceptualize occupational groups in the strict terms of the social polarization theory has led to many inaccurate measurements of changes in the division of labour.

Another methodological feature of this study is that it has entailed a rejection of the positivist model of establishing proof of causation by using statistical correlations. To the contrary, following the insights of critical realism, I have viewed statistical correlations as the object to be explained rather than as evidence for a hypothesized causal mechanism. As an alternative, the evidence of causal mechanisms has been sought in the qualitatively defined properties of the labour market and housing market and the policies and practices that brought them about.

In the case of research on racial residential segregation, I have argued that the dissimilarity index is not a valid measure of the extent of the racial desegregation of the formerly whites-only neighbourhoods of Johannesburg. The idea of a summary statistic, such as the dissimilarity index, is tempting but it is not justified on methodological grounds. The problem with the dissimilarity index is that it measures more than one phenomenon simultaneously. As such, the dissimilarity index is a 'chaotic concept' (Sayer, 2010: p.93) in the sense that it measures two distinct real phenomena as if they were one and the same thing. The result is that the trends in racial segregation as measured by the dissimilarity index are a composite of two distinct phenomena or processes, namely the changes in the relative size of racially defined populations, on the one hand, and changes in their residential segregation, on the other. The result is that the dissimilarity index is incapable of measuring solely the latter. In the context of Johannesburg, where there has been a large increase in the number of blacks-only neighbourhoods compared with no increase in the size of the white population, this has resulted in high dissimilarity indices. The use of the dissimilarity index as a measure of changes in racial residential segregation should therefore only be used in cities in which the racial proportions of the total population remain substantially the same over time.

As an alternative, I have used descriptive statistics to measure the relative and absolute racial composition of neighbourhoods that I conceptualized in terms of *Apartheid*-period Group Areas designations and in terms of the character of the housing. This approach enabled me to measure both the changes in the extent of desegregation in the formerly whites-only neighbourhoods and the geographical character of these changes. This approach requires a qualitative research method to establish precisely which neighbourhoods were legally designated as white Group Areas. It also required the conceptualization of the different kinds of housing found in the formerly white neighbourhoods in order to avoid inflating the measurement of desegregation by including black domestic workers, black residents of shack settlements and black tenants of backyard rooms and hostels. Such an approach is completely different to the logic of the dissimilarity index, which treats all neighbourhoods as if they were the same and, by implication, as if they have no distinct properties and therefore no powers and liabilities, which have distinct social consequences. The positivist approach, which tends to overlook the relevance of conceptualizing the qualitative nature of phenomena, therefore has little to say about what causes or obstructs racial residential desegregation.

REFERENCES

Abrahams, G. (1992) *A History of Conflict: The Relocation of the Zevenfontein Squatters*. Johannesburg: Urban Foundation.

Adler, J., Beetge, M. and Sher, S. (1984) 'The "New" Illegality. Squatters with Urban Rights but No Houses: A Case Study of Grasmere Squatter Camp', *Indicator SA* 2(2), pp.8–10.

Ahmad, P. and Pienaar, H. (2014) 'Tracking Changes in the Urban Built Environment: An Emerging Perspective from the City of Johannesburg', in P. Harrison, G. Gotz, A. Todes and C. Wray (Eds.), *Changing Space, Changing City: Johannesburg after Apartheid*. Johannesburg: Wits University Press, pp.101–16.

Andersen, H., Andersen, H. and Ærø, T. (2000) 'Social Segregation in Greater Copenhagen', *Danish Journal of Geography* 100(1), pp.71–83.

Atzema, O. and De Smidt, M. (1992) 'Selection and Duality in the Employment Structure of the Randstad', *Tijdschrift voor Economische en Sociale Geografie* 83(4), pp.289–305.

Autor, D., Katz, L. and Kearney, M. (2006) 'The Polarization of the U.S. Labor Market', *American Economic Review* 96, pp.189–94.

Autor, D., Levy, F. and Murnane, R. (2003) 'The Skill Content of Recent Technological Change: An Empirical Exploration', *Quarterly Journal of Economics* 118(4), pp.1279–333.

Badcock, B. (2000) 'The Imprint of the Post-Fordist Transition on Australian Cities', in P. Marcuse and R. Van Kempen (Eds.), *Globalizing Cities: A New Spatial Order?* Oxford: Blackwell Publishers, pp.211–27.

Bailey, T. and Waldinger, R. (1991) 'The Changing Ethnic/Racial Division of Labour', in J. Mollenkopf and M. Castells (Eds.), *Dual City: Restructuring New York*. New York: Russell Sage Foundation, pp.43–78.

Ballard, R., and Hamann, C. (2021) 'Socio-Economic Segregation and Income Inequality in the City of Johannesburg', in M. Van Ham, T. Tammaru, R. Ubarevičiene and H. Janssen (Eds.), *Urban Socio-Economic Segregation and Income Inequality: A Global Perspective*. New York: Springer, pp.91–109.

Ballard, R., Hamann, C. and Mkhize, T. (2021a) 'Johannesburg: Repetitions and Disruptions of Spatial Patterns', in A. Lemon, R. Donaldson and G. Visser (Eds.), *South African Urban Change Three Decades after Apartheid: Homes (Still) Apart?* Cham: Springer, pp.35–55.

Ballard, R., Jones, G. and Ngwenya, M. (2021b) 'Trickle-out Urbanism: Are Johannesburg's Gated Estates Good for Their Poor Neighbours?', *Urban Forum* 32(2), pp.165–82.

Barchiesi, F. (1999) 'Kelvinator: Restructuring, Collapse and Struggle', *South African Labour Bulletin*, 23(6), pp.65–70.

Barchiesi, F. (2005) 'Social Citizenship and the Transformations of Wage Labour in the Making of Post-Apartheid South Africa, 1994–2001', Doctoral Thesis, University of the Witwatersrand, Johannesburg.

Baum, S. (1997) 'Sydney, Australia: A Global City? Testing the Social Polarisation Thesis', *Urban Studies* 34(11), pp.1881–01.

Baum S. (1999) 'Social Transformations in the Global City: Singapore', *Urban Studies* 36(7), pp.1095–117.

Bauman, T. (1995) *An Industrial Strategy for the Household Electrical Durable Goods Sector*. Cape Town: Industrial Strategy Project, UCT Press.

Beall, J., Crankshaw, O. and Parnell, S. (2002) *Uniting a Divided City: Governance and Social Exclusion in Johannesburg*. London: Earthscan.

Beall, J., Crankshaw, O. and Parnell, S. (2006) 'A Matter of Timing: Urbanisation and Housing Access in Metropolitan Johannesburg', in D. Bryceson and D. Potts (Eds.), *African Urban Economies: Viability, Vitality or Vitiation of Major Cities in East and Southern Africa?* Basingstoke: Palgrave MacMillan, pp.229–51.

Beauregard, R. and Haila, A. (2000) 'The Unavoidable Continuities of the City', in P. Marcuse and R. Van Kempen (Eds.), *Globalizing Cities: A New Spatial Order?* Oxford: Blackwell, pp.22–36.

Beavon, K. (2004) *Johannesburg: The Making and Shaping of the City*. Pretoria: UNISA Press.

Beavon, K. and Larsen, P. (2014) 'Sandton Central, 1969–2013: From Open Veld to New CBD?', in P. Harrison, G. Gotz, A. Todes and C. Wray (Eds.), *Changing Space, Changing City: Johannesburg after Apartheid*. Johannesburg: Wits University Press, pp.370–94.

Bekker, S. and Humphries, R. (1985) *From Control to Confusion: The Changing Role of Administration Boards in South Africa, 1971–1983*. Pietermaritzburg: Shuter & Shooter.

Bell, J. and McKay, T. (2011) 'The Rise of "Class Apartheid" in Accessing Secondary Schools in Sandton, Gauteng', *Southern African Review of Education* 17, pp.27–48.

Bénit, C. (2002) 'The Rise or Fall of the "Community"? Post-apartheid Housing Policy in Diepsloot, Johannesburg', *Urban Forum* 13(2), pp.47–66.

Black Sash (1989) *Nearly an A-Z Guide to Homelessness on the Witwatersrand*. Johannesburg: Black Sash Transvaal Region Urban Removals and Homelessness Group, and Community Research and Information Network.

Black, A. (1994) *An Industrial Strategy for the Motor Vehicle Assembly and Component Sector*. Cape Town: Industrial Strategy Project, UCT Press.

Black, A. and Hasson, R. (2016) 'Capital-Intensive Industrialisation, Comparative Advantage and Industrial Policy', in A. Black (Ed.), *Towards Employment-Intensive Growth in South Africa*. Cape Town: UCT Press, pp.286–306.

Bonner, P. and Nieftagodien, N. (2008) *Alexandra: A History*. Johannesburg: Wits University Press.

Bonner, P. and Segal, L. (1998) *Soweto: A History*. Cape Town: Maskew Miller/Longman.

Borel-Saladin, J. (2012) 'Testing the Social Polarization Hypothesis in Johannesburg, South Africa', Doctoral Thesis, University of Cape Town, Cape Town.

Borel-Saladin, J. (2013) *Social Polarisation and Migration to Johannesburg*. Falmer: Migrating out of Poverty Research Programme Consortium, University of Sussex.

Borel-Saladin, J. and Crankshaw, O. (2009) 'Social Polarisation or Professionalisation? Another Look at Theory and Evidence on Deindustrialisation and the Rise of the Service Sector', *Urban Studies* 46(3), pp.645–64.

Branson, N. (2006) *The South African Labour Market 1995–2004: A Cohort Analysis*. Working Paper No.06/07. Cape Town: Southern Africa Labour and Development Research Unit, University of Cape Town.

Burgers, J. and Musterd, S. (2002) 'Understanding Urban Inequality: A Model Based on Existing Theories and an Empirical Illustration', *International Journal of Urban and Regional Research* 26(2), pp.403–13.

Butcher, S. (2016) 'Infrastructures of Property and Debt: Making Affordable Housing, Race and Place in Johannesburg', Doctoral Dissertation, University of Minnesota.

Butcher, S. (2020) 'Appropriating Rent from Greenfield Affordable Housing: Developer Practices in Johannesburg', *Environment and Planning A: Economy and Space* 52(2), pp.337–61.

Butcher, S. (2021) 'New Ward for a New Johannesburg? Reformatting Belonging and Boundaries in the City's South', *Urban Forum* 32(2), pp.183–204.

Carrim, N. (1990) *Fietas: A Social History of Pageview, 1948–1988.* Johannesburg: Save Pageview Association.

Carruthers, J. (1993) *Sandton: The Making of a Town.* Rivonia: Celt Books.

Castells, M. (2002) 'Information Technology, the Restructuring of Capital-Labour Relationships, and the Rise of the Dual City', in I. Susser (Ed.), *The Castells Reader on Cities and Social Theory.* Oxford: Blackwell Publishers, pp.285–313.

Ceruti, C. (2013) 'Contemporary Soweto: Dimensions of Stratification', in P. Alexander, C. Ceruti, K. Motseke, M. Phadi and K. Wale (Eds.), *Class in Soweto.* Scottsville: University of KwaZulu-Natal Press, pp.55–95.

Charlton, S. (2014) 'Public Housing in Johannesburg', in P. Harrison, G. Gotz, A. Todes and C. Wray (Eds.), *Changing Space, Changing City: Johannesburg after Apartheid.* Johannesburg: Wits University Press, pp.176–93.

Charlton, S. (2017) 'Poverty, Subsidised Housing and Lufhereng as a Prototype Megaproject in Gauteng', *Transformation: Critical Perspectives on Southern Africa* 95, pp.85–110.

Chipkin, C. (1998) 'The Great Apartheid Building Boom: The Transformation of Johannesburg in the 1960s', in H. Judin and I. Vladislavic (Eds.), *Architecture, Apartheid and after.* Rotterdam: NAi Publishers, pp.249–67.

Chipkin, I. (2013) 'Capitalism, City, Apartheid in the Twenty-First Century', *Social Dynamics* 39(2), pp.228–47.

Chiu, S. and Lui, T. (2004) 'Testing the Global City-Social Polarisation Thesis: Hong Kong since the 1990s', *Urban Studies* 41(10), pp.1863–88.

Christopher, A. (2001) 'Urban Segregation in Post-*Apartheid* South Africa', *Urban Studies* 38(3), pp.449–66.

Christopher, A. (2005) 'Further Progress in the Desegregation of South African Towns and Cities, 1996–2001', *Development Southern Africa* 22(2), pp.267–76.

Cirolia, L. (2016) 'Reframing the Gap Market: Lessons and Implications from Cape Town's Gap Market Housing Initiative', *Journal of Housing and the Built Environment* 31(4), pp.621–34.

Clark, W. (2003) *Immigrants and the American Dream: Remaking the Middle Class.* New York: The Guilford Press.

Clark, W. (2007) 'Race, Class and Place: Evaluating Mobility Outcomes for African Americans', *Urban Affairs Review* 42(3), pp.295–314.

Clark, W. and McNicholas, M. (1996) 'Re-Examining Economic and Social Polarisation in a Multi-Ethnic Metropolitan Area: The Case of Los Angeles', *Area* 28(1), pp.56–63.

Coetzee, G. (2018) 'The Role of the Private Sector in Providing Gap Housing in Johannesburg', Master's Thesis, University of the Witwatersrand, Johannesburg.

CoJ (2011) *The Remaking of Soweto: End of Term Report, 2006–2011.* Johannesburg: City of Johannesburg Metropolitan Municipality.

Cooper, D. (2015) 'Social Justice and South African University Student Enrolment Data by "Race", 1998–2012: From "Skewed Revolution" to "Stalled Revolution"', *Higher Education Quarterly* 69(3), pp.237–62.

Cortese, C., Falk, R. and Cohen, J. (1976) 'Further Considerations of the Methodological Analysis of Segregation Indices', *American Sociological Review* 41(4), pp.630–7.

Crankshaw, O. (1986) 'Theories of Class and the Emerging African Middle Class in South Africa, 1969–1985', *Africa Perspective* 1(1&2), pp.3–30.

Crankshaw, O. (1990) 'Apartheid and Economic Growth: Craft Unions, Capital and the State in the South African Building Industry, 1945–1975', *Journal of Southern African Studies* 16(3), pp.503–26.

Crankshaw, O. (1993) 'Squatting, Apartheid and Urbanisation on the Southern Witwatersrand', *African Affairs* 92(366), pp.31–51.

Crankshaw, O. (1996) 'Changes in the Racial Division of Labour during the Apartheid Era', *Journal of Southern African Studies* 22(4), pp.633–56.

Crankshaw, O. (1997) *Race, Class and the Changing Division of Labour under Apartheid.* London: Routledge.

Crankshaw, O. (2005) 'Class, Race and Residence in Black Johannesburg, 1923–1970', *Journal of Historical Sociology* 18(4), pp.353–92.

Crankshaw, O. (2008) 'Race, Space and the Post-Fordist Spatial Order of Johannesburg', *Urban Studies* 45(8), pp.1692–711.

Crankshaw, O. (2012) 'Deindustrialization, Professionalisation and Racial Inequality in Cape Town', *Urban Affairs Review* 48(6), pp.836–62.

Crankshaw, O. (2014) 'Causal Mechanisms, Job Search and the Labour Market Spatial Mismatch: A Realist Criticism of the Neo-Positivist Method', *The Journal of Critical Realism* 13(5), pp.498–519.

Crankshaw, O. (2017) 'Social Polarisation in Global Cities: Measuring Changes in Earnings and Occupational Inequality', *Regional Studies* 51(11), pp.1612–21.

Crankshaw, O. and Borel-Saladin, J. (2014) 'Does De-Industrialisation Cause Social Polarisation in Global Cities?', *Environment & Planning A* 46(9), pp.1852–72.

Crankshaw, O., Gilbert, A. and Morris, A. (2000) 'Backyard Soweto', *International Journal of Urban and Regional Research* 24(4), pp.841–57.

Crankshaw, O. and Hart, T. (1990) 'The Roots of Homelessness: Causes of Squatting in the Vlakfontein Squatter Settlement South of Johannesburg', *South African Geographical Journal* 72(2), pp.65–70.

Crankshaw, O., Heron, G. and Hart, T. (1992) 'The Road to Egoli: Urbanization Histories from a Johannesburg Squatter Settlement', in D. Smith (Ed.), *The Apartheid City and Beyond: Urbanization and Social Change in South Africa.* London: Routledge, pp.136–46.

Crankshaw, O. and Parnell, S. (1999) 'Interpreting the 1994 African Township Landscape', in H. Juden and I. Vladislavic (Eds.) *Blank Architecture after Apartheid.* David Philip: Cape Town, pp.439–43.

Crankshaw, O. and Parnell, S. (2004) 'Johannesburg: Race, Inequality and Urbanisation', in J. Gugler (Ed.), *World Cities beyond the West: Globalisation, Development and Inequality.* Cambridge: Cambridge University Press, pp.348–70.

Crankshaw, O. and White, C. (1992) *Results of the Johannesburg Inner City Survey.* Contract Report C/Pers 451. Pretoria: Human Sciences Research Council.

Crankshaw, O. and White, C. (1995) 'Racial Desegregation and Inner-City Decay in Johannesburg', *International Journal of Urban and Regional Research* 19(4), pp.622–38.

Crompton, R. (1995) *An Industrial Strategy for the Commodity Plastics Sector.* Cape Town: UCT Press.

De Coning, C., Fick, J. and Olivier, N. (1986) *Residential Settlement Patterns: A Pilot Study of Socio-Political Perceptions in a Grey Area of Johannesburg.* Johannesburg: Department of Development Studies, Rand Afrikaans University.

De Kadt, J., Norris, S., Fleisch, B., Richter, L. and Alvanides, S. (2014) 'Children's Daily Travel to School in Johannesburg-Soweto, South Africa: Geography and School Choice in the Birth to Twenty Cohort Study', *Children's Geographies* 12(2), pp.170–88.

De Vos, T. (1986) *Housing Requirements and Affordability with Special Reference to Johannesburg*. Pretoria: Council for Scientific and Industrial Research.

Debnar, M., Yasui, D. and Tarohmaru, H. (2014) 'Global Cities and Social Polarization in Japan: Industries, Occupations and Inequality in Comparison with Other Regions', *Kyoto Journal of Sociology* 22, pp.23–48.

Donaldson, R. and Kotze, N. (2006) 'Residential Desegregation Dynamics in the South African City of Polokwane (Pietersburg)', *Tijdschrift voor Economische en Sociale Geografie* 97(5), pp.567–82.

Donaldson, S. and Van Der Merwe, I. (1999a) 'Residential Segregation and the Property Market in Pietersburg, 1992–1997', *Urban Forum* 10(2), pp.235–58.

Donaldson, S. and Van Der Merwe, I. (1999b) 'Urban Transformation and Social Change in Pietersburg during Transition', *Society in Transition* 30(1), pp.69–83.

Donaldson, R., Jürgens, U. and Bähr, J. (2003) 'Inner-City Change in Pretoria: Social and Spatial Trends', *Acta Academica Supplementum* 1, pp.1–33.

DoL (2004) *Annual Report of the Unemployment Insurance Fund for the Period 1 April 2003–31 March 2004*. Pretoria: Department of Labour.

Doyal, L. and Harris, R. (1986) *Empiricism, Explanation and Rationality: An Introduction to the Philosophy of the Social Sciences*. London: Routledge & Kegan Paul.

Duca, F. (2013) 'New Community in a New Space: Artificial, Natural, Created, Contested. An Idea from a Golf Estate in Johannesburg', *Social Dynamics* 39(2), pp.191–209.

Duncan, O. and Duncan, B. (1955) 'A Methodological Analysis of Segregation Indexes', *American Sociological Review* 20(2), pp.210–17.

Emdon, E. (1993) 'Privatisation of State Housing: With Special Focus on the Greater Soweto Area', *Urban Forum* 4(2), pp.1–13.

Esping-Anderson, G., Assimakopoulou, Z. and Van Kersbergen, K. (1993) 'Trends in Contemporary Class Structuration: A Six-Nation Comparison', in G. Esping-Anderson (Ed.), *Changing Classes: Stratification and Mobility in Post-Industrial Societies*. London: Sage, pp.32–57.

Falkof, N. (2016) 'Out the Back: Race and Reinvention in Johannesburg's Garden Cottages', *International Journal of Cultural Studies* 19(6), pp.627–42.

Fick, J., De Coning, C., and Olivier, N. (1988) 'Ethnicity and Residential Patterning in a Divided Society: A Case Study of Mayfair in Johannesburg', *South Africa International* 19(1), pp.1–27.

Fieldhouse, E. (1999) 'Ethnic Minority Unemployment and Spatial Mismatch: The Case of London', *Urban Studies* 36(9), pp.1569–96.

Fiske, E. and Ladd, H. (2004) 'Balancing Public and Private Resources for Basic Education: School Fees in Post-Apartheid South Africa', in L. Chisholm (Ed.), *Changing Class: Education and Social Change in Post-Apartheid South Africa*. Pretoria: HSRC Press, pp.57–88.

Fleetwood, S. (2001) 'Causal Laws, Functional Relations and Tendencies', *Review of Political Economy* 3(2), pp.201–20.

FM (1983) 'Soweto: A Survey', Supplement to the *Financial Mail*, 25th March.

Friedmann, J. and Wolff, G. (1982) 'World City Formation: An Agenda for Research and Action', *International Journal of Urban and Regional Research* 6(3), pp.309–44.

Gardner, D. and Rubin, M. (2016) 'The "Other Half" of the Backlog: (Re)Considering the Role of Backyarding in South Africa', in L. Cirolia, T. Görgens, M. Van Donk, W. Smit and S. Drimie (Eds.), *Upgrading Informal Settlements in South Africa: A Partnership-Based Approach*. Cape Town: UCT Press, pp.77–95.

Geyer, H. and Mohammed, F. (2016) 'Hypersegregation and Class-Based Segregation Processes in Cape Town 2001–2011', *Urban Forum* 27(1), pp.35–58.

Gilbert, A. and Crankshaw, O. (1999) 'Comparing South African and Latin American Experience: Migration and Housing Mobility in Soweto', *Urban Studies* 36(13), pp.2375–400.

Gilbert, A., Mabin, A., McCarthy, M. and Watson, V. (1997) 'Low-Income Rental Housing: Are South African Cities Different?', *Environment and Urbanization* 9(1), pp.133–47.

Ginsberg, R. (1996) 'Now I Stay in a House: Renovating the Matchbox in Apartheid-Era Soweto', *African Studies* 55(2), pp.127–39.

Ginsburg, R. (2000) '"Come in the Dark": Domestic Workers and Their Rooms in Apartheid-Era Johannesburg, South Africa', *Perspectives in Vernacular Architecture* 8, pp.83–100.

Gnad, M., Bähr, J. and Jürgens, U. (2002) 'Residential Succession in Johannesburg: The Case of Yeoville', in R. Donaldson and L. Marais (Eds.), *Transforming Rural and Urban Spaces in South Africa during the 1990s: Reform, Restitution, Restructuring*. Pretoria: Africa Institute of South Africa, pp.249–84.

Goldthorpe, J. (1996) 'Class Analysis and the Reorientation of Class Theory: The Case of Persisting Differentials in Educational Attainment', *The British Journal of Sociology* 47(3), pp.481–505.

Goldthorpe, J. and Knight, A. (2006) 'The Economic Basis of Social Class', in S. Morgan, D. Grusky and G. Fields (Eds.), *Mobility and Inequality*. Stanford: Stanford University Press, pp.109–36.

Goos, M. and Manning, A. (2007) 'Lousy and Lovely Jobs: The Rising Polarization of Work in Britain', *The Review of Economics and Statistics* 89(1), pp.118–33.

Gorard, S. (2009) 'Does the Index of Segregation Matter? The Composition of Secondary Schools in England since 1996', *British Educational Research Journal* 35(4), pp.639–52.

Grant, G. and Flinn, T. (1992) *Watershed Town: The History of the Johannesburg City Engineer's Department*. Johannesburg: Johannesburg City Council.

Grimes, S. (1996) 'Economic Change, Immigration and Social Polarization in Sydney', in J. O'Loughlin and J. Friedrichs (Eds.), *Social Polarisation in Post-Industrial Metropolises*. New York: Walter de Gruyter, pp.173–93.

Grinker, D. (2000) *Inside Soweto: The Inside Story of the Background to the Unrest*. Johannesburg: Eastern Enterprises.

Gu C. (2001) 'Social Polarisation and Segregation in Beijing', *China Geographical Sciences* 11(1), pp.17–26.

Gu, C. and Liu, H. (2002) 'Social Polarization and Segregation in Beijing', in J. Logan (Ed.), *The New Chinese City: Globalization and Market Reform*. Oxford: Blackwell Publishers, pp.198–211.

Gu, C., Chan, R., Liu, J., Kesteloot, C. (2006) 'Beijing's Socio-Spatial Restructuring: Immigration and Social Transformation in the Epoch of National Economic Reformation', *Progress in Planning* 66, pp.249–310.

Guillaume, P. (2001) *Johannesburg: Géographies de l'exclusion*. Paris: Karthala.

Guillaume, P. and Houssay-Holzschuch, M. (2002) 'Territorial Strategies of South African Informal Dwellers', *Urban Forum* 13(2), pp.86–101.

Gunter, A. and Massey, R. (2017) 'Renting Shacks: Tenancy in the Informal Housing Sector of the Gauteng Province, South Africa', *Bulletin of Geography. Socio-Economic Series* 37, pp.25–34.

Haferburg, C. (2013) 'Townships of To-Morrow? Cosmo City and Inclusive Visions for Post-Apartheid Urban Futures', *Habitat International* 39, pp.261–8.

Hamnett, C. (1986) 'The Changing Socio-Economic Structure of London and the South East, 1961–1981', *Regional Studies* 20(5), pp.391–406.

Hamnett, C. (1994) 'Social Polarisation in Global Cities: Theory and Evidence', *Urban Studies* 31(3), pp.401–24.

Hamnett, C. (1996) 'Social Polarisation, Economic Restructuring and Welfare State Regimes', *Urban Studies* 33(8), pp.1407–30.

Hamnett, C. (1998) 'Social Segregation and Social Polarization', in R. Paddison (Ed.), *The Urban Studies Handbook*. London: Sage, pp.162–76.

Hamnett, C. (2003) *Unequal City: London in the Global Arena*. London: Routledge.

Hamnett, C. (2010) 'Urban Inequality and Polarization', in F. Wu and C. Webster (Eds.), *Marginalization in Urban China: Comparative Perspectives*. Houndmills: Palgrave MacMillan, pp.17–28.

Hamnett, C. (2012) 'Urban Social Polarization', in B. De Rudder, M. Hoyler, P. Taylor and F. Witlox (Eds.), *The International Handbook of Globalization and World Cities*. Cheltenham: Edward Elgar Publishing, pp.361–8.

Hamnett, C. (2015) 'The Changing Occupational Class Composition of London', *City: Analysis of Urban Trends, Culture, Theory, Policy, Action* 19(2–3), pp.239–46.

Hamnett, C. (2020) 'The Changing Social Structure of Global Cities: Professionalisation, Proletarianisation or Polarisation', *Urban Studies* 58(5), pp.1050–66.

Hamnett, C. and Randolph, B. (1986) 'The Role of Labour and Housing Markets in the Production of Geographical Variations in Social Stratification', in K. Hoggart and E. Kofman (Eds.), *Politics, Geography and Social Stratification*. London: Croom Helm, pp.213–46.

Harber, A. (2011) *Diepsloot*. Johannesburg: Jonathan Ball.

Harrison, B. and Bluestone, B. (1988) *The Great U-Turn: Corporate Restructuring and the Polarizing of America*. New York: Basic Books.

Harrison, P. and Harrison, K. (2014) 'Soweto: A Study in Socio-Spatial Differentiation', in P. Harrison, G. Gotz, A. Todes and C. Wray (Eds.), *Changing Space, Changing City: Johannesburg after Apartheid*. Johannesburg: Wits University Press, pp.293–318.

Harrison, P. and Zack, T. (2014) 'The Wrong Side of the Mining Belt? Spatial Transformations and Identities in Johannesburg's Southern Suburbs', in P. Harrison, G. Gotz, A. Todes and C. Wray (Eds.), *Changing Space, Changing City: Johannesburg after Apartheid*. Johannesburg: Wits University Press, pp.269–92.

Harrison, P., Masson, A. and Sinwell, L. (2014) 'Alexandra', in P. Harrison, G. Gotz, A. Todes and C. Wray (Eds.), *Changing Space, Changing City: Johannesburg after Apartheid*. Johannesburg: Wits University Press, pp.351–62.

Hart, G. (1968) 'An Introduction to the Anatomy of Johannesburg's Southern Suburbs', *South African Geographical Journal* 50, pp.65–72.

Hart, T. (1975) 'The Factorial Ecology of Johannesburg', Occasional Paper No.5, Urban and Regional Research Unit. Johannesburg: University of the Witwatersrand.

Hart, T. (1976) 'The Evolving Pattern of Élite White Residential Areas in Johannesburg, 1911–1970', *South African Geographical Journal* 58(1), pp.68–75.

Hart, T. and Browett, J. (1976) 'A Multi-Variate Spatial Analysis of the Socio-Economic Structure of Johannesburg, 1970', Occasional Paper No.13, Urban and Regional Research Unit. Johannesburg: University of the Witwatersrand.

Heller, P. (2017) 'Growth and Inclusion in the Mega-Cities of India, South Africa and Brazil', in G. Bhan, S. Srinivas and V. Watson (Eds.), *The Routledge Companion to Planning in the Global South*. London: Routledge, pp.37–47.

Hellmann, E. (1948) *Rooiyard: A Sociological Survey of an Urban Native Slum Yard*. Cape Town: Oxford University Press.

Hlatshwayo, M. (2015) 'Unpacking Numsa's Responses to Technological Changes at the ArcelorMittal Vanderbijlpark Plant', *South African Review of Sociology* 46(2), pp.77–96.

Hlatshwayo, M. and Buhlungu, S. (2017) 'Work Reorganisation and Technological Change: Limits of Trade Union Strategy and Action at ArcelorMittal, Vanderbijlpark', *African Sociological Review* 21(1), pp.126–53.

Hodge, D. (2009) 'Growth, Employment and Unemployment in South Africa', *South African Journal of Economics* 77(4), pp.488–504.

Hodge, J. (1998) 'The Midrand Area: An Emerging High-Technology Cluster? *Development Southern Africa* 15, pp.851–73.

Hoogendoorn, G. and Visser, G. (2007) 'The Evolving South African Neighbourhood: The Case of Westdene, Bloemfontein', *Urban Forum* 18(4), pp.329–349.

Hooghiemstra, G. and Cloete, C. (2018) 'A Century of Contested Ownership: Land Tenure in Alexandra, South Africa 1912–2011', *International Journal of Real Estate and Land Planning* 1, pp.197–214.

Hook, D. and Vrdoljak, M. (2002) 'Gated Communities, Heterotopia and a "Rights" of Privilege: A "Heterotopology" of the South African Security Park', *Geoforum*, 33(2), pp.195–219.

Horn, A. and Ngcobo, J. (2003) 'The Suburban Challenge: (De)segregation, Opportunity, and Community in Akasia, City of Tshwane', *Urban Forum* 14(4), pp.320–46.

Horrell, M. (1982) *Race Relations as Regulated by Law in South Africa, 1948–1979*. Johannesburg: South African Institute of Race Relations.

Howe, L. (2018) 'Paradigm Johannesburg: Control and Insurgency in South African Urban Development', *Independent Development Planning Review* 40(4), pp.349–69.

Howe, L. (2021) 'The Spatiality of Poverty and Popular Agency in the GCR: Constituting an Extended Urban Region', *Urban Geography*, published online only.

Huchzermeyer, M. (2005) 'Housing Subsidies and Urban Segregation: A Reflection on the Case of South Africa', in D. Varady (Ed.), *Desegregating the City: Ghettos, Enclaves and Inequality*. Albany: State University of New York Press, pp.213–20.

Huchzermeyer, M., Karam, A. and Maina, M. (2014) 'Informal Settlements', in P. Harrison, G. Gotz, A. Todes and C. Wray (Eds.), *Changing Space, Changing City: Johannesburg after Apartheid*. Johannesburg: Wits University Press, pp.154–75.

Hunter, M. (2010) 'Racial Desegregation and Schooling in South Africa: Contested Geographies of Class Formation', *Environment and Planning A* 42(11), pp.2640–57.

Hunter, M. (2015) 'Schooling Choice in South Africa: The Limits of Qualifications and the Politics of Race, Class and Symbolic Power', *International Journal of Educational Development* 43, pp.41–50.

ILO (2012) *2012 International Standard Classification of Occupations: ISCO-08*. Geneva: International Labour Office.

Joffe, A., Kaplan, D., Kaplinsky, R. and Lewis, D. (1995) *Improving Manufacturing Performance in South Africa: The Report of the Industrial Strategy Project*. Cape Town: UCT Press.

Jürgens, U. and Gnad, M. (2002) 'Gated Communities in South Africa: Experiences from Johannesburg', *Environment and Planning B*, 29(3), pp.337–53.

Jürgens, U. and Landman, K. (2006) 'Gated Communities in South Africa', in G. Glasze, C. Webster and K. Frantz (Eds.), *Private Cities: Global and Local Perspectives*. London: Routledge, pp.105–22.

Jürgens, U., Gnad, M. and Bähr, J. (2002) 'Residential Dynamics in Yeoville, Johannesburg in the 1990s after the End of Apartheid', in A. Osmanovic (Ed.), *Transforming South Africa*. Hamburg: Institute of African Affairs, pp.172–206.

Jürgens, U., Gnad, M. and Bähr, J. (2003a) 'New Forms of Class and Racial Segregation: Ghettos or Ethnic Enclaves?' in R. Tomlinson, R. Beauregard, L. Bremner and X. Mangcu (Eds.), *Emerging Johannesburg: Perspectives on the Postapartheid City*. London: Routledge, pp.56–70.

Jürgens, U., Marais, L., Barker, C. and Lombaard, M. (2003b) 'Socio-Demographic Transformation in the Bloemfontein Inner-City Area', *Acta Academica Supplementum* 1, pp.34–54.

Kasarda, J. (1989) 'Urban Industrial Transition and the Underclass', *Annals of the American Academy of Political and Social Science* 501, pp.26–47.

Kasarda, J. (1995) 'Industrial Restructuring and the Changing Location of Jobs', in R. Farley (Ed.), *State of the Union: America in the 1990s, Volume One: Economic Trends*. New York: Russell Sage Foundation.

Kenny, B. (2019) 'The Sprawl of Malls: Financialisation, Service Work and Inequality in Johannesburg's Urban Geography', *Transformation* 101, pp.36–60.

Kerr, A. (2013) *Dataset Overview, PALMS v2.1 (1994–2012)*. Cape Town: DataFirst, University of Cape Town.

Kerr, A., Lam, D., and Wittenberg, M. (2014) *South Africa: Post Apartheid Labour Market Series 1994–2012*. Cape Town: DataFirst, University of Cape Town.

Kerr, A. and Wittenberg, M. (2020) 'The Post-Apartheid Labour Market Series', *Research Data Journal for the Humanities and Social Sciences* 5(1), pp.39–49.

Kesteloot, C. (1994) 'Three Levels of Socio-Spatial Polarization in Brussels', *Built Environment* 20(3), pp.204–17.

Kesteloot, C. (2000) 'Brussels: Post-Fordist Polarization in a Fordist Spatial Canvas', in P. Marcuse and R. Van Kempen (Eds.), *Globalizing Cities: A New Spatial Order?* Oxford: Blackwell, pp.186–210.

Kesteloot, C. (2005) 'Urban Socio-Spatial Configurations and the Future of European Cities', in Y. Kazepov (Ed.), *Cities of Europe: Changing Contexts, Local Arrangements, and the Challenge to Urban Cohesion*. Oxford: Blackwell, pp.123–47.

Khanyile, S. and Ballard, R. (2018) 'Shopping Malls and Centres in Gauteng', GCRO Map of the Month Series, September 28, 2018. Johannesburg: Gauteng City-Region Observatory.

Kloosterman, R. (1996) 'Double Dutch: Polarization Trends in Amsterdam and Rotterdam after 1980', *Regional Studies* 30(5), pp.467–76.

Kracker Selzer, A. and Heller, P. (2010) 'The Spatial Dynamics of Middle-Class Formation in Post-Apartheid South Africa: Enclavization and Fragmentation in Johannesburg', *Power and Social Theory* 21, pp.171–208.

Krige, D. (2012) 'The Changing Dynamics of Social Class, Mobility and Housing in Black Johannesburg', *Alternation* 19(1), pp.19–45.

Lam, D., Leibbrandt, M. and Mlatsheni, C. (2008) 'Education and Youth Unemployment in South Africa', Working Paper No.22. Cape Town: Southern Africa Labour and Development Research Unit, University of Cape Town.

Landman, K. and Badenhorst, W. (2012) *The Impact of Gated Communities on Spatial Transformation in the Greater Johannesburg Area*. Johannesburg: School of Architecture and Planning, University of the Witwatersrand.

Larsen, P. (2004) 'The Changing Status of the Sandton Business District, 1969–2003', Master's Thesis, University of Pretoria.

Lee, P. and Murie, A. (1999) 'Spatial and Social Divisions within British Cities: Beyond Residualisation', *Housing Studies* 14(5), pp.625–40.

Lemanski, C. (2006) 'Desegregation and Integration as Linked or Distinct? Evidence from a Previously "White" Suburb in Post-Apartheid Cape Town', *International Journal of Urban and Regional Research* 30(3), pp.564–86.

Lemanski, C., Landman, K. and Durington, M. (2008) 'Divergent and Similar Experiences of "Gating" in South Africa: Johannesburg, Durban and Cape Town', *Urban Forum* 19(2), pp.133–58.

Lemon, A. and Clifford, D. (2005) 'Post-Apartheid Transition in a Small South African Town: Interracial Property Transfer in Margate, KwaZulu-Natal', *Urban Studies* 42(1), pp.7–30.

Lodge, T. (1981) 'The Destruction of Sophiatown', *The Journal of Modern African Studies* 19(1), pp.107–32.

Lupton, M. (1991) 'Urban Policy in the Johannesburg Region: The Case of Eldorado Park and Ennerdale', African Studies Seminar Paper, University of the Witwatersrand, Johannesburg.

Lupton, M. (1993) 'Collective Consumption and Urban Segregation in South Africa: The Case of Two Colored Suburbs in the Johannesburg Region', *Antipode* 25(1), pp.32–50.

Mabin, A. (2005a) 'Suburbs and Segregation in South African Cities: A Challenge for Metropolitan Governance in the Early Twenty-First Century', in D. Varady (Ed.), *Desegregating the City: Ghettos, Enclaves and Inequality.* Albany: State University of New York Press, pp.221–32.

Mabin, A. (2005b) 'Suburbs on the Veld, Modern and Postmodern', Unpublished Paper, University of the Witwatersrand.

Mabin, A. (2013) *The Map of Gauteng: Evolution of a City-Region in Concept and Plan.* Johannesburg: Gauteng City-Region Observatory.

Mager A. (2010) *Beer, Sociability and Masculinity in South Africa.* Bloomington: Indiana University Press.

Maharaj, B. and Mpungose, J. (1994) 'The Erosion of Residential Segregation in South Africa: The "Greying" of Albert Park in Durban', *Geoforum* 25(1), pp.19–32.

Malala, J. (2019) 'Why Are South African Cities Still so Segregated 25 Years after Apartheid?', *The Guardian*, 21st October.

Mandy, N. (1984) *A City Divided: Johannesburg and Soweto.* Johannesburg: Macmillan.

Manicas, P. (2006) *A Realist Philosophy of Social Science: Explanation and Understanding.* Cambridge: Cambridge University Press.

Marcuse, P. (1997) 'The Enclave, the Citadel and the Ghetto: What Has Changed in the Post-Fordist U.S. City', *Urban Affairs Review* 33(2), pp.1–27.

Marcuse, P. and Van Kempen, R. (Eds.) (2000) *Globalizing Cities: A New Spatial Order?* Oxford: Blackwell.

Mashabela, H. (1988) *Townships of the PWV.* Johannesburg: South African Institute of Race Relations.

Masondo, D. (2005) 'Trade Liberalisation and Work Restructuring in Post-Apartheid South Africa: A Case Study of BMW', in E. Webster and K. Von Holdt (Eds.), *Beyond the Apartheid Workplace: Studies in Transition.* Durban: University of KwaZulu-Natal Press, pp.149–72.

Mather, C. and Parnell, S. (1990) 'Upgrading the "Matchboxes": Urban Renewal in Soweto, 1976–86', in D. Drakakis-Smith (Ed.), *Economic Growth and Urbanisation in Developing Areas.* London: Routledge, pp.238–50.

Matlapeng, A. (2011) 'Bommastandi of Alexandra Township', Doctoral Thesis, University of the Witwatersrand, Johannesburg.

Metcalfe, M. (1991) *Desegregating Education in South Africa: White School Enrolments in Johannesburg, 1985–1991*. Johannesburg: Education Policy Unit, University of the Witwatersrand.

Meth, P. and Charlton, S. (2017) 'Lived Experiences of State Housing in Johannesburg and Durban', *Transformation* 93, pp.91–115.

Moore, W. (2016) '"Class D Coloureds": The Establishment of Noordgesig, 1939–1948', *New Contree* 77, pp.1–22.

Morris, A. (1994) 'The Desegregation of Hillbrow, Johannesburg, 1978–82', *Urban Studies* 31(6), pp.821–34.

Morris, A. (1998) 'Fighting against the Tide: The White Right and Desegregation in Johannesburg's Inner City', *African Studies* 57(1), pp.55–78.

Morris, A. (1999) *Bleakness and Light: Inner-City Transition in Hillbrow, Johannesburg*. Johannesburg: Witwatersrand University Press.

Morris, A., Bozzoli, B., Cock, J., Crankshaw, O., Gilbert, L., Lehutso-Phooko, L., Posel, D., Tshandu, Z. and Van Huysteen, E. (1999) *Change and Continuity: A Survey of Soweto in the Late 1990s*. Johannesburg: Department of Sociology, University of the Witwatersrand.

Morris, M. and Hindson, D. (1997) 'Class and Household Restructuring in Metropolitan Durban', *Society in Transition* 1(4), pp.101–21.

Morris, P. (1980) *Soweto: A Review of Existing Conditions and Some Guidelines for Change*. Johannesburg: Urban Foundation.

Morris, P. (1981) *A History of Black Housing in South Africa*. Johannesburg: South Africa Foundation.

Moser, C. and Kalton, G. (1971) *Survey Methods in Social Investigation*. Dartmouth: Aldershot.

Murray, M. (2011) *City of Extremes: The Spatial Politics of Johannesburg*. Johannesburg: Wits University Press.

Musiker, N. and Musiker, R. (1999) *Historical Dictionary of Greater Johannesburg*. Oxford: Scarecrow Press.

Myburgh, D. (1996) 'The Transformation of Social Space in the Tygerberg, Cape Town', in R. Davies (Ed.), *Contemporary City Structuring*. Cape Town: International Geographical Union on Urban Development and Society for South African Geographers, pp.200–9.

Nattrass, N. (1998) 'Globalisation and the South African Labour Market', *Journal for Studies in Economics and Econometrics* 22(3), pp.71–90.

Nattrass, N. (2013) 'A South African Variety of Capitalism?', *New Political Economy* 19(1), pp.56–78.

Nattrass, N. (2014) 'Macro-Economic Visions and the Labour-Market Question', in T. Meyiwa, M. Nkondo, M. Chitiga-Mabugu, M. Sithole and F. Nyamnjoh (Eds.), *State of the Nation: South Africa 1994-2014: A Twenty-Year Review of Freedom and Democracy*. Pretoria: HSRC Press, pp.129–41.

Nattrass, N. and Seekings, J. (2001) '"Two Nations"? Race and Economic Inequality in South Africa Today', *Daedalus* 130(1), pp.45–70.

Nattrass, N. and Seekings, J. (2019) *Inclusive Dualism: Labour-Intensive Development, Decent Work, and Surplus Labour in Southern Africa*. Oxford: Oxford University Press.

Nauright, J. (1998) '"The Mecca of Native Scum" and "A Running Sore of Evil": White Johannesburg and the Alexandra Township Removal Debate, 1935-1945', *African Historical Review* 30(1), pp.64–88.

Ndaba, B. (2002) 'Mandelaville Squatters Begin Forced Move', *The Star* 7ᵗʰ January.

Nell, M., Bertoldi, A., Taljaard, R., Gordon, R., Holmes, T., Pretorius, R., Di Lollo, A. (2011) *Housing Subsidy Assets: Exploring the Performance of Government Subsidised Housing in South Africa*. Rosebank: Shisaka Development Management Services.

Ngoasheng, M. (1995) *An Industrial Strategy for the Building Materials Supplies Sector*. Cape Town: UCT Press.

Nieftagodien, N. and Gaule, S. (2012) *Orlando West Soweto: An Illustrated History*. Johannesburg: Wits University Press.

Nijman, J. and Wei, Y. (2020) 'Urban Inequalities in the 21st Century Economy', *Applied Geography* 117, pp.1–8.

Onatu, G. (2010) 'Mixed-Income Housing Development Strategy: Perspective on Cosmo City, Johannesburg, South Africa', *International Journal of Housing Markets and Analysis* 3(3), pp.203–15.

Ownhouse, S. and Nel, E. (1993) 'The "Greying" of Central: A Case Study of Racial Residential Desegregation in Port Elizabeth', *Urban Forum* 4(1), pp.81–92.

Palmer, I., Moodley, N. and Parnell, S. (2017) *Building a Capable State: Service Delivery in Post-Apartheid South Africa*. London: Zed Books.

Pandy, W. and Rogerson, C. (2012) 'The Economic Geography of South Africa's Call Centre Industry', *Urban Forum* 23(1), pp.23–42.

Parnell, S. (1988) 'Racial Segregation in Johannesburg: The Slums Act, 1934–1939', *South African Geographical Journal* 70(2), pp.112–26.

Parnell, S. (1991) 'The Ideology of African Home-Ownership: The Establishment of Dube, Soweto, 1946-1955', *South African Geographical Journal* 73, pp.69–76.

Parnell, S. (2003) 'Race, Power and Urban Control: Johannesburg's Inner City Slum-Yards, 1910-1923', *Journal of Southern African Studies* 29(3), pp.615–37.

Parnell, S. and Pirie, G. (1991) 'Johannesburg', in A. Lemon (Ed.), *Homes Apart: South Africa's Segregated Cities*. London: Paul Chapman Publishing, pp.129–45.

Parry, K. and Van Eeden, A. (2015) 'Measuring Racial Residential Segregation at Different Geographic Scales in Cape Town and Johannesburg', *South African Geographical Journal* 97(1), pp.31–49.

Pernegger, L. (2021) *The Agonistic City? State-Society Strife in Democratic Johannesburg*. London: Zed Press.

Pickard-Cambridge, C. (1988) *The Greying of Johannesburg: Residential Desegregation in the Johannesburg Area*. Braamfontein: South African Institute of Race Relations.

Pieterse, E. (2019) 'Urban Governance and Spatial Transformation Ambitions in Johannesburg', *Journal of Urban Affairs* 41(1), pp.20–38.

Pilger, J. (2006) *Freedom Next Time*. London: Bantam.

Pongoma, L. (2009) 'Mshengu is No More', *Sowetan Live* 21ˢᵗ July. https://www.sowetanlive.co.za/news/2009-07-21-mshengu-is-no-more/

Porpora, D. (2008) 'Sociology's Causal Confusion', in R. Groff (Ed.), *Revitalizing Causality: Realism about Causality in Philosophy and Social Science*. London: Routledge, pp.195–204.

Posel, D. (2001) 'What's in a Name? Racial Categorisations under Apartheid and Their Afterlife', *Transformation* 47, pp.50–74.

Randolph, B. (1991) 'Housing Markets, Labour Markets and Discontinuity Theory', in J. Allen and C. Hamnett (Eds.), *Housing and Labour Markets: Building the Connection*. London: Unwin Hyman, pp.16–51.

Roberts, S. (2014) 'Industrialization Strategy', in H. Bhorat, A. Hirsch, R. Kanbur and M. Ncube (Eds.), *The Oxford Companion to the Economics of South Africa*. Oxford: Oxford University Press, pp.185–90.

Rogerson, C. (1996) 'Dispersion within Concentration: The Changing Location of Corporate Headquarter Offices in South Africa', *Development Southern Africa* 13(4), pp.567–79.

Rogerson, C. (2000) 'Manufacturing Change in Gauteng 1989–99: Re-examining the State of the Manufacturing Heartland', *Urban Forum* 11(2), pp.311–40.

Rogerson, C. and Rogerson, J. (1995) 'The Decline of Manufacturing in Inner-City Johannesburg, 1980–1994', *Urban Forum* 6(1), pp.17–42.

Rogerson, C. and Rogerson, J. (1997) 'Intra-Metropolitan Industrial Change in the Witwatersrand, 1980–1994', *Urban Forum* 8(2), pp.194–223.

Rogerson, C. and Rogerson, J. (1999) 'Industrial Change in a Developing Metropolis: The Witwatersrand 1980–1994', *Geoforum* 30(1),pp.85–99.

Rogerson, J. (1995) 'The Changing Face of Retailing in the South African City: The Case of Inner-City Johannesburg', *Africa Insight* 25(3), pp.163–71.

Rogerson, J. (2014) 'Hotel Location in Africa's World Class City: The Case of Johannesburg, South Africa', in D. Szymańska and S. Środa-Murawska (Eds.), *Bulletin of Geography. Socio-economic Series*, No.25. Toruń: Nicolaus Copernicus University Press, pp.181–96.

Rose, D. and Pevalin, J. (2005) *The National Statistics Socio-Economic Classification: Origins, Development and Use*. Houndmills: Palgrave Macmillan.

Rubin, M. and Charlton, S. (2020) 'Living with Strangers: Backyarding, Density and Intimacy in Johannesburg', in M. Rubin, A. Todes, P. Harrison, A. Applebaum (Eds.), *Densifying the City?: Global Cases and Johannesburg*. Cheltenham: Edward Elgar, pp.190–201.

Rule, S. (1988) 'Racial Residential Integration in Bertrams, Johannesburg', *South African Geographical Journal* 70, pp.69–72.

Rule, S. (1989) 'The Emergence of a Racially Mixed Residential Suburb in Johannesburg: Demise of the Apartheid City?', *Geographical Journal* 155, pp.196–203.

Rule, S. (1993) 'Propinquitous Social Diversity in Diepkloof, Soweto', *South African Journal of Sociology* 24(1), pp.9–13.

Rule, S. (2002) 'Post-apartheid Parkhurst: Gentrification and Deracialisation', in: R. Donaldson and L. Marais (Eds.), *Transforming Rural and Urban Spaces in South Africa during the 1990's: Reform, Restitution, Restructuring*. Pretoria: Africa Institute of South Africa, pp.225–48.

Rule, S. (2006) 'Suburban Transformation in Johannesburg', *Kieler Geographische Schriften* 111, pp.553–68.

Rust, K. and Steedley, A. (2013) *Tracking Affordable Housing Markets with Credit Data*. Johannesburg: Affordable Land and Housing Data Centre.

Saff, G. (1998) *Changing Cape Town: Urban Dynamics, Policy and Planning during the Political Transition in South Africa*. Lanham: University Press of America.

SAHO (2019) 'Indian Community in Lenasia', South African History Online, https://www.sahistory.org.za/article/indian-community-lenasia (accessed 6 March 2019).

SAIRR (1979) *Survey of Race Relations in South Africa 1978*. Johannesburg: South African Institute of Race Relations.

SAIRR (1984) *Survey of Race Relations in South Africa 1983*. Johannesburg: South African Institute of Race Relations.

SAIRR (1987) *Survey of Race Relations in South Africa 1986*. Johannesburg: South African Institute of Race Relations.

SAIRR (1992) *Survey of Race Relations in South Africa 1991/92*. Johannesburg: South African Institute of Race Relations.

SAIRR (1993) *Survey of Race Relations in South Africa 1992/93*. Johannesburg: South African Institute of Race Relations.

SAIRR (2004) *South African Survey 2003/2004*. Johannesburg: South African Institute of Race Relations.

Sapire, H. (1990) *Report on the Social and Political Ecology of Free-Standing Settlements on the PWV*. Johannesburg: Urban Foundation and Centre for Policy Studies.

Sapire, H. (1992) 'Politics and Protest in Shack Settlements of the Pretoria-Witwatersrand-Vereeniging Region, South Africa, 1980–1990', *Journal of Southern African Studies* 18(3), pp.670–97.

Sapire, H. and Schlemmer, L. (1990) *Results of the Survey of 3071 Black Households on the PWV*. Johannesburg: The Urban Foundation and Centre for Policy Studies.

Sarakinsky, M. (1984) *Alexandra: From 'Freehold' to 'Model' Township*. Johannesburg: Development Studies Group, University of the Witwatersrand.

Sassen, S. (1990a) 'Economic Restructuring and the American City', *Annual Review of Sociology* 16, pp.465–90.

Sassen, S. (1990b) *The Mobility of Labor and Capital: A Study in International Investment and Labor Flow*. New York: Cambridge University Press.

Sassen, S. (1998) *Globalisation and Its Discontents*. New York: The New Press.

Sassen, S. (2000) *Cities in a World Economy* (2nd Ed.). Thousand Oaks: Pine Forge Press.

Sassen, S. (2001) *The Global City: New York, London, Tokyo* (2nd Ed.). Princeton: Princeton University Press.

Sassen-Koob, S. (1984) 'The New Labor Demand in Global Cities', in M. Smith (Ed.), *Cities in Transformation: Class, Capital and the State*. Beverly Hills: Sage, pp.139–71.

Sayer, A. (2010) *Method in Social Science: A Realist Approach*. London: Routledge.

Sayer, A. and Walker, R. (1992) *The New Social Economy: Reworking the Division of Labour*. Blackwell: Cambridge.

Schensul, D. and Heller, P. (2011) 'Legacies, Change and Transformation in the Post-Apartheid City: Towards an Urban Sociological Cartography', *International Journal of Urban and Regional Research* 35(1), pp.78–109.

Schlemmer, L. and Stack, S. (1990) *Black, White and Shades of Grey: A Study of Responses to Residential Segregation in the Pretoria-Witwatersrand Region*. Braamfontein: Centre for Policy Studies, University of the Witwatersrand.

Seekings, J. (2011) 'Race, Class, and Inequality in the South African City', in G. Bridge and S. Watson (Eds.), *The New Blackwell Companion to the City*. Oxford: Wiley-Blackwell, pp.532–46.

Seekings, J. and Nattrass, N. (2005) *Class, Race and Inequality in South Africa*. New Haven: Yale University Press.

Seekings, J. and Nattrass, J. (2015) *Policy, Politics and Poverty in South Africa*. Basingstoke: Palgrave Macmillan.

SERI (2011) *Towards a Synthesis of the Political, Social and Technical in Informal Settlement Upgrading in South Africa: A Case Study of Slovo Park Informal Settlement, Johannesburg*. Braamfontein: Socio-Economic Rights Institute of South Africa.

SERI (2013) *Thembelihle: Engaging an Unresponsive State*. Braamfontein: Socio-Economic Rights Institute of South Africa.

Shapurjee, Y. and Charlton, S. (2013) 'Transforming South Africa's Low-Income Housing Projects through Backyard Dwellings: Intersections with Households and the State in Alexandra, Johannesburg', *Journal of Housing and the Built Environment* 28(4), pp.653–66.

Simkins, C. and Hindson, D. (1979) 'The Division of Labour in South Africa, 1969–1977', *Social Dynamics* 5(2), pp.1–12.

Soja, E., Morales, R. and Wolff, G. (1983) 'Urban Restructuring: An Analysis of Social and Spatial Change in Los Angeles', *Economic Geography* 59(2), pp.195–230.

Solomon, J. (2019) 'Living Side-by-Side? An Analysis of the Changing Relationship between Race, Space and Class in Cape Town, 1980–2011', Doctoral Thesis, University of Cape Town, Cape Town.

Southall, R. (2016) *The New Black Middle Class in South Africa*. Auckland Park: Jacana Media.

Spaull, N. (2013) *South Africa's Education Crisis: The Quality of Education in South Africa 1994–2011*. Johannesburg: Centre for Development and Enterprise.

Stadler, A. (1979) 'Birds in the Cornfield: Squatter Movements in Johannesburg, 1944–1947', *Journal of Southern African Studies* 6(1), pp.93–123.

Stanback, T. and Noyelle, T. (1984) *The Economic Transformation of American Cities*. New Jersey: Rowman and Allanheld.

StatsSA (2007) *Using the 2001 Census: Approaches to Analysing Data*. Pretoria: Statistics South Africa.

StatsSA (2008) *Concepts and Definitions Used in the Quarterly Labour Force Survey: Report Number 02-11-01*. Pretoria: Statistics South Africa.

Stevens, L. and Rule, S. (1999) 'Moving to an Informal Settlement: The Gauteng Experience', *South African Geographical Journal* 81(3), pp.107–18.

Stickler, L. (1982) 'Aspects of the Socio-Economic and Spatial Organisation of the Coloured Population on the Witwatersrand', Master of Arts Dissertation, University of the Witwatersrand, Johannesburg.

Storper, M. and Walker, R. (1983) 'The Theory of Labour and the Theory of Location', *International Journal of Urban and Regional Research* 7(1), pp.1–43.

Sujee, M. (2004) 'Deracialisation of Gauteng Schools: A Quantitative Analysis', in M. Nkomo, C. McKinney and L. Chisholm (Eds.), *Reflections on School Integration*. Cape Town: Human Sciences Research Council, pp.43–60.

Tai, P. (2005) 'Social Polarization and Income Inequality: Migration and Urban Labour Markets', in R. Kwok (Ed.), *Globalizing Taipei: The Political Economy of Spatial Development*. London: Routledge, pp.141–66.

Tai, P. (2006) 'Social Polarisation: Comparing Singapore, Hong Kong and Taipei', *Urban Studies* 43(10), pp.1737–56.

Thale, T. (2004) 'Old Diepkloof Shackland Is Now Prime Property', Johannesburg News Agency, 5th August. www.joburg.org.za

Todes, A., and Robinson, J. (2020) 'Re-Directing Developers: New Models of Rental Housing Development to Re-Shape the Post-Apartheid City?' *Environment and Planning A: Economy and Space*, 52(2), pp.297–317.

Tomlinson, M., Bam, S. and Mathole, T. (1995) *More than Mielies and Marigolds: From Homeseekers to Citizens in Ivory Park*. Doornfontein: Centre for Policy Studies.

Tomlinson, R. (1996) 'The Changing Structure of Johannesburg's Economy', in N. Harris and I. Fabricius (Eds.), *Cities and Structural Adjustment*. London: UCL Press, pp.175–199.

Tomlinson, R. and Larson, P. (2003) 'The Race, Class and Space of Shopping', in R. Tomlinson, R. Beauregard, L. Bremner and X. Mangcu (Eds.), *Emerging Johannesburg: Perspectives on the Post-apartheid City*. London: Routledge, pp.43–53.

Van Der Berg, S. (2007) 'Apartheid's Enduring Legacy: Inequalities in Education', *Journal of African Economies* 16(5), pp.849–89.

Van Ham, M., Uesugi, M., Tammaru, T., Manley, D. and Janssen, H. (2020) 'Changing Occupational Structures and Residential Segregation in New York, London and Tokyo', *Nature Human Behaviour* 4, pp.1124–34.

Vlok, E. (1999) 'Rose-Tinted Glasses: Kelvinator's Liquidation', *South African Labour Bulletin*, 23(6), pp.59–64.

Wacquant, L. (2008) *Urban Outcasts: A Comparative Sociology of Advanced Marginality*. Cambridge, MA: Polity Press.

Wagner, M. (2014) 'A Place under the Sun for Everyone: Basis for Planning through the Analysis of Formal and Non-Formal Space Practices in the Housing Area Cosmo City', Paper presented to the Southern African City Studies Conference, University of the Witwatersrand, Johannesburg.

Wagner, M. (2018) 'A Place under the Sun for Everyone: Planunsgrundlagen für integrative stadtplanung und angepasste architekture anhand der analyse formeller und nicht-formeller raumpraktiken in der satelitenstadt Cosmo City, Johannesburg', Master's Thesis, Vienna University of Technology.

Waldinger, R. and Bozorgmehr, M. (1996) 'The Making of a Multicultural Metropolis', in R. Waldinger and M. Bozorgmehr (Eds.), *Ethnic Los Angeles*. New York: Russell Sage Foundation, pp.3–38.

Webster, E. (1985) *Cast in a Racial Mould: Labour Process and Trade Unionism in the Foundries*. Johannesburg: Ravan Press.

Webster, E., Benya, A., Dilata, X., Joynt, K., Ngoepe, K. and Tsoeu, M. (2008) *Making Visible the Invisible: Confronting South Africa's Decent Work Deficit*. Johannesburg: Sociology of Work Unit, University of the Witwatersrand.

Wilson, W. (1987) *The Truly Disadvantaged: The Inner City, the Underclass and Public Policy*. Chicago: University of Chicago Press.

Wilson, W. (1996) *When Work Disappears: The World of the New Urban Poor*. New York: Alfred A. Knopf.

Wilson, W. (2003) 'Race, Class and Urban Poverty: A Rejoinder', *Ethnic and Racial Studies* 26(6), pp.1096–114.

Wilson, W. (2009) *More than Just Race: Being Black and Poor in the Inner City*. New York: W. W. Norton & Company.

Wood, L. (2000) 'Residential Real Estate Transfers in Pietermaritzburg–Msunduzi, South Africa', *Tijdschrift voor Economische en Sociale Geografie* 91(3), pp.263–77.

Wright, E. (1997) *Class Counts: Comparative Studies in Class Analysis*. Cambridge: Cambridge University Press.

Wright, E. and Dwyer, R. (2003), 'The Patterns of Job Expansions in the United States: A Comparison of the 1960s and 1990s', *Socioeconomic Review* 1, pp.289–325.

INDEX

www.ingramcontent.com/pod-product-compliance
Lightning Source LLC
Chambersburg PA
CBHW050431280326
41932CB00013BA/2070